CW01403453

This book is to be returned o~
the last date ~

WITHDRAWN

DONCASTER COLLEGE

00242915

Sociolinguistic Metatheory

LANGUAGE & COMMUNICATION LIBRARY
Series Editor: Roy Harris, *University of Oxford*

Related Pergamon Journals

Language & Communication*

An Interdisciplinary Journal
Editors: Roy Harris, *University of Oxford,* and Talbot Taylor, *College of William & Mary*

The primary aim of the journal is to fill the need for a publicational forum devoted to the discussion of topics and issues in communication which are of interdisciplinary significance. It will publish contributions from researchers in all fields relevant to the study of verbal and non-verbal communication. Emphasis will be placed on the implications of current research for establishing common theoretical frameworks within which findings from different areas of study may be accommodated and interrelated. By focusing attention on the many ways in which language is integrated with other forms of communicational activity and interactional behaviour it is intended to explore ways of developing a science of communication which is not restricted by existing disciplinary boundaries.

Language Sciences*
Editor: Paul Hopper

Studies in History & Philosophy of Science*
Editors: Nicholas Jardine and Andrew Cunningham

*Free specimen copy available on request

Sociolinguistic Metatheory

ESTHER FIGUEROA

PERGAMON

UK   Elsevier Science Ltd, The Boulevard, Langford Lane, Kidlington,
            Oxford OX5 1GB, UK

USA   Elsevier Science Inc., 660 White Plains Road, Tarrytown,
            New York 10591-5153, USA

JAPAN   Elsevier Science Japan, Tsunashima Building Annex, 3-20-12 Yushima,
            Bunkyo-ku, Tokyo 113, Japan

Copyright © 1994 Elsevier Science Ltd

All Rights Reserved. No part of this publication may be reproduced, stored in a retrieval system or transmitted in any form or by any means: electronic, electrostatic, magnetic tape, mechanical, photocopying, recording or otherwise, without permission in writing from the publishers.

First edition 1994

Library of Congress Cataloging in Publication Data

Figueroa, Esther.
Sociolinguistic metatheory / Esther Figueroa.
p. cm.– (Language & communication library ; v. 14)
Includes bibliographical references (p.) and index.
1. Sociolinguistics. 2. Metalanguage. I. Title. II. Series.
P40.F54 1994
306.4'4–dc20
94-14272

British Library Cataloguing in Publication Data

A catalogue record for this book is available from the British Library

ISBN 0 08 042399 X

Doncaster College
HIGH MELTON LEARNING
RESOURCE CENTRE

| Classification Number | 401.9 |
| Accession Number | 115908 |

Printed in Great Britain by Galliard (Printers) Ltd, Great Yarmouth

to
my parents
with gratitude

&

to
my brother Thomas
in loving memory

Table of Contents

Acknowledgements

Thanks first to the ones who gave me life and consciousness: my mother, father, sisters and brothers. I am the lucky one. As the youngest of seven I could not have asked for more fertile soil to grow in. I was lucky to come from a large family and thank my many aunts for showing me such diversity of womanhood.

Thanks to my second family – my friends with whom I am so blessed. I thank you for entertaining me, telling me stories, inspiring me, feeding me and keeping me alive these many years. A special thanks to those who got me through the growing-up years: Pine Dubois, Kate Missett, Sheila Hoben.

Thanks to my teachers from whom I learned a great deal, especially Deborah Schiffrin, Deborah Tannen and Ralph Fasold. Thanks to Hsieh Hsin-I for unwittingly starting me down this path years ago. Thanks also to Julie Andresen, Frank Dinneen, Maria Garcia, Rom Harre, Vivienne Holt, John Joseph, Charles Kreidler, Carolyn Nocella, Jame Vincent, Walt Wolfram. Thanks to my fellow Georgetown students without whom I would not have made it through graduate school, especially Shay Auerbach. Special thanks to my saving graces: Mary Coit, Mayotte Michaud, Lisa Smith. And to my number one saving grace, Talbot Taylor whose generosity got me to this book, many, many thanks.

Thanks to Roy Harris for this opportunity. Thanks to Chris Pringle for his patience. Thanks to Carolyn Cooper. And thanks to Michele Eff for her computer smarts.

And finally to the one who makes everything possible, to Heather Haunani Giugni, my undying love and gratitude.

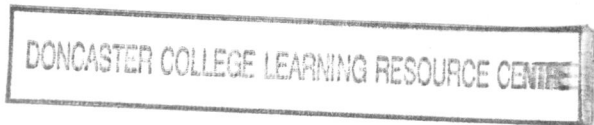

DONCASTER COLLEGE LEARNING RESOURCE CENTRE

1

Introduction

The Problem

Background

By many accounts, sociolinguistics, in what may be called its modern and primarily American state, has been in existence for approximately four decades. (See, for example, Currie, 1981; Shuy 1988.) In 1952, Haver Currie published an article in *Southern Speech Journal* entitled, "A projection of sociolinguistics: the relationship of speech to social status." It is this article upon which Currie (1981) bases his claim that he was the first person to use the term sociolinguistics and to suggest sociolinguistics as an independent discipline. From other perspectives, sociolinguistics is more often seen as developing in the United States in the early sixties, partly out of dialectology, partly out of anthropology, motivated by reaction against linguistic formalism and spurred on by changes in the society, especially the Black civil rights movement. (See, Gieshers 1985 for an example of this version of the development of sociolinguistics.)

The above views as to the development of sociolinguistics are rather narrow and American centered, and do not consider what Peng (1982, p. 26) has called "the historical depth of the discipline." The issues which are often associated with sociolinguistics (for example, language diversity, the relationship between language and society) are issues which have been around since attention has been paid to language and languages. Making this point, Neubert (1976, p. 152) writes, "practical questions of how language is an integral part of society and, above all, how social or rather extralinguistic factors have shaped and are shaping language...were in fact the concern of linguistic research long before the term sociolinguistics was coined, so that linguistics has always had a social aspect." Verberg (1974, p.193), for one, traces the two main trends in doctrinal theories of language (what this study will be calling linguistic formalism and functionalism, see Chapter Two) back to "the old philosophical opposition between Heraclitus (c.540-c.480BC) and the Eleatic school (Parmenides, c.40BC.)." And Taylor (1990b, p. 12) proposes that "the issues and puzzles facing linguistic theory today are in almost every case contemporary retreads of issues and puzzles that have appeared and reappeared in Western linguistic thought since it was first written down. (...)

1

contemporary theory remains entranced by the same problems our ancestors have been attempting to solve for over two thousand years."

The history of sociolinguistics obviously does not start with the first person who used the term, nor the first institutional use of the term; nor is the field defined by any one person or point of view. But what *does* define sociolinguistics remains a problem. In Hymes' (1974a, p. 195) words: "The term 'sociolinguistics' means many things to many people, and of course no one has a patent on its definition. Indeed not everyone whose work is called 'sociolinguistic' is ready to accept the label, and those who do use the term include and emphasize different things."

A review of working definitions of the field shows a family resemblance, but it is very difficult to pinpoint what is causing this resemblance. Sociolinguistics is "the study of the characteristics of language varieties, the characteristics of their functions, and the characteristics of their speakers as these three constantly interact, change and change one another within a speech community" (Fishman, 1971, p. 4). Sociolinguistics "should be regarded as a new effort to deal more realistically and comprehensively with the facts of language. One of these basic facts is that language is part of social life" (Neubert, 1976, p. 154). Sociolinguistics "attempts to make a coherent statement about the relationship between language use and social patterns or structures of various kinds" (Romaine, 1982, p. 1). Sociolinguistics places "stress on *parole*, on the speech act in all its social dimensions" (Giglioli, 1972, p. 8). Sociolinguistics "studies the varied linguistic realizations of socio-cultural meanings...the currency of everyday social interactions which are nevertheless relative to particular cultures, societies, social groups, speech communities, languages, dialects, varieties, styles" (Pride, 1970, p. 301). Sociolinguistics "is that part of linguistics which is concerned with language as a social and cultural phenomenon" (Trudgill, 1974, p. 32). Sociolinguistics is the interplay between the fact that language varies and the fact that variation is used to define the social situation, defining the speaker in terms of "what her group loyalties are, how she perceives her relationship to her hearer, and what sort of speech event she considers herself to be engaged in" (Fasold, 1984, p.ix). Sociolinguistics is "the study of language in relation to society" (Hudson, 1980, p. 1).

What might these various interpretations of sociolinguistics have in common and how would these definitions delimit sociolinguistics as a discipline? They seem to emphasize variation and diversity; the socio-cultural nature of language; and that the focus of sociolinguistics should be on *parole*/language use, interaction and meaning. These definitions are broad enough to include a wide range of topics as proper concern for sociolinguistics, from the choice of varieties on the part of governments or institutions (language policy, language planning) and on the part of groups of individuals (variation studies), to the choice of discourse strategies in specific situations (discourse analysis, pragmatics), to the choice of linguistic genre in speech events (the ethnography of communication, stylistics). This is not an exhaustive list, nor is it non-controversial. Levinson (1983), for example, spends an entire section of a chapter defining pragmatics in such a way that it would not be subsumed under sociolinguistics and most of these headings (discourse analysis, pragmatics etc.) are listed separately from sociolinguistics in library catalogues, publishing catalogues and annotated bibliographies.

Sociolinguistics may be seen as a special type of linguistic method (for example, "secular linguistics"; see Trudgill 1974a for that term); an application or extension of existing linguistic theory (for example, studies in linguistic variation as originally proposed by Labov); a unique sort of interdisciplinary field (something Hymes has suggested, see Chapter Three); a sub-field of sociology or anthropology; or a separate linguistic paradigm.

This problem of definition is in no way unique to sociolinguistics. Parret (1983, p. 1), for example, notes that "semiotics strikes skeptics as having neither a precise object nor a method of its own, thus as *not* being a *discipline* but rather a vaguely defined field of studies, a repertoire of interests that is not at all unified" (Emphasis in original). This sort of discontent with the state of sociolinguistics has been frequently expressed. In 1970, de Camp states that "at present, sociolinguistics is at worst a poorly-defined interdisciplinary activity, at best an empirical discipline without a theoretical basis" (de Camp, 1970, p. 158). And in 1974, some ten years after establishing a theoretical framework for sociolinguistics, Hymes (1974a, p. 194) cautions that "sociolinguistics might drift indefinitely, profuse and shallow, a mile wide and an inch deep." In 1980, Durmuller continues this critical trend seeing "the need for an integrating theory", and suggesting that "one of the tasks awaiting American sociolinguistics in the 80's...is to provide us with a unifying perspective on its many and diverse branches" (Durmuller, 1980, p. 5). Currie in 1981, almost thirty years after his initial call for a sociolinguistic discipline notes that "it is now time for sociolinguistics to devote more exacting consideration toward theoretical accuracy and sufficiency. We are in danger of finding ourselves abstracted in a frustrating area of speculative profusion insufficiently controlled by definition and inadequately guided by empirically tested hypothesis and systematic theory" (Currie, 1981, p. 5). And in 1985, Muysken complains that "it seems as if the enormous development of linguistics in the last twenty years has passed by sociolinguistics, and also as if the developments in sociology have not been incorporated" (Muysken, 1985, p. 13).

Why all this discontent? Why the need for a unified theory, "empirically tested hypothesis", "systematic theory," and the like? What do sociolinguists want? Underneath these types of complaints are certain assumptions about what a discipline should be like, therefore what sociolinguistics should be like. Underneath the definitions of sociolinguistics above lie assumptions about what language is, what linguistics is, what linguistics should focus on, and so forth. It is the unquestioned assumptions which underlie these types of statements which are of special interest to this study.

Purpose of Study

This study is concerned with two connected metatheoretical problems in sociolinguistics: what defines sociolinguistics as a field either within or apart from linguistics generally, and how does a definition of sociolinguistics relate to the development and application of sociolinguistic theoretical models. The purpose of this study is not so much to trace the origins or development of sociolinguistics (though this would be a useful endeavor) but to ask the following question: what is modern sociolinguistics in relationship to modern received linguistics? Part of answering this question requires also answering another question: what is sociolinguistics? But in attempting to define sociolinguistics one becomes entangled in prior metatheoretical questions having to do with larger issues of epistemology, ontology, ideology and historical developments in philosophy, science and the humanities. It becomes difficult to separate out the web of prior unanswered questions when attempting to define sociolinguistics in a non-trivial way.

For this reason this study approaches the question of sociolinguistics from the vantage point of metatheory. By metatheory is meant the underlying beliefs which generate a particular approach. Another word for metatheory, may be ideology or theoretical presupposition. In attempting to understand sociolinguistics from a metatheoretical perspective this study places sociolinguistics within a tradition of longstanding discourse on the nature of reality, knowledge, description and explanation.

However, the point of this study is not to define sociolinguistics, but rather to examine how leading sociolinguists have defined sociolinguistics and what this might add to an understanding of theories of language. Specifically, this study looks in detail at three leading sociolinguists, Dell Hymes, William Labov, and John Gumperz. The three different approaches that they have proposed are reviewed in terms of what these approaches express about a sociolinguistic theory of language and therefore what they say about a sociolinguistic theory of linguistics. As will be elaborated below, this is a rather narrow, though representative, sampling of sociolinguistic theory.

The Approach

Content

This study will look in detail at the work of Dell Hymes, William Labov and John Gumperz. In each case (a separate chapter for each individual's work) how they have defined sociolinguistics is examined, including how they compare their approach with other sociolinguistic approaches, then their sociolinguistic theory is placed in relation to received linguistic theory. In this way their work is placed in a dialogue with other contemporary linguistic theories. Important aspects of their theories are then examined in order to highlight the diversity of theories of language and diversity of methods available in the field of linguistics.

This study in no way claims to represent the true, absolute or correct interpretation of the works of Hymes, Labov, and Gumperz (or anyone else under review). Nor does it claim to represent the actual beliefs or feelings of anyone being addressed. This study is based on a rather narrow, public, and to a great part, decontextualized representation of the positions held by these sociolinguists, in that interpretations are based solely on their writings – writings which span three decades and which were written for different purposes and within different contexts.

In addition to the above stated procedure, this study also discusses larger metatheoretical questions which frame the work of these individual linguists. These are questions of philosophy having to do with such things as the nature of knowledge in relation to the world. These sorts of questions exist within the longstanding tradition in Western discourse of competing theories such as realism versus relativism, rationalism versus empiricism, and so forth. These general questions are addressed in Chapter Two on traditional Western metatheory, but each chapter on the individual sociolinguists is also framed in terms of these sorts of questions. Thus, Hymes is framed in terms of relativism, Labov in terms of realism, and Gumperz in terms of intentionality.

As mentioned earlier, the point of this study is not to define sociolinguistics; however, a particular way of looking at sociolinguistics is suggested (see Chapter Six). It is suggested that sociolinguistics be defined in terms of a linguistics of particularity and that this particularity is based on the nature of utterance/*parole* discourse.[1]

Fasold (1986) has noted that there are three kinds of linguistic analyses based on, one, a biological definition where the concern is with the "language acquisition device" or the "language faculty" in the brain (Chomsky, 1986); two, a social definition of language where the concern is with language users and language in "context" (see, e.g. Schiffrin 1987); and three, a platonic definition of language where the concern is not with mental states, knowledge or social action but abstract objects and mathematical principles (Katz 1981). Fasold notes, however, that *in practice* the first and third types of linguistic analyses, despite their theoretical differences, end up being the same (Fasold, 1983, pp. 8-9). A primary reason why the two are the same in practice is because their object of study is the same: sentences (whether abstract without reference to psychology or idealized but psychologically real), and that why they differ (or should differ) from the contextual approach, is that this approach is concerned with utterance, which by its very nature is contextualized.

In this study, therefore, in addition to discussing the general metatheoretical issues which surround linguistic theory, as well as looking in detail at the work of Hymes, Labov and Gumperz, there is also a development of a specific perspective on sociolinguistics; a perspective which is particularistic and which is utterance based. This is certainly not an original perspective (see, for example Giglioli's definition of sociolinguistics above as placing "stress on *parole*"), but it is one which can do with further argument.

Context: Linguistic Historiography

Though this study is not purely historiographic, it is informed by linguistic historiography and it is based on a historical approach.

Both Andresen (1990) and Taylor (1990b) have made the point that the field of linguistic historiography is undergoing growth. There are international and regional organizations dedicated to the study of the history of linguistics and a great number of publications on the subject.[2] Andresen and Taylor suggest that there are a number of reasons for doing linguistic historiography. These reasons include the recording of linguistic history; the uncovering of hitherto undiscovered or forgotten "facts"; the need for preventive measures – a historically informed field will not attempt to reinvent the wheel; the need for the historiographer as referee or mediator between competing schools of thought (Andresen, 1990, pp. 243-244); and the better understanding of contemporary theory through understanding the historical foundations of that theory (Taylor, 1990b, p. 2).

Andresen's preferred reason for doing linguistic historiography, is:

> to lay bare the sometimes unconscious assumptions that linguists bring to their theories of language and to follow the consequences of those assumptions through the elaboration of the theories, often over long periods of time. If we choose, we might also simultaneously reconstruct the philosophical and sociological contexts within which particular periods of linguistic activity take place. This examination of the historical record provides us with a broad perspective on the variety of factors which contribute to the construction of a theory of language. (Andresen, 1987, p. 647.)

Similarly, Taylor (1990b, pp. 13-14) suggests that "linguistic historiography as a mode of intellectual inquiry...comes naturally to address the topic of the foundations of linguistic theories, whether these foundations are sought in narrative of historical influence, in accounts of social or political contexts, or in rhetorical analyses of the conceptual features of the practice of theorizing itself." Taylor's preferred reason for doing linguistic historiography is to understand the nature of theorizing itself.

There are therefore many reasons for doing linguistic historiography, including one given by Breky (1986, p. 2) which differs from those mentioned above: "Every generation of linguists will, in so far as there is a necessity for historiographical research at all, write its own history." The historiographic basis of this study is partly motivated by Breky's claim that each generation will write its own history. But primarily it follows Andresen and Taylor's concern with understanding the foundations of linguistic theory and the nature of theorizing itself. Therefore, though the writings examined are placed within a philosophical context, they are usually not placed within a sociological context; nor are they placed within historical contexts which are not directly linguistic.

Context: Kuhn and the History of Science

In addition to this general historiographic context, this study is framed in terms of Thomas Kuhn's (1962, 1977) work on the history of science and on his three levels of paradigm. Though Kuhn's notion of the way science develops is deficient, his notion of paradigms and his distinction between "normal science" and "revolutionary science" is interesting.

Thomas Kuhn's book *The Structure of Scientific Revolutions*, published in 1962, has had an immense impact on the philosophy of science, the sociology of knowledge and on the development of non-positivist perspectives generally. (See Gutting (ed) 1980 for appraisals of Kuhn's work.) One of Kuhn's major contributions is to portray science and scientists not as transcendent of ordinary socio-historical processes but as participants in these processes. Therefore, rather than the history of science being portrayed as a linear progression to ever greater knowledge and progress, and the scientific community portrayed as some objective and ideal entity, Kuhn portrays the history of science in terms of conflict: a scientific community made up of conflicting social values. Not only did Kuhn bring value into a scientific discourse which typically excluded value as an element in science, but to make matters more controversial, Kuhn introduced a relativist notion of value. (For a discussion of relativism and value see Herrnstein Smith 1988.) Kuhn portrays the history of science as one of competing systems of incompatible values. He proposes that the structure of scientific revolutions is the complete replacement of one competing system with another. These value systems Kuhn calls paradigms.

In *The Structure of Scientific Revolutions* Kuhn uses the term paradigm in a number of different ways. He uses the term initially to refer to the traditional examples that a novice in a scientific field is exposed to and which she must master to become a full member of that field. Kuhn later termed this use of paradigm "exemplars". Kuhn also uses the term to mean the shared beliefs of a community of practitioners as to how one goes about practicing in their field (what counts as data, good methodology, valid argument, etc.). This Kuhn went on to term a "disciplinary matrix". In addition, Kuhn uses the term paradigm to refer to what one might term a world view. This world view, or perceptual framework, Kuhn (1962, p. 112) considered "prerequisite to perception itself. What a man sees depends both upon what he looks at and also upon what his previous visual-conceptual experience has taught him to see."

Eckberg and Hill (1980) take these three usages of paradigm and show that they may be said to exist on three different levels, the metaphysical (paradigm as world view), the sociological (paradigm as disciplinary matrix) and the concrete (paradigm as exemplar). These three levels of paradigm are integral and are related in a complex way. Hypothetically, it is possible that the exemplars that one is exposed to as a novice implicitly introduce one to the values of the disciplinary matrix, the matrix itself then instills and polices these values, and these values become the perceptual framework with which one views the world. It is also possible that one starts out with a particular world view which the disciplinary matrix supports, and that the exemplars with which one works, as well as the disciplinary matrix, further reinforce this world view. In looking at sociolinguistics this study considers all three levels to be of interest, and is structured in terms of these three levels.

I support Kuhn's relativist beliefs that knowledge and values are contingent rather than objective or independent. I also support Kuhn's anti-positivism which considers scientific behavior as behavior which should be viewed, like any other behavior, as following the social constraints of much of behavior generally while having particular tendencies of its own. Therefore, this study examines sociolinguistics not as an ever progressive accumulation of knowledge approaching some ideal, but as a diverse, multiplex, loosely related and emergent entity. It therefore looks at different approaches to sociolinguistics from the perspective of paradigm differences rather than from the assumption of universality or uniformity.

However, I do not subscribe to Kuhn's notion of how a change from one scientific paradigm to another takes place. Kuhn's work is within the "hard" sciences, in particular physics. He is concerned with, for example, how we got from Newton's physics to Einstein's physics. Kuhn's explanation for major paradigm shifts, "scientific revolutions" as he calls them, is that there is a process whereby normal science breaks down; it is unable to account for more and more important data; and a new paradigm takes over, one which, paradoxically, may in fact not address the questions of the previous paradigm.

In Kuhn's scheme, under normal science the basic presuppositions of the field are not questioned and the same exemplars are recreated over and over. When problems arise, they are not seen as fundamentally challenging the paradigm but instead adjustments are made. In contrast, under revolutionary science, the presuppositions of the field are questioned and rejected. A paradigm of irreconcilable difference then takes the place of the previous paradigm and a revolution has taken place. Kuhn maintained that a mature science has only one dominant paradigm at a time but immature sciences have simultaneous competing paradigms.

Kuhn's version of history is too categorical and lacking in attention to developmental processes. Whether this is a correct assessment or not, Kuhn's scheme does not adequately account for the history of linguistics where one finds throughout its history, co-existence of competing paradigms. (Of course in Kuhn's defense one could simply claim that linguistics is and always has been an "immature" science, hence the existence of various approaches at any given time.) Hyme's (1974b) assessment of the history of the linguistics as competing cynosures is therefore more appealing. Hymes' (1974b, p. 10) writes of the competing "paradigmatic communities":

> In their political aspect each approach in turn has dominated journals, professional meetings, textbooks and the like. But neither has been exclusive holder of the stage. Each has had the center, but not the whole....In the case of linguistics, at least, other approaches than the dominant ones continued, and indeed sometimes emerged contemporaneously. One can say that each dominant approach was successively the *cynosure* of its discipline. One can say that its participants, and others around them, had a *consciousness* of a revolutionary change, and that there was indeed a *paradigmatic community* [emphasis in original]. The paradigmatic community, however, has never come to be equivalent to the whole of the discipline....Each new 'paradigm' simply has not succeeded in establishing complete authority.

Nevertheless, when attempting to place a scholar or a school of thought in relation to other scholars or schools of thought within linguistics, Kuhn's notion of normal science is useful. Whether someone sets out to continue or reform a tradition and does not question the fundamental tenets of that tradition, or whether someone sets out to radically question or reformulate a tradition, is an interesting way to make historical comparisons. This study therefore uses the notion of normal and revolutionary science as a means for comparing the sociolinguists reviewed. Did they set out to make their approach more or less like received linguistics? Did they see the goal of sociolinguistics as belonging to normal science or revolutionary science?

Related to Kuhn's notion of normal and revolutionary science, as well as to Hymes' notion of a paradigmatic community and cynosures, are the terms *received linguistics* and *received linguistic theory* which will be used throughout this study. Recall above Hymes' (1974b, p. 10) proposition that certain linguistic traditions have "in their political aspect...dominated journals, professional meetings, textbooks and the like." The terms received linguistics/received linguistic theory are meant to reflect this political reality. The received position is that which under normal science is accepted as authoritative and true. It is quite simply that which has the most institutional power. However, received theory has a much longer historical existence than any specific manifestation of it. For example, at various times Saussure's linguistics, Bloomfield's linguistics, or Chomsky's linguistics will be referred to as received, though the linguistics of Saussure, Bloomfield and Chomsky have fundamental differences. However, it is in their fundamental similarities that we find the received position.

First there is the question of institutional power. At various times in recent history the views represented by these men have dominated linguistic discourse as well as dominated major areas within the linguistic community in terms of journals, jobs, etc. (See Newmeyer 1986 and Taylor 1990a for two different views on the political dominance of generative linguistics.) In addition, the work of sociolinguists is often an ongoing discourse with received linguistics, often in direct and indirect dialogue with these men, for example, Hymes in dialogue with Chomsky over the nature of competence. (See Chapter Three.)

However, there is a second more powerful reason why Saussure, Bloomfield and Chomsky, despite their differences as to the nature of language, may be considered practitioners of received linguistic theory. This is because the three demonstrate certain fundamental similarities as to the scientific basis of linguistics: that there is an objective entity which linguists study, that it is independent of the humans who use it, and that it is only the "core" aspects of this entity, i.e. formal grammar, which is the object of linguistic enquiry. That this is the received linguistic position can be witnessed by opening any college catalogue for courses offered and requirements to be met, or by scanning titles in linguistic journals.[3]

Received linguistics, then, is the normal science assumptions about the object of linguistic enquiry, the core values of linguistics, in relation to which sociolinguistics is usually positioned on the periphery. (A more detailed explanation of received linguistics can be found in Chapter Two in the discussion on Formalist Linguistics.)

Overview of Study

Structure

As already mentioned, this study is structured in terms of Kuhn's three levels of paradigm. It is therefore divided into three parts. Part One, which corresponds with Chapter Two, is the metaphysical level – a paradigm as a world view. First, an argument is presented as to why it is important to consider paradigm assumptions which underlie theoretical discourse. Then using Markova 1982, traditional divisions in Western thought, between what Markova calls the Cartesian and Hegelian Frameworks, are discussed. These opposing world views are then related to the historical division in linguistic theory between what is often known as the formalist and functionalist linguistic paradigms. Finally, sociolinguistics is related to both the larger questions raised by Markova and the traditional division in linguistics between formalism and functionalism.

Part Two, which corresponds with Chapters Three through Five, is the disciplinary matrix level – paradigm as a sociological entity, what Hymes referred to earlier as a "paradigmatic community". In Chapter Three, the work of Dell Hymes and his approach to sociolinguistics, which is related to the disciplinary matrix usually known as the ethnography of communication, is reviewed. This chapter is framed in terms of relativism, both philosophical relativism and linguistic relativism. In Chapter Four, the work of William Labov and his approach to sociolinguistics, which is related to the disciplinary matrix usually known as linguistic variation, is reviewed. This chapter is framed in terms of realism, both philosophical realism and scientific realism. In Chapter Five, the work of John Gumperz and his approach to sociolinguistics, which is related to the disciplinary matrix usually known as interactional sociolinguistics, is reviewed. This chapter is framed in terms of intentionality and the interpretation of social meaning.

Part Three, which corresponds with Chapter Six, is the construct level – paradigm as a unit of analysis or exemplar. This chapter argues that sociolinguistics is based on the study of utterance. Utterance is defined in terms of context, universals and particulars, and the sentence/utterance distinction. Using Bakhtin and Wittgenstein as frames, a linguistics of particularity based on the study of utterance is suggested.

In Chapter Seven, the concluding chapter, the disciplinary matrixes under discussion are briefly compared in terms of what they have to say about sociolinguistics as linguistics, what they have to say about theories of language, and in terms of Kuhn's notion of normal and revolutionary science. The chapter concludes with questions about the future of sociolinguistics.

Limited Range of Focus

Fasold (1984, 1990), in writing two separate texts on the field of sociolinguistics, makes a distinction between what he calls the sociolinguistics of society and the sociolinguistics of language. Trudgill in his editor's preface to the 1990 volume explains that the *Sociolinguistics of Society* is concerned with "those areas of the subject that lie towards the societal end of the language and society continuum. The *Sociolinguistics of Language*...[concentrates] on those aspects of sociolinguistics which are more central concern to linguists(...)."

If one follows this distinction, this study is focused on the sociolinguistics of language rather than the sociolinguistics of society: on what sort of linguistics is sociolinguistics – what does sociolinguistics say about theories of language. However, one could equally ask what sort of sociology or anthropology is sociolinguistics. Instead of looking at the works of Hymes, Labov and Gumperz in terms of linguistic constructs, or theories of language, one could have looked at the social and cultural constructs and theories of society that these works reveal. Indeed there are many important questions to ask along these lines. Likewise, one could look at works traditionally done within the sociolinguistics of society and ask what sort of linguistics do they reveal. It is not that there are no theories of language in the former and no theories of society in the latter; quite on the contrary, it is simply a matter of what one chooses to focus on.

The three sociolinguists, on whom this study concentrates, represent a cross section of the field of sociolinguistics but they in no way represent the field generally. Both Hymes and Gumperz have backgrounds in anthropological linguistics, and the early collaboration between Gumperz and Hymes (cf. Gumperz and Hymes 1964, 1972) created much of the foundation for their respective sociolinguistic theories, (for example, Hymes' and Gumperz's notion of communicative competence), so, though there are important differences between their two approaches to sociolinguistics there is also much continuity. My choice of Hymes and Gumperz therefore weights my analysis of sociolinguistics heavily to one side.

There are many important sociolinguists and approaches to sociolinguistics which are not discussed in this study. For example, Halliday and systemics; C-J Bailey and developmental linguistics; Joshua Fishman and the sociology of language. Pidgin and creole studies are not discussed, nor is linguistic variation except as it applies to the work of William Labov, nor applied sociolinguistics, nor stylistics except as it applies to the work of Hymes and Gumperz.[4] This focus is of course ultimately limited by time and space. However, these three approaches, which span developments in sociolinguistics of over thirty years, are representative of both sociolinguistics as an institution and sociolinguistics as a diverse body of theory.

Review of Related Sociolinguistic Literature

There is certainly no lack for general purviews of the field of sociolinguistics as can be witnessed by the many textbooks devoted to the description of the field, (e.g., Fishman 1971; Trudgill 1974a, Hudson 1980; Downes 1983; Fasold 1984, 1990; Wardhaugh 1986) as well as general works not necessarily intended as textbooks (e.g. Dittmar 1976; Bell 1976), and edited collections of general scope (e.g. Bright 1966; Giglioli 1972; Gumperz and Hymes 1972; Shuy 1973; Baugh and Sherzer, 1984; Ammon, et al. 1987). These general works include discussions of critical theory to varying degrees, dependent greatly on the purpose of the publication. Broadly speaking, however, general works have tended to spend less time on general discussions of theory and more time on specific details of description, or specific questions of definition be it, for example, defining a speech community, or defining languages and dialects in relation to each other in discussions of multilingualism.

Likewise, though there does exist a diverse body of critical theoretical work, this work has tended to concentrate on specific problems. These problems may be of a definitional nature (for example, the now traditional discussions over the term "speech community" such as Romaine, 1982). Problems may be methodological (e.g. Milroy 1987), or related to constructs such as class (e.g. Dittmar 1976; Svejcer and Nikol'skij 1986), or frameworks, such as arguments over "interactional" versus "correlational" approaches (e.g. Gumperz and Hymes [1972] 1986).

Neubert 1976, Aracil 1978, Durmiller 1980, Miller, 1981, Peng 1982, Giesbers 1985, Muysken 1985, and Van de Craen 1985 are all examples of sociolinguists who have addressed issues of sociolinguistic metatheory, attempting to define sociolinguistics in relation to linguistic theory; but their works are in article form, and are therefore not able to explore the problem in depth.

There are also sociolinguists who have developed complete theories of sociolinguistics which include the types of metatheoretical questions raised in this study, as well as an explicit theory of language and an explicit methodology. Fasold (1990:157-164) proposes Charles-James Bailey as such a sociolinguist. Michael Halliday (1978, 1985) is another sociolinguist who has developed a complete theory of sociolinguistics. Though they do not present the degree of formal explicitness that Bailey and Halliday have developed, Dell Hymes, William Labov and John Gumperz have also developed complete theories of sociolinguistics.[5] (There are no doubt other sociolinguists of the modern era that are here overlooked.)

By looking at these three sociolinguists in detail, the nature of their sociolinguistic theories (or more correctly this interpretation of their theories) may be more easily accessible to those looking for (and often not finding) sociolinguistic theory. What is hoped is a return to critical theoretical discourse in sociolinguistics: an acknowledgement that there is a very deep and rich body of sociolinguistic theory which when framed in a metatheoretical light can become not only accessible but can highlight the important, and overlooked, place of the contribution of sociolinguistic theory to general linguistic discourse. This discussion of Hymes, Labov, and Gumperz and the foundations of sociolinguistic theory may be to many minds slightly off or downright wrong, but such detailed discussion will at least stimulate a reassessment of sociolinguistic theory and a stimulation of questions for the future. In this way, those beginning in the field of sociolinguistics may find a historical and philosophical background in which to place the exemplars into which they are being socialized.

Notes

[1] The terms "*parole*", "utterance" and "discourse" are related but not always interchangeable. See Chapter Six for a detailed discussion of utterance and the relationship of utterance to *parole* and discourse. I prefer to use the term utterance over the term "language use" which implies that there is a discrete entity "language" which exists independently and which is somehow being "used" (itself a vague notion). However, I do use the term "language use" in this study because it becomes difficult when discussing issues raised by those who present their arguments in terms of language use not to also use it.

[2] There are, for example, the International Association for the History of the Language Sciences and the North American Association for the History of the Language Sciences. Konrad Koerner, one of the leading linguistic historiographers, is the editor of a series *Studies in the History of the Language Sciences* which is published by John Benjamins Publishing Company and which has over fifty titles. There are also other series including one edited by Talbot Taylor on the *History of Linguistic Thought* which is published by Routledge.

[3] Leonard Bloomfield (1933) in writing about linguistics as a discipline distinguishes between "main stream" and "not in the main stream". (See Andresen 1990, p. 12 for this reference.) Though the "core" of linguistics has shifted over the century and certain aspects of the field, such as the importance of historical linguistics, have waxed and waned, there has remained a fairly stable core, though it may have had different labels over the years. The core consists of the study of sentence form/structure, in specific, the aspects of grammar which in current parlance may be listed as segmental phonology, morphology and syntax. Semantics is less marginal than it once was and linguistic pragmatics has made some inroads. Undergraduate (and graduate) requirements reflect this notion of core. At Georgetown University, for example, graduate students at the Masters level are required to take a "core" exam which has four basic areas of questioning: phonetics or phonology, morphology or syntax, historical linguistics, and semantics or pragmatics.

[4] Deborah Cameron (1990, p. 83) rhetorically asks if the fact that Fasold (1984) titled his first volume the sociolinguistics of society rather than the sociology of language is because "perhaps the term 'sociology of language' no longer sells books to linguists?" Cameron who is arguing against the lack of social theory in sociolinguistics, asserts that there has been a collapse of Fishman's distinction between the sociology of language and a linguistics focused sociolinguistics. Cameron interprets this collapse as being "a shift in the consensus about what properly constitutes the study of language in society, and it is a shift away from the sociological towards the more purely linguistic. (ibid)." Though this study is focused on the linguistic end of the spectrum it is

in no way suggesting that the social end is not at least equally important. In fact it is somewhat ironical that sociolinguistics might be seen as moving away from the sociology of language because my experience is that most work listed under the title sociolinguistics in library and publishing catalogues is of an obvious social and not always obvious linguistic nature. Since this study does not include a chapter on the sociology of language, here is a brief outline of the work done in the sociology of language and applied sociolinguistics.

One of the foundational works in the field of sociolinguistics is Fishman's "The sociology of language." According to Fishman, "The sociology of language examines the interaction between these two aspects of human behavior: use of language and the social organization of behavior. Briefly put, the sociology of language focuses upon the entire gamut of topics related to the social organization of language behavior, including not only language usage per se but also language attitudes, overt behavior toward language and toward language user." (Fishman in Giglioli, 1972, p. 45).

Fishman includes within the sociology of language, descriptive sociolinguistics which "seeks to provide an answer to the question 'who speaks (or writes) what language (or what language variety) to whom and when and to what in end?'"; dynamic sociolinguistics which "tries to explain why and how the social organization of language use and behavior toward language have become selectively different in the same social networks or communities on two different occasions. (...) and why and how two once similar social networks or communities have arrived at a quite different social organization of language use and behavior toward language"; and applied sociolinguistics which is the application of the sociology of language to "topics normally considered within the field of applied linguistics" and applied sociology (Fishman in Giglioli, 1972, p. 45-57).

The sociology of language is therefore both synchronic and diachronic and has a very broad focus including such areas as language attitudes, language planning and policy, multilingualism and speech communities, language and politics, and situational use of language such as code switching. In addition, applied sociolinguistics has developed into a wide range of concerns including, language and education, language and the professions, language and communication. (See, Shuy 1984; Trudgill 1984; Fasold 1990).

[5] By a complete theory is not meant that the theory is without problems, inconsistencies, or holes, nor that it is finalized or exhaustive. Rather, by "complete" is meant that it is whole and presents a somewhat complex and integrated theory of language. There is also no *a priori* criteria for whether or not a theory can count as a theory, for example, that it must be predictive, have universals, and have mathematical or logical formulae. A complete theory, is more simply a means of understanding and explaining phenomena in a thorough and metatheoretically motivated way.

Part One — Paradigms: The Metaphysical Level

2

Foundations of Sociolinguistic Theory

Paradigms may be prior to, more binding, and more complete than any set of rules for research that could be unequivocally abstracted from them.

Thomas Kuhn,1962, p. 46

It thus seems that it is both conceptually and psychologically impossible to develop a scientific framework that owes nothing to philosophical preconceptions concerning the nature of the world and the nature of man, and nothing to epistemological assumptions.

Ivana Markova, 1982, p. 5

The Need for "Metaworries"[1]

This chapter is concerned with the following types of questions: On what basis do linguists make decisions over such issues as what does or does not count as linguistics? What is or is not "good" linguistics? What is the best way to do linguistics? How do linguists value one type of linguistic analysis over another, or one type of linguistic model over another?

These types of questions, which concern decision making, choice and value amongst linguists, like questions of value and taste generally, are answered based upon fundamental assumptions as to what is normal, good, bad, pleasing, elegant, expedient, and so on, and in the case of scientific linguistics, what is normal, good, bad, pleasing, elegant, expedient in science.

When viewing internal theoretical arguments within the field of linguistics, such as over what are or are not valid ways of doing, conceiving of, or talking about linguistics, it becomes clear that these arguments are not based solely on specific differences as to what constitutes valid linguistic principles or linguistic methods, but are more deeply found in basic differences in underlying metatheoretical assumptions. These are often incompatible assumptions as to the nature of the world, the nature of knowledge, the nature of society, the nature of "scientific" enquiry, the role of linguists, and so forth. These basic differences hold far greater weight than can be captured in the particularities of any one specific argument within the field of linguistics. Because these differences are metatheoretical, to not approach them from a metatheoretical perspective is to analyze differences in linguistic theory in a shallow way, one which will not add much insight to understanding general developments in the field of linguistics.

17

If paradigm assumptions profoundly influence our choices and values, then the fundamental assumptions underlying a particular work, or field, should be considered. Paradigm presuppositions: "the set of background assumptions which one makes about the nature and limits of one's subject matter, the method of studying it, and what counts as evidence, and which determines the form that theories take"(Leech, 1983, p. 3) are the motivational forces from which a work is derived.

Ivana Markova (1982) in her book *Paradigms, Thought and Language*, notes that we become oblivious to the presuppositions upon which our norms, beliefs and routines are based. And she adds: "In fact, some ways of cognizing and believing, such as prejudging, stereotyping and religious and political believing, are often so deeply rooted in our social realities that even the suggestion of an alternative way of seeing the social world may provoke violent reactions" (Markova, 1982, p. 1).

According to Markova, there are dangers in not considering paradigm assumptions: "First, being unaware of our presuppositions, we are unable to reflect upon them and consequently unable to consider alternatives to the adopted ways of thinking and researching. Secondly, we are liable to make unjustified generalizations across different subjects" (Markova, 1982, p. 3).

The first danger suggested by Markova can be witnessed in one's inability to acknowledge the existence of work done from a fundamentally different perspective, or to grasp its import or its meaning. This leads to a dogmatic approach which is dismissive and exclusive, unable to acknowledge or encourage alternative ways of perceiving and acting. This may lead to a stifling of dialogue or dissent, to stagnation and uncritical orthodoxy. The second danger is the tendency to over-generalize, to extend one's program universally, without questioning whether one's point of view may be universally applicable or not. This tendency may lead to the willful exclusion of data, results, etc. which do not conform to one's presupposed notions of reality. Or it may lead to the inclusion of data, results, etc. which initially do not conform but which are then transformed in some way to conform to one's presuppositions.

In addition to these risks outlined by Markova, there are a number of useful reasons for considering metatheory. It is at the paradigm level that we are able to see fundamental differences, or fundamental similarities, in works which may or may not seem similar or different on the more concrete level of theoretical models, methods, or applications. In this way, for example, one can compare works across history, because the paradigm level allows one to make comparisons across time, place and specific theoretical models. It is also at this paradigm level that one can explain problems or inconsistencies in particular models, methods or applications. For example, a particular work may reveal certain tensions between competing paradigms which have led to certain anomalous elements in that particular model.[2]

Roger Lass (1980) has complained that most linguists seem to avoid "metaworries", that there is some kind of distaste for concerning oneself with metatheory which should be left to philosophers while real linguists get on with **DOING** linguistics. Lass (1980, p. ix) points out that the separation between 'real' linguistics and 'metalinguistics' is untenable. He suggests that it is untenable because linguistics is "one of these argument based subjects...about anything interesting that linguists come up with is the result of a complex interaction between argumentative strategies and (ultimately largely theory-defined) 'data'". Given then that the work linguists do is deeply influenced by paradigm assumptions, the relationship between linguistics and metatheory is an important one to study.

Markova's Frameworks

Despite what has been said above, paradigms are not deterministic. One can change one's beliefs and one can maintain conflicting beliefs at the same time. In addition, one must get beyond the paradigm level and look very closely at the specifics of any given theory in order to understand that theory within its own boundaries. Nevertheless, when attempting to go across individual theories, and across time, to study a field as a whole, it becomes necessary to be able to identify tendencies, trends, and clusters of defining beliefs. Given that linguistics is not itself a metatheory, in understanding linguistics in terms of general developments, it is useful to look to the philosophical and cultural frameworks which have defined its development.

Markova (1982), has traced the relationship of metatheory, in the form of two Western philosophical-cultural frameworks, to the development of the field of psychology. In doing so she demonstrates how philosophical preconceptions have guided the development of psychological models and methodology, and how given a different set of presuppositions, a different emphasis or explanation could have been reached.

In order to discuss developments in psychology, Markova isolates two large-scale world views or philosophical-cultural frameworks which have remained quite consistent over the time-span of what one might call the Western intellectual tradition. She names these the Cartesian and Hegelian frameworks.[3] She isolates the following distinctions between the two frameworks:

Markova's Cartesian and Hegelian Frameworks

CARTESIAN FRAMEWORK	HEGELIAN FRAMEWORK
Nature of mind is individualistic	Nature of mind is social
Mind is static and passive in acquisition of knowledge	Mind is dynamic and active in acquisition of knowledge
Knowledge is acquired through algorithms	Knowledge is acquired through a 'circle returning within itself'

The criterion of knowledge is external (Markova, 1982, p. 6)	The criterion of knowledge is internal

In contrasting the Cartesian and Hegelian frameworks, Markova concentrates on the nature of mind, and the nature of knowledge. The Cartesian framework maintains a theory of knowledge which has as its aim to identify that which is certain. This leads to a search for invariants known as universals. The means by which knowledge (certainty = truth) is attained is through intuition which perceives truth immediately, or through a series of deductive steps in the form of algorithms. Cartesian dualism separates the mind (consciousness) from the body (unconsciousness), and "the inner world [is] epistemologically prior to the outer world." Therefore, "interaction between the thinking subject and the rest of the world [is] not considered by the Cartesian paradigm" (Markova, 1982, p. 20,23).

Evolutionary and developmental processes in the Cartesian framework are considered in terms of innate predetermined structures and functions, and are viewed therefore as ahistorical states. The laws of thought are pure logic (separate from other cognitive activities such as feeling) and consist most importantly of the law of identity (a thing is what it is), the law of non-contradiction (a thing cannot be something and not be something at the same time) and the law of the excluded middle (a thing has a property or does not have a property and there is no third possibility) (Markova, 1982, p. 24).

In contrast, the Hegelian framework rejects body-mind duality and instead insists on an integrationist approach: "mind and body, mind and medium, are dependent on each other, for their growth and their very existence" (Markova, 1982, p. 136). It is through interaction with the world that consciousness develops, and the subject object relationship is not unconnected: "both partners in the interaction, both the knowing subject and the object of his knowing, are gradually transformed" (Markova, 1982, p. 178). Knowledge is not acquired through algorithms, but through the reflexive process of a circle returning within itself; that is, with each experience our consciousness is altered. There is an innate basis for structures and functions, but it is a potential which emerges and changes within a particular interactive context.

The Hegelian framework is therefore significantly historical and developmentally orientated. It rejects the "laws of thought" (the laws of identity, non-contradiction, and the excluded middle) as being purely formal, outside reality, and replaces them with the notion of the dialectic nature of being, whereby it is only through contradiction that things change: "If anything is to develop it must have internal contradiction." (Markova, 1982, p. 164).

Unlike the Cartesian framework, the search is not for invariants but universals realized in particulars. The focus, therefore, is not to "discover the particular features of entities" (as is the Cartesian concern with universals) but to "discover the particular expressions of common features in particular situations or in particular individuals" (Markova, 1982, p. 122).

The Cartesian and Hegelian frameworks are opposing views of the world. In the Cartesian framework, what is of concern are abstract universals which are discrete, essential, objective, eternal and unaffected by human actions. In the Hegelian framework, what is of concern are concrete particulars which are non-discrete, changeable, relative, temporal, and dependent upon human actions. How would these opposing world views relate to such basic issues in linguistics as: the locus of language, the nature of language acquisition, the functions of language, and the relationship between linguistic form and language use?

The Formalist and Functionalist[4] Linguistic Paradigms

It is now common in linguistics to make a distinction between two different types of linguistic frameworks. Lass (1980) has called these "speaker free" and "speaker centered", Peng (1982) "narrow" and "broad" linguistics, Lyons (1977a,b) "micro-linguistics" and "macro-linguistics", Harris (1981) "autonomous" linguistics versus "integrational linguistics", and Hopper (1988) the "A Priori Grammar attitude" and the "Emergence of Grammar attitude". In addition, there is the long standing distinction between "formalist linguistics" and "functionalist linguistics".

Each distinction made between the two types of linguistic frameworks, such as those listed above, captures a different element of comparison, a different historical context, a different emphasis; therefore one cannot be simply substituted for the other. In Lass's distinction, "speaker-free" linguistics is concerned with an abstract platonic linguistic system which exists without reference to the particularities of individual speakers or instances of speech. In contrast, "speaker-centered" linguistics is concerned with the totality of actual language use by real language users. This basic distinction is repeated: "narrow- linguistics", "micro-linguistics" and "autonomous linguistics" are also only concerned with an abstract linguistic system, while "broad-linguistics", "macro-linguistics" and "integrational linguistics" consider language in terms of a wide range of phenomena, both linguistic and non-linguistic.

The important distinction here is between concern with essentials, invariants and the notion of pure thought unimpeded by human intervention and concern with particularity and the interactive, context dependent nature of consciousness. Autonomous linguistics has therefore been the study of formal objects or formal systems, either without reference to language users or with reference to idealized language users. In contrast, integrative linguistics has been the study of a broad array of factors related to human existence and the inter-relatedness of language to that existence.

Leech (1983), makes a brief comparison of linguistic formalism and functionalism. Given our previous discussion of the two perceptual frameworks, Leech's following two points are of particular interest:

Formalists (e.g. Chomsky) tend to regard language primarily as a mental phenomenon. Functionalists (e.g. Halliday) tend to regard it primarily as a societal phenomenon. (...)

...Formalists study language as an autonomous system...functionalists study it in relation to its social functions. (Leech, 1983, p. 46.)

Dik (1978), makes a more detailed comparison between formalism and functionalism:

Linguistic Formalism and Linguistic Functionalism

FORMAL PARADIGM	FUNCTIONAL PARADIGM
1. a lg. is a set of sentences	a lg. is an instrument of social interaction
2. the primary function of a lg. is expression of thoughts	the primary function of a language is communication
3. the psychological correlate of language is competence: the capacity to produce, interpret and judge sentences	the psychological correlate of language is communicative competence: the ability to carry on social interaction by means of language
4. the study of competence has logical and methodological priority over the study of performance	the study of the language system must take place within the frame-work of the system of language use
5. the sentences of a lg. must be described independently of the setting (context and of functioning in given situation) in which they are used	the description of linguistic elements of language use must provide points of contact for the description of their settings
6. lg. acquisition is innate input is restricted & unstructured – poverty of stimulus theory	child discovers the system underlying lg. & lg. use aided by extensive & highly structured input of linguistic data presented in natural settings
7. lg. universals are innate properties of the human organism biological and psychological	lg. universals are constraints inherent in the goals of communication, the constitution of lg. users and the settings where language is used

8. syntax is autonomous with respect to semantics; syntax and semantics are autonomous with respect to pragmatics and the priorities run from syntax via semantics to pragmatics
(Dik; 1978, p. 4)[5]

pragmatics is the framework within which semantics and syntax must be studied; semantics is subservient to pragmatics & the priorities run from pragmatics via semantics to syntax

A cursory look at Dik's list quickly shows a striking correspondence between the Formal paradigm and the Cartesian framework and between the Functional paradigm and the Hegelian framework.

Item one: The early Chomskyian definition of a language as a set of sentences expanded to mean something more general, such as an abstract formal system, compared to Dik's functionalist definition of a language as an instrument of social interaction provides a good example of the differing perspectives within not only formalist and functionalist linguistics but also between the Cartesian and Hegelian frameworks. The emphasis of formalist linguistics is on the formal properties of language without reference to function. This is in keeping with the Cartesian preference for platonic objects and the individuality of mind (the mind therefore need not be explained in relation to other minds or to functional manifestations of the mind). The emphasis of functionalist linguistics is on the social interactive properties of language, and therefore form is not considered excluded from function. This is in keeping with the Hegelian preference for interactive explanation and the social nature of mind.

Item two: In line with the Cartesian framework, formalist linguistics holds that the primary function of language is thought (thought existing in abstract logical form above the level of human interaction). In line with the Hegelian framework, functionalist linguistics states that the primary function of language is communication, language used by individuals in particular settings, for particular interactive purposes.

Item three: Again, there is this distinction between abstract formal properties and human interaction. In considering the psychological correlate, the formalist linguistic notion is competence as a *formal capacity*, while the functionalist linguistic notion is competence as a *social ability*.

Items four and five: The Cartesian emphasis on what the individual "knows" rather than what the individual does, and the Cartesian emphasis on universals over particulars. Formalist linguistics therefore gives priority to competence over the study of performance, and the formal system (sentences) is described without reference to the context in which it is used. Functionalist linguistics, in keeping with the Hegelian framework, is concerned with the particular contexts of language use.

Items six and seven: The Cartesian emphasis on universals, as well as the Cartesian emphasis on the innateness of knowledge and the relationship between this innateness and language universals. In formalist linguistics, language acquisition is a matter of an innate species endowment. Language is a given, pre-existing in platonic form, which the child then acquires. In functionalist linguistics, language is not a given; it has to be actively acquired through use in specific settings. As with the Hegelian framework, knowledge is acquired socially. Language, in this way, is a potential which is only realized through dynamic social interaction. In functionalist linguistics, therefore, language universals are not simply a matter of innate biological endowment but are related to a number of constraints having to do with the goals of communication, the settings of language use and the psychological make up of language users.

Item eight: Formalist linguistics divides the linguistic system into separate and distinct parts with ontological priority going to syntax. This is in keeping with the Cartesian priority given to the "inner" world, the world of innate platonic knowledge, and the priority of abstract form over human functions. In functionalist linguistics, there is an integrational approach with the emphasis on pragmatic concerns over abstract form.

The formalist linguistic paradigm therefore parallels closely the Cartesian framework, while the functionalist linguistic paradigm parallels the Hegelian framework. The Cartesian framework stresses the autonomy of form over function, the individual nature of the mind, the innateness of ideas and capacities, and the central place of thought in the form of pure logic. Thus, in formal linguistics there is the autonomy of syntax, the role of intuition in explanation, the focus on innate universals, and the centrality of language as thought.

The Hegelian framework stresses the inter-relationship between form and function, the social nature of the mind, the developmental nature of knowledge and capacities, and the central place of reflexivity and interaction. Thus, in functional linguistics there is systemic inter-relatedness rather than formal autonomy, an emphasis on language development and change, the notion of emergent forms and functions, and the centrality of social communication.

How do these general principles relate to specific issues within linguistics? Returning to the questions of linguistic theory asked at the end of the section titled "Markova's Framework's":

One: The locus of language – the Cartesian framework/formal linguistic approach places the locus of language in the individual brain; the Hegelian framework/functional linguistic approach places the locus of language in the social mind.

Two: Language acquisition – the Cartesian framework/formal linguistic approach places language acquisition in the individual brain based on innate species mental structures; the Hegelian framework/functional linguistic approach places language acquisition in the social mind based on interactive social processes.

Three: Functions of language – the Cartesian framework/formal linguistic approach considers the primary function of language to be abstract thought;

the Hegelian framework/functional linguistic approach considers the primary function of language to be communication.

Four: The relationship between form and function – the Cartesian framework/formal linguistic approach considers form prior to and unrelated to use; the Hegelian framework/functional approach considers form and function to be complexly and interestingly inter-related.

Sociolinguistic Metatheory

How does sociolinguistics fit into our discussion of metatheory? Though sociolinguists have not been consistent in application of the types of metatheoretical principles isolated thus far, it is safe to place sociolinguistics within both the Hegelian framework and the functionalist linguistic paradigm. It is safe to do so for two reasons: the theoretical issues historically raised in sociolinguistics, and, the subject matter of sociolinguistics are consistent with such an approach.

Sociolinguistics is "the study of language in relation to society" (Hudson, 1980, p. 1). Sociolinguistics "attempts to make a coherent statement about the relationship between language use and social patterns or structures of various kinds" (Romaine, 1982, p. 1). Sociolinguistics "is that part of linguistics which is concerned with language as a social and cultural phenomenon" (Trudgill, 1974, p. 32). Sociolinguistics is "the study of language as a social phenomenon" (Svejcer and Nikol'skij, 1986, p. 1). Sociolinguistics is "the study of the characteristics of language varieties, the characteristics of their functions, and the characteristics of their speakers as these three constantly interact, change and change one another within a speech community" (Fishman, 1971, p. 4). Sociolinguistics "studies the varied linguistic realizations of socio-cultural meanings...the currency of everyday social interactions which are nevertheless relative to particular cultures, societies, social groups, speech communities, languages, dialects, varieties, styles" (Pride, 1970, p. 301).

Starting with the historical theoretical concerns of sociolinguistics, from these definitions isolatable principles include at least the fundamental principle of the social nature of language. Areas of concern include social and cultural phenomena such as social patterns and structures, language varieties such as dialects and styles, social groups such as language communities, language functions in society, language change, socio-cultural meaning, social interaction.

Without getting into a fruitless attempt at sharply delineating sociolinguistic boundaries, it is non-controversial that sociolinguistic research has been historically concerned with at least communication and interaction, linguistic variation and language varieties, the social functions of language, situationally defined language use, language change and development. This incomplete list would include work done in the ethnography of communication, discourse analysis, dialectology, sociolinguistic variation, the sociology of language, pragmatics, stylistics, pidgins and creole studies.

Recall Dik's functional linguistic paradigm in which language is considered an instrument of social interaction. The focus of sociolinguistics is on language as communication, the study of language is related to its use within a society (including the study of acquisition and language structure), and linguistic description includes description of function. It is obvious that sociolinguistics, in the unrefined sense of the term that we are using for our purposes here, fits within functionalist linguistics. Functionalist linguistics, as has already been argued, conforms with the metatheoretical assumptions Markova has grouped within the Hegelian framework, thus sociolinguistic metatheory may also be categorized within Markova's Hegelian framework.

What is the subject matter of sociolinguistics? Aracil (1978, p. 4) defines the subject matter of sociolinguistics as follows: "The proper concern of sociolinguistics is language *use*...the sociolinguistic approach obviously differs from that of linguistics proper in that it centers on the *existential conditions*...whereas linguistics proper detaches language from nonlinguistic sociocultural structures, sociolinguistics *relates* it to them" (emphasis in original). Also in this vein, Romaine (1982, p. 7) writes: "The contrast between linguistics proper and sociolinguistics lies in the fact that language structure constitutes the subject matter of linguistics, while language use is left to sociolinguistics. A sociolinguistic theory, however, presupposes a linguistic theory; if it is to be truly integrative, it must relate both structure and use."

What, is meant by "the subject matter of sociolinguistics is language use"?[6] A number of things which can be rather clumsily narrowed down to the following statement: sociolinguistics is the study of utterance (spoken, written, signalled). An utterance is language performed in a particular context. There cannot be an adequate contextualized description of utterance which excludes those producing the utterances nor excludes the contexts of the utterance. (See Chapter Six for a discussion of utterance.)

Aracil (1978, p. 7) makes the following points about language use (which is concretized above as "utterance"):

1. language use is not a "thing", but a set of connections ...
2. language use is dynamic by definition ...The dynamic nature of use probably accounts for the fact that use seems to be definitely less substantializable than structure...
3. even though we assume language use to be a coherent whole, it is extremely complex and certainly not directly accessible in its entirety...
4...language use is both diverse and variable.

The Hegelian framework is based on the principles of the interactive, variant, particular, and dynamic nature of phenomena. It is also based on the active nature of consciousness and the social nature of mind. It is also an approach which attempts to be integrative, relating interdependent parts to an overall whole. The Hegelian framework supplies a means of describing and accounting for language use/utterance without having to resort to abstraction to ideal objects, as is the case when working within the Cartesian framework.

Within the framework of sociolinguistic metatheory, there is a subject matter which is dynamic rather than static. There is a basic principle of integration which leads to the consideration of language use as part of human behavior generally. There is, on a more specific level, the concern of sociolinguistics with language as a cultural and societal entity (in addition to it being a biological phenomenon, see Dik above #7) and, concern with language variation rather than, or in addition to, language invariation.

Recall Lass's "speaker-free" versus "speaker-centered" linguistics: sociolinguistics is a speaker-centered linguistics. The study of language use by definition includes the study of those using language. Sociolinguistics belongs to Lyons' "macro-linguistic" typology, Pengs' "broad linguistics" and Harris' "integrational linguistics". Because sociolinguistics considers more than the linguistic system, it takes into consideration the contexts of use, the participants and the communicative constraints of the situation. To state the obvious, therefore, sociolinguistics on a metatheoretical level is not well served by the Cartesian framework nor is it part of the formalist linguistic paradigm.[7]

Conclusion

Markova (1982) has pointed out that the normal science paradigm in psychology, and in all "scientific" fields for that matter including linguistics, has traditionally been the Cartesian framework and not the Hegelian framework. This fact has important ramifications for the historical development of the field of sociolinguistics.

Recall Kuhn's notion of normal science. According to Kuhn (1962, p. 5), normal science which is "predicted on the assumption that the scientific community knows what the world is like" is the accepted assumptions of the scientific community which supply "the foundation for its further practice" (Kuhn, 1962, p. 10). Under normal science the exemplars of the field are repeated and there is no fundamental questioning of normal science assumptions. According to Kuhn, it is therefore only under revolutionary science when fundamental tenets are exposed and questioned that paradigm changes may occur. The normal science paradigm for academic scholarship has been traditionally Cartesian.

The received linguistic paradigm has been Cartesian and formalist. Given these facts, sociolinguistics may be seen as part of an evolving revolutionary science paradigm, one which offers an alternative to the normal Cartesian assumptions. It is very difficult to participate in normal science (as do all participants at least during their academic training) and to also question it, and it is also difficult to find alternative ways of argument to those which are received and to which one has been acculturated. Paradigm changes, like any changes in belief systems, are neither painless nor orderly. It requires amongst other things the development of a revised language and a new or revised discourse.

One of the more lasting points to be taken from Kuhn's work on paradigm differences is the incompatible nature of competing paradigms. Kuhn points out that there can be no real dialogue between competing paradigms because, to put it colloquially, each side is missing the point of the other side. Though they might seemingly be speaking the same "language", they are not talking about the same thing. The logical progression of argument in one paradigm is irrelevant or nonsensical in another because it is based on assumptions which are not held by, or are rejected, by the other paradigm.

This is important to keep in mind given the often contentiousness of differing positions held by linguists who are arguing from completely different starting points and therefore have very little, if any, common ground. Rather than insisting that there be only one authentic way of doing linguistics, or that there be a scalar hierarchy of more to less linguistic, it is more accurate to admit genuine diversity based on differences.

Notes

[1] The term "metaworries" comes from the work of Roger Lass, 1980.

[2] One can often explain apparent anomalies in a theoretical model, method or practice by noting an extension of a paradigm beyond its limits or a tension between competing paradigms. As will be discussed in Chapter Four, William Labov's development of variable rules may be seen as an attempt to extend Chomskyian generative phonology beyond the notion of categorical and optional rules. However, if one considers that Chomskyian rules were based on Cartesian categorical principles, the attempt to bring in variability into a non-variant model led not to an extension of the paradigm but the inability of the paradigm (Chomskyian/Cartesian linguistics) to absorb variable rules and therefore the rejection of such rules.

[3] It is unfortunate that Markova chose to name the two frameworks Cartesian and Hegelian since there is such a large, diverse and uneven body of work by both Descartes and Hegel and such a broad body of scholarship on both men and their work. One can find great disagreement as to what either men really stood for. Markova's frameworks are adopted in this study as representing real divisions in Western thought, but with the caveat that no claims are being made about either Descartes or Hegel, rather the frameworks are considered useful abstractions.

[4] The term functionalist is often negatively linked with a now unpopular school of sociology which saw society as made up of mutually functioning parts of a whole. It was thought that this functionalist position justified societal inequalities and exploitation while ignoring real social conflict. In terms of linguistics, many practitioners of what this study is calling functionalist linguistics would reject the term (see for example Hopper 1988). The term functionalism has had a varied history across a number of disciplines and those practicing as functionalists in any one discipline have in no way been a unified body. The term is often related to a teleological form of explanation. It is at other times related to the notion of system and the internal workings of a system. In this way the Prague school practitioners such as Jakobson were functionalists who were concerned with, for example, the internal functioning of phonology from a structural perspective. More recent functional grammarians such as Givón and Halliday are concerned with how internal language structure is influenced by and related to external factors such as social interaction and cognitive processes.

[5] Dik's Formal and Functional paradigms are framed in terms of his functional grammar and Chomsky's generative grammar. Point one, the formal paradigm definition of a language as "a set of sentences", is a typical structuralist definition of language, one which one can find in Chomsky 1957 but which he now rejects (see Chomsky 1986). Chomsky makes a distinction

between an I (internal) language and an E (external) language. An E-language definition of a language would be something like a set of sentences, or a set of actions or behaviors. Chomsky holds that his definition of language (I-language) is more profound being representative of the mental structure of a language rather than any external manifestation. In point three, Dik takes the term communicative competence from Hymes. In point eight, Dik contrasts the role of pragmatics, semantics and syntax vis-a-vis each other. For Dik, the hierarchical relationship is one going from pragmatics to semantics and then syntax as part of the functional paradigm. Functionalists have sought to integrate semantics and syntax within a pragmatic framework (social and cognitive constraints of language processing/production) but not necessarily in this hierarchical manner.

[6] "Language use" is one of many inadequate theory laden terms this study has to make do with. The term language use is meant in opposition to the study of language structure (i.e. grammar) without reference to use.

[7] Though sociolinguistics is not part of the autonomous formal linguistic paradigm because its subject matter is wedded to non-autonomous phenomena, much work done in sociolinguistics derives its formalism from formal linguistics and therefore shares many features with formal linguistics, using the same units of analysis of language, and so forth.

The fact that the Hegelian framework provides a perceptual frame which is suited to studying language use/utterance, and provides a metalanguage for describing and explaining language use/utterance does not mean that work done in sociolinguistics has been done from this perspective. Likewise, the fact that the functional linguistic paradigm and sociolinguistics have been historically linked does not mean that all work in sociolinguistics has been within the functional linguistic paradigm.

Though speaking in terms of these metatheoretical frameworks is a useful abstraction for theoretical argument, it is not possible to define any one individual's work as simply fitting into one or another framework. Markova explains this well when she states that it is not true that science develops "in a neat and orderly way, that concepts are precisely defined from the beginning, or that the history of science follows a straight line. The conceptual frameworks of research workers are not tidy showrooms where everything is in place. It may well be that a researcher accepts the presupposition that the mind is individualistic while at the same time holding that the mind is dynamic; or that the criterion of knowledge is external while claiming that the mind is active in the acquisition of knowledge; and so on" (Markova, 1982, p. 8).

3

Dell Hymes and the Ethnography of Communication—Sociolinguistic Relativism

> *Speech and writing are means, resources, which different groups and individuals make different use of, and what these uses and meanings are must be established empirically in the given case.*
>
> Dell Hymes, 1986, p. 51

> *...the role of language as a device for categorizing experience and its role as an instrument of communication cannot be separated, and indeed, the latter includes the former.*
>
> Dell Hymes, 1974a, p. 19

Sociolinguistics According to Dell Hymes

> *Certainly it is a sociolinguistic perspective, uniting theory and practice, that is most appropriate to a vision of the future of mankind as one in a world of peace(....). Linguistics as sociolinguistics, if it will, can envisage and work toward a unity that is yet to come.*
>
> Hymes, 1974a, p. 209

> *...it is not linguistics, but ethnography, not language, but communication, which must provide the frame of reference within which the place of language in culture and society is to be assessed.*
>
> Hymes, 1974a, p. 4

In 1972, Dell Hymes presented a paper at the Georgetown Annual Round Table on Languages and Linguistics in which he distinguishes between three "orientations" in sociolinguistics: "(1) the social as well as the linguistic; (2) socially realistic linguistics; (3) socially constituted linguistics" (Hymes, 1974a, p. 195). According to Hymes, the first two orientations do not fundamentally challenge received linguistics. The first orientation is an application of linguistic theory to practical problems such as education. And the second orientation challenges existing linguistic methodology but the "expressed theoretical goals are not distinct from those of normal linguistics..." (Hymes, 1974a, p. 196).

In contrast, the third orientation "cannot leave normal linguistic theory unchallenged.., nor limits challenge to reform, because its own goals are not allowed for by normal theory, and cannot be achieved by 'working in the system'... Its task is the thoroughgoing critique of received notions and practices, from the standpoint of social meaning, that is, from a functional perspective" (Hymes, 1974a, p. 197). It is this third orientation within sociolinguistics, the redefining of linguistics, that Hymes has firmly placed himself as a leading advocate.

Hymes' background is in the tradition of American Indian linguistics with its descriptivist character and its strong links to anthropology and folklore. Hymes is also a historian of linguistics (see Hymes 1974b, 1981, 1984) this gives him an awareness of where his own work fits into the history of linguistics, and how it might relate to future developments. In this way Hymes is able to see sociolinguistics not as an isolated or recent development, but as a ongoing trend within the history of linguistics which takes different forms and has different strengths in relationship to other trends at different points in time. He acknowledges his own work as building on that of other linguists, in particular in the modern era that of Sapir, Firth and Jakobson. Hymes sees his work as a renewal of Prague Circle functionalism, Firth's contextualization and Sapir's relativism (Hymes, 1974a, p. 5). In addition, he places his work in a larger non-linguistic framework: "I accept an intellectual tradition adumbrated in antiquity, and articulated in the course of the Enlightenment, which holds that mankind cannot be understood apart from the evolution and maintenance of its ethnographic diversity" (Hymes, 1974a, p. 33).[1]

For Hymes there is a direct link between one's ideology, linguistic metatheory, and the development of a particular linguistic model. Hymes does not separate the role of the academic scholar from the role of the individual in a moral social order. The principles which guide the way one lives one's life therefore are not separate principles from those which guide the way one approaches research. Following this logic, Hymes sees the linguist as an activist who must integrate social knowledge with linguistic knowledge. Hymes criticizes Chomsky in this regard, pointing out that there is little or no linguistics in Chomsky's work on sociopolitical issues, and little or no social consciousness in Chomsky's work on linguistics. Hymes complains that "such principled schizophrenia besets linguistics today; the scientific and social goals of its practitioners are commonly compartmentalized" (Hymes, 1980, p. 19). His vision of sociolinguistics is clearly one which rejects the notion that the practitioner is somehow able to transcend socio-political content and context. Instead, he requires that sociolinguistic knowledge be applied to solving socio-political problems.[2]

Hymes proposes that for sociolinguistics to be a meaningful label, in distinction to linguistics proper, it cannot be by default but must be purposeful. He isolates three areas of definition which would make sociolinguistics a meaningful term: the scope of sociolinguistics, the requirements ("dependencies") of this scope, and the effect this scope has on the foundations of linguistics (Hymes, 1974a, p. viii).

According to Hymes, the scope of sociolinguistic enquiry is language broadly defined within the parameters of communication rather than language narrowly defined as grammar. Hymes (1974a, p. vii) writes, "(...)

there is a mode of organization of language that is a part of the organization of communicative conduct in a community, whose understanding requires a corresponding new mode of description of language(...)." Language so conceived is not separate from the other social and cultural systems at work in the community, therefore types of description developed within linguistics which are exclusively grammatical are not sufficient.

For Hymes there is a direct consequence of this broad scope for sociolinguistics: the need for a multidisciplinary approach. He maintains that "the recognition of this mode of organization leads one to recognize that the study of language is a multidisciplinary field, a field to which ordinary linguistics is indispensable, but to which other disciplines, such as sociology, social anthropology, education, folklore, and poetics, are indispensable as well..." (Hymes, 1974a, p. vii,viii). In considering language as an integrated part of general socio-cultural organization and behavior, linguistic theory by itself is ill equipped to account for this organization and behavior, hence Hyme's call for a multidisciplinary approach.

This leads Hymes to the reconsideration of the foundations of linguistic theory. Hymes writes that the "study of this mode of organization leads one to reconsider the bases of linguistics itself" (Hymes, 1974a, p. viii). If one considers language not simply in terms of formal grammar but in terms of communication, then one is left with whole areas of language which are problematic for received linguistic description. For example, Hymes (1974a, p. viii) points out that there are stylistic features of speech such as "details of articulation, intonation, pitch, tempo, lexical choice, syntactic choice that go together in a fashion or way of speaking, a style [which]...may not be part of a standard description of the language."

Given the scope of Hymes' approach to sociolinguistics and the consequences of this scope, Hymes advocates "a science that would approach language neither as abstracted from nor an abstract correlate of a community, but as situated in the flux and pattern of communicative events. It would study communicative form and function in integral relation to each other." (Hymes; 1974a, p. 5)

Socially Constitutive Linguistics

According to Hymes (1974a, p. 196): "the phrase 'socially constituted' is intended to express the view that social function gives form to the ways in which linguistic features are encountered in actual life. This being so, an adequate approach must begin by identifying social functions, and discover the ways in which linguistic features are selected and grouped together to serve them."

A socially constituted linguistics questions received linguistic premises because these premises are based on the exclusion of social meaning. In this way, a socially constituted linguistics "reverses the structuralist tendency of most of the twentieth century, toward the isolation of referential structure, and the posing of questions of social functions from that standpoint" (Hymes, 1974a, p. 197).

Hymes (1974a, p. 206) isolates seven themes which he sees as central to a socially constituted linguistics:

1. Linguistic theory as theory of language, entailing the organization of speech (not just of grammar).

2. Foundations of theory and methodology as entailing questions of function (not just of structure).

3. Speech communities as organizations of ways of speaking (not just equivalent to the distribution of the grammar of a language).

4. Competence as personal ability (not just grammatical knowledge, systemic potential of a grammar, superorganic property of a society, or, indeed, irrelevant to persons in any other way).

5. Performance as accomplishment and responsibility, investiture and emergence (not just psycholinguistic processing and impediment).

6. Languages as what their users have made of them (not just what human nature has given).

7. *Liberté, Egalité, Fraternité* of speech as something achieved in social life (not just postulated as given as a consequence of language).

Point one maintains that a sociolinguistic theory of language must entail not just formal grammar ("*langue*" or "competence") but speech ("*parole*").[3] Speech consists of both what are traditionally considered linguistic properties and non-linguistic properties. To be able to describe or explain speech therefore requires a linguistic theory equipped with more than linguistic elements.

Point two has to do with the inherent functionalism of Hymes' approach. The socially constitutive approach anchors language within society. It is not enough to study the structure of a language, instead a socially constitutive approach requires that the functions language or language varieties play in a society, or a context, also be considered.

Point three has to do with the question of how one defines a speech community. In Hymes' approach the social matrix from which language evolves is the speech community and the speech community is defined in terms of social rather than linguistic factors.

Point four has to do with definitions of competence – the knowledge that an individual has of language and language use. Hymes disagrees with Chomsky's definition of competence.[4] Hymes maintains that competence is a question of individual ability not *a priori* universal endowment.

Point five is again in disagreement with Chomsky's linguistic theory, this time Chomsky's notion of performance. Here Hymes defines performance in terms of volitional, moral, situated behavior rather than psychological processing or mechanistic behavior.

Point six similarly has to do with the active role that individuals have in creating language, rather than language being simply a matter of biological endowment.

Point seven has to do with Hymes' notion of linguistic relativism whereby the equality of speech may be an ideological position held by linguistics but is not the experience of individual speakers of language. This final point also suggests the political nature of language.

How does this socially constituted linguistics compare with the other approaches to sociolinguistics which Hymes has isolated? Hymes (1974a, p. 195) defines "the social as well as the linguistic" as "ventures into social problems involving language and the use of language, which are not seen as involving a challenge to existing linguistics." This type of work is sometimes called applied sociolinguistics or the sociology of language and would include such issues as language policy and linguistic applications to problems in education.

The other approach to sociolinguistics which Hymes calls socially realistic linguistics "extends and challenges existing linguistics with data from the speech community. (...) The expressed theoretical goals are not distinct from those of normal linguistics, e.g., the nature of linguistic rules, the nature of sound change, but the method of work, and the findings, differ sharply" (Hymes, 1974a, p. 196). This type of work which is best exemplified by the work of William Labov, which will be discussed in detail in the following chapter, is fundamentally concerned with questions of empiricism having to do with issues pertaining to methodology rather than fundamentally challenging received linguistic theory.

For Hymes sociolinguistics is a meaningful label only if it is part of revolutionary science rather than normal science. He writes:

> 'Sociolinguistics' could be taken to refer to use of linguistic data and analyses in other disciplines, concerned with social life, and conversely, to use of social data and analysis in linguistics. The word could also be taken to refer to correlations between languages and societies, and between particular linguistic and social phenomena. These worthwhile activities would not really require a special name. They leave linguistics and the other disciplines as they are. (Hymes, 1974a, p. vii)

Hymes (ibid.) suggests that the two approaches to sociolinguistics, "the social as well as the linguistic" and "socially realistic linguistics", in not challenging the basic assumptions underlying the separation of disciplines "presuppose a science of mankind among whose departments human life has been accurately and completely apportioned." He (ibid.) suggests instead that sociolinguistics:

merits our attention just insofar as it signals an effort to change the practice of linguistics and other disciplines, because their present practice perpetuates a fragmented, incomplete understanding of humanity. Sociolinguistics, so conceived, is an attempt to rethink received categories and assumptions as to the bases of linguistic work, and as to the place of language in human life.

The goal of Hymes' sociolinguistics therefore goes far beyond questions solely concerning linguistics.

Ethnography of Communication

Hymes has used a number of different terms for his approach to sociolinguistics including (but not limited to) the "ethnography of communication", the "ethnography of speaking", "ethno-linguistics", and as discussed above, "socially constituted linguistics". These terms are somewhat dependent on Hymes' audience and the context surrounding his discourse, whether for example he is addressing anthropologists, folklorists, sociologists or linguists. Sociolinguistics, as "socially constituted linguistics", is the broadest representation of Hymes' sociolinguistic program; that is, Hymes' sociolinguistics at its most metatheoretical. The ethnography of communication/speaking is at a more specific level, one more historically related to anthropology and other issues to be addressed below.

The choice of additional labels for sociolinguistics by Hymes is revealing. Hymes introduces the term "ethnography of speaking" in an article of the same name in 1962. In 1964, he uses the term "ethnography of communication" in an article in a collection edited with John Gumperz titled *The Ethnography of Communication*. Both terms continued to be used interchangeably for over a decade before the ethnography of communication became established as the dominant term. Though work done under both labels is without theoretical or methodological difference, the two terms speak to two related but historically separated issues in linguistic discourse. The important distinctions here are of course in the choice of the words "speaking" and "communication".

The choice of the word "speaking" is addressed to the Saussurian dichotomy between *langue* and *parole* whereby *langue* (the supra-individual socially instituted grammatical system) is the concern of linguistics and not *parole* (situated context bound speech.) (Saussurian linguistics is discussed in greater detail in the following chapter.) By choosing the term "speaking", Hymes is claiming the priority of speech (not speech in contrast to writing but *parole* in contrast to *langue*). Similarly, the choice of the word "communication" is directed against a narrow definition of language as grammar, rather than language more complexly defined in relation to communication. Here Hymes' choice of the word "communication" is directed at Chomskyian linguistics and the narrow focus of generative linguistic theory at the time he coined the term (the first half of the 1960's). It is important to note that both choices of words signify Hymes' intentional break from received linguistic beliefs and practices.

Hymes (1974a, p. 4) has proposed that it is communication not language, and ethnography not linguistics "which must provide the frame of reference within which the place of language in culture and society is to be assessed." Ethnography is a branch of cultural anthropology which is primarily descriptive in nature. It is, according to Hymes (1974a, p. 10), "the structural analysis of cultural behavior...viewed as the development of theories adequate to concrete cases." According to Agar (1986, p. 12), "Ethnographers set out to show how social action in one world makes sense from the point of view of another." Or as explained by Hymes, both the ethnographer and any person in any given culture "must formulate from finite experience theories adequate to predict and judge as appropriate or inappropriate what is, in principle, an infinite amount of cultural behavior" (Hymes, 1974a, p. 11). The role of the ethnographer therefore is parallel to the role of the ordinary person developing theories which explain everyday perceptions and experience.

The significance of ethnography to the ethnography of communication is multi-fold. This significance includes on the level of metatheory the principles of relativism, holism and emergence, and on the level of methodology participant observation.

Traditionally the most common procedure used in ethnography, and the most common procedure used in the ethnography of communication, has been participant observation. This is a practice whereby the investigator involves herself in the community, or with the subjects she is studying, in such a way as to have access to a means of arriving at a common-sense understanding of what is taking place around her. This understanding, or at least the means of arriving at such an understanding, is supposed to be reflective of the understanding of the ordinary person in the everyday world. (See Schutz 1970 for a view on "common-sense" versus "expert" understanding.) The importance of this type of methodological procedure is that it is particularistic (each investigation is considered as a concrete case rather than an abstract universal). In theory it requires that the investigator pay attention to the actualities of the situation irrespective of prior theorizing.

Two principles of anthropological metatheory guide ethnography: holism and emergence. As applied to the ethnography of communication, the principle of holism would require that linguistic issues not be divorced from human experience and behavior generally. And the principle of emergence would require that one discover structure rather than pre-assign or impose structure. In this way one may have a general concept of what social organization is, and general terms for describing such organization, but one is not supposed to predetermine categories, events, the meaning of interactions, and so on. One is instead supposed to follow discovery procedures which will lead one from an outside to an inside view of cultural phenomena.

Relativism

An important motivation for the particularity of ethnography is the relativist framework that guides most anthropological work. Bauman and Sherzer (1974/1989, p. 7) say of the ethnography of speaking that it draws on the basic relativism of anthropology: "the understanding that speaking, like other systems of behavior – religious, economic, political, etc. – is organized in each society in culture specific ways, which are to be discovered." Both the relativistic nature of the ethnography of communication and the importance of this relativism for Hymes' sociolinguistic theory is significant.

In questions of epistemology, there are longstanding arguments as to whether there are universals of knowledge or whether knowledge is particularistic due to the intrusion of each person's individual experience. Framed another way, the question is whether or not there are ideal platonic universals which our own individual knowledge may or may not be able to approach. In questions of ethics, there is ongoing discussion as to whether or not there is absolute truth, absolute right and wrong, or whether notions of value are contingent. And in linguistics there are questions as to whether languages are fundamentally the same or different and whether differences in language lead to (or are evidence of) differences in perception and knowledge.

Realism holds that "there are things and events in the world which exist independently" (Gifford, 1983, p. x) so that things and events exist independent of our cognition of them. The relativist position in contrast maintains that "what we know will vary with the unique features of a person, or of a context or of a culture... (ibid)" so that the existence of things and events is not independent of our cognition of them.

Put another way, knowledge, values, reality, the self, are contingent not objective. Contingency, in the words of Herrnstein Smith:

> is a function not of 'the way the world is' but of the states of numerous particular systems interacting at a particular time and place. This conception of the world requires that there be 'something' other than itself, other than the process of conceiving-the-world; but it cannot conceive of a single other thing to say, or nay to think, about that 'something' – not a single feature to predicate of it, or any way to describe, analyze, or manipulate any of its properties – that would be independent of that process (Herrnstein Smith, 1988, p. 183).

Herrnstein Smith describes her own relativism as "a general conceptual style or taste," it is:

> (a) a conceptualization of the world as continuously changing, irreducibly various, and multiply configurable, (b) a corresponding tendency to find cognitively distasteful unsatisfying, or counterintuitive any conception of the world as fixed and integral and/or as having objectively determinate properties, and (c) corresponding disinclination

or inability to use terms such as "reality", "truth", "meaning", "reason", or "value" as glossed by the latter objectivist conceptions (Herrnstein Smith, 1988, p. 151).

Another notion used to explain relativity is economy. Communities and individuals have different communicative economies, that is different linguistic (and other) resources available to them and different currency (i.e. value) assigned to the distribution and use of these resources. In Hymes (1974a, p. 4) words:

> The same linguistic means may be made to serve various ends; the same communicative ends may be served, linguistically, by various means. Facets of the cultural values and beliefs, social institutions and forms, roles and personalities, history and ecology of a community may have to be examined in their bearing on communicative events and patterns (...).

Value within the economies of the community and the individual are contingent, and therefore the relationship between the linguistic code and behavior is not a determined relationship, "all elements that constitute the communicative economy of a group, are conditioned, to be sure, by properties of the linguistic codes within the group, but are not controlled by them (ibid)." (See, Bourdieu 1977 for the application of economics to linguistics.)

In writing about the particularity of discourse, Hymes acknowledges the dominance of universals in received linguistic theory, but argues for relativism:

> Dichotomies and frameworks with few categories attract us because they offer order in a complex sphere, yet it is the hard truth that what goes on in given situations escapes such categorization. There is a particular tendency today to seek the satisfaction of universal frameworks without realizing the empirical inadequacy of them. Our sense of historical and cultural relativism and diversity seems attenuated, if not lost. The appeal of universal grounding tends to overcome any fear of ethnocentric origin, yet differences of social structure, ecology, class, region, historically derived character give rise to very distinctive cuts of cloth grounded in fundamental concerns and motives of difference kinds.
> (Hymes, 1986, p. 49.)

For Hymes knowledge and values are contingent: "speech and writing are means, resources, which different groups and individuals make different use of, and what those uses and meanings are must be established empirically in the given case" (Hymes, 1986, p. 51). Nevertheless, though knowledge and values are contingent Hymes does not mean that every situation is unique and thus cannot be described or compared. Hymes (1986, p. 65) writes:

The lack of strict order, however, is not the absence of any order at all. To abandon the fixity of *a priori* general categories is not to be lost in a sea of exceptions. Persons, events and groups have characteristic tendencies, dispositions, and styles, recognizable to others in principle describable by investigators. We do not experience conversational interaction as chaos ordinarily. This is so for at least three kinds of reasons: a. There are some recurrent types of sequences b. Persons, events, and groups have recognizable patterns, even though each sequence may not be predictable in advance c. Persons and groups bring to conversation expectations and resources which contribute to a sense of its orderliness.

The fact that Hymes' approach is relativist therefore does not preclude the ability to describe or explain contingent (i.e. contextualized) behavior.

Sociolinguistic Theory and Linguistic Theory

It remains that sociolinguistics, conceived in terms of the ethnography of speaking, is ultimately part of the study of communication as a whole.

Hymes, 1974a, p. 6

To put it in grossly simplified form: in seeking structure, Saussure is concerned with the word, Chomsky with the sentence, the ethnography of speaking with the act of speech.

Hymes, 1974a, p. 90

Linguistic Relativism, Universals and Linguistic Theory

Relativism begins with the observation of diversity.

Meiland and Krauz, 1972, p. 1

We need to transcend the liberal assumption built into so much of linguistic thought, that all sets of communicative means are equal in the eyes of linguistic theory. They are not equal in the eyes of history.

Hymes, 1980;vi

In considering the question of linguistic relativity, at least two important questions come to mind: what does it mean to say that two languages or language varieties are different? And to what extent do differences in languages, language varieties or individual linguistic abilities affect mental processes? The first question has to do with the universality of language, and the second has to do with the relationship between language and mental processes.

In relation to the first question, Hymes (1974a, p. 18) writes: "Languages, like other cultural traits, will be found to vary in the degree and nature of their integration into the societies and cultures in which they occur...what is necessary is to realize that the functional relativity of languages is general, applying to monolingual situations too."

For Hymes, the universality of language can be defended only if one remains at a level of abstraction which does not include the situated nature of speech. He suggests that language conceived "exclusively in terms of the vast potentiality of formal grammar" encourages us "to think of that potentiality exclusively in terms of its universality. But a perspective which treats language only as an attribute of Man leaves language as an attribute of men unintelligible. In actuality language is in large part what users have made of it" (Hymes, 1973, p. 60).

Universals in received linguistic theory are of two sorts, Chomskyian universals which are biological in nature and the universals of the Greenberg (1963) sort which don't seem to have one single source.[5] It is the former type of universals which Hymes is addressing above. In arguing against a grammatical definition of language, Hymes argues that language is more than a attribute of the species through biology. Rather, language is complexly linked to history, societal, and cultural evolution and the particularities of the individual actually speaking, "because people themselves are never abstract mind, but participants in specific communities, changing, and in need of change" (Hymes, 1974a, p. 172).

Hymes therefore stresses the diversity of languages:

> First, languages differ in their makeup as adaptive resources. The linguistic resources of speech communities differ in what can be done with them ...
> Second, linguistic resources differ as an aspect of persons and personalities. In addition to the variability inevitable on genetic grounds, there is the variability due to social patterning.
> Third, linguistic resources differ according to the institutions of a community.
> Fourth, linguistic resources differ according to the values and beliefs of a community (Hymes, 1974c, pp. 78,79).

Hymes writes that "we know that people who speak different languages do to some extent live in distinct worlds, not merely the same experiential world with different labels attached (...)" (Hymes, 1966, p. 116). And again: "Peoples do not all everywhere use language to the same degree, in the same situations, or for the same things; some peoples focus upon language more than others. Such differences in the place of a language in the communicative system of a people cannot be assumed to be without influence on the depth of a language's influence on such things as world view" (Hymes, 1974c, p. 79).

This view of language, that different languages influence such things as world view, is a type of linguistic relativity often associated with Benjamin Whorf.[6] However, Whorf's linguistic relativity is most often associated with the claim that differences in linguistic structure lead to differences in perceptions and other cognitive structuring of the world. Hymes (1966, p. 114) claims that this type of linguistic relativity is "associated with inference from linguistic data to other aspects of culture." For example, great weight is placed upon the fact that "Eskimo" has many words for specific types of snow but no general word for snow collectively. Somehow this lexical evidence is assumed to be culturally significant. Hymes argues that this approach is superficial and that there is a prior and more important form of linguistic relativity going on at a functional rather than formal level. Hymes (1966, p. 114) writes: "Less studied, but, I think, theoretically prior, notion is a relativity that has to do with the use of language. The notion of a second type of linguistic relativity calls attention to differences in cultural pattern and to their importance for linguistic experience and behavior."

It is not the linguistic form which creates the social pattern, therefore, but the social pattern which informs the linguistic form. In this case, the inference is from the ethnographic data to language functions. For Hymes, "the cognitive significance of a language depends not only on structure but also on patterns of use" (Hymes, 1966, p. 116). This is because: "linguistic habits are in part constitutive of cultural reality. My contention is that people who enact different cultures do to some extent experience distinct communicative systems, not merely the same natural communicative condition with different customs affixed. Cultural vales and beliefs are in part constitutive of linguistic reality (ibid)."

What is the significance of Hymes' linguistic relativity in terms of received linguistics? First, linguistic relativity is based on the principle of diversity rather than homogeneity or invariance. Second, for Hymes, the *a priori* universals found in received linguistics are not sufficient. Ethnography requires that one focus on specific cases. Third, the received assumption of linguistic equality between languages or between individuals is rejected. Hymes maintains that the differences in the evolution of languages, the disapportionate functional load of language in different communities and in different situations, as well as the political nature of interaction, leads to inequality among speakers (See Hymes 1973.)

Hymes has stated that "just as a theory of grammar must have its universal terms, so must a theory of language use" (Hymes, 1974a, p. 43). He has also stated that "there is no quarrel with the Cartesian concern for universals and the human mind. There is much concern with the Herdian stress upon individuation and emergent form" (Hymes, 1974a, p. 124). Hymes, then, does not categorically reject universals but he does consider the search for universals not necessarily the pinnacle of linguistic enquiry:

> Chomsky's interest is in moving from what is said to what is most abstract and elementary in grammar, and from what is social to what is innate in human nature. That, so to speak, is but half a dialectic. A thoroughgoing linguistics must move in the other direction as well, from what is potential in human nature, and elementary in a grammar, to what is realizable and realized (Hymes, 1974a, p. 93).

In addition, it would seem that Hymes has a broader definition of universals and the role that they should play in a theory than does Chomsky:

> The use of universals...is not to extricate language, as abstract mind, from human history, but to enrich our understanding of history. The abstract potentialities of language, the undubitable common properties of all languages, the contingencies of interactions among kinds of provence, human nature, and kinds of use – one seeks to weave such things into a general theory of language, because people themselves are never abstract mind, but participants in specific communities, changing, and in need of change (Hymes, 1974a, pp. 171,172).

Hymes' theory is therefore based on a dialectic which requires that both universals and particulars be taken into account.

Hymes states that a theory of language use must have universal terms; he does not say that a theory of language use must be based on universals. To have universal terms means that one can make generalizations across particular cases, something which a field must do to achieve acceptance in received science. (See, for example Sherzer 1977 on criticism against the ethnography of communication for lack of universal terminology.) However, universal terms are not the same as universals. There is a difference, for example, between the claim that all human beings are endowed with the ability to learn language as an innate species faculty, and the claim that all languages have "adjectives".

In calling for universal terms, Hymes would seem to be acknowledging the need for generalization and the ability to make comparisons across cases. In this way Hymes is concerned with "concrete universals, such that language could be described in terms relevant to a specific system, yet applicable to all terms, that is, free of bias due to a particular context, and mediating between given systems and general theory, doing justice to both" (Hymes, 1974b, p. 434). For example, Hymes suggests that one can distinguish between a variety ("major speech styles associated with social groups"), and a personal, situational or genre style ("major speech styles associated with persons, particular situations, and genres") (Hymes, 1974b, p. 440). The terms "variety" and "genre" would therefore be "concrete universals" which one could use to compare across cases.

Beyond the question of general terminology, Hymes also tries to expand what counts as a universal. He does this by claiming that there is another basis to universals other than the essentialist one which underlies received linguistic theory. He terms this other basis "existential" or "experiential" (Hymes, 1974a, p. 170). According to Hymes, the constraints which direct language use are the universal constraints of "human nature", but they are also those of "provenance" (historical tradition) and "use" (purposes of language use) (ibid). In this way he suggests that there are language universals which are not related to formal constraints, or the referential function, but which are related to non-referential functions such as the stylistic function. Hymes (1974b, p.

438), for example, suggests the following as candidates for the status of linguistic universals "vowel length, reduplication, pitch accent, syllabification, word order, and properties such as a minimal vowel system."

Here there is some confusion over what is meant by a universal. There are two separate types of universals in received linguistic theory; Chomsky's universals which are based on a theory of the structure of the mind – on the supposition that language acquisition and use is a species specific entity and therefore all humans share the same mental linguistic structures – and Greenberg's universals, which have to do with observed tendencies in languages based on empirical data as to word order, the existence and definition of linguistic units such as nouns and verbs, and the possible or typical combinations of linguistic units.

Hymes' expansion of universals to include not only biological universals but historical universals is addressed at universals in the Chomskyian sense, but the addition of stylistic universals of the sort in the list above is addressed at universals in the Greenberg sense. Hymes does not always maintain this distinction. This leads to potential unclarity as to the role of universals in his theory, and as to what he is critiquing when he addresses universals in received linguistic theory.

In sum, Hymes has raised the question of universals in terms of the role of generalization in his theory and has granted universals a place though not a predominant one. He has also attempted to expand what counts as universals, both in terms of species universals and language universals. By adding the notion style to the realm of a universal, Hymes integrates rather than separates form and function and he carves out for sociolinguistics a large area of language study which received linguistic theory is not concerned with.

For Hymes a universal is a potential which only gets realized in actual instances of language use. But the realization of the potential is not a causal or predetermined one. That is, the universal does not cause or create the particular (such as an utterance being created from an abstract sentence through some kind of transformation). There is no *a priori* form or function which gets imposed on language use; instead, forms and functions emerge within the context of the utterance. It is not that the context is defined by metaphysical universals; rather it is the context which defines the utterance. The role of the ethnography of communication is therefore to describe and to understand these particular, context bounded, instances of language.

Hymes has defined the ethnography of speaking as "a theory of speech as a system of cultural behavior; a system not necessarily exotic, but necessarily concerned with the organization of diversity" (Hymes, 1971, p. 51). Elsewhere Hymes has pointed out that diversity is the cornerstone of sociolinguistics (Hymes, 1974a, p. 29). Hymes explains individual diversity in the following way: "social life shapes communicative competence and does so from infancy onward. Depending on gender, family, community, and religion, children are raised in terms of one configurations of the use and meaning of language rather than another" (Hymes, 1980, p. vi).

In contrast to sociolinguistics, because of the search for essential form or structure, received linguistic theory removes diversity (variation). This is done via the separation of form from use whereby use is considered inessential. It is this emphasis on universals in received theory which has led to the exclusion of the diversity of situated factors in linguistic analysis. (See, for example, Bloomfield's (1933) exclusion of semantics from the realm of linguistics, Saussure's (1922) exclusion of *parole* from the scientific study of language, and Chomsky's (1980) exclusion of creative language use from his theory of linguistics.)

In opposition to received theory, Hymes believes that a thorough understanding of language must go in two simultaneous directions, outward towards universals and inwards towards particulars. This is partly because Hymes believes that there is a dialectic relationship between form and function. It is also because Hymes believes that, taken holistically, there is an ongoing dialectic relationship between the largest of structures (universals) and the smallest of actions (particulars).

Functionalism

Hymes' approach to linguistics is a functionalist approach. For Hymes "speech is prior to code, function to structure, context to message, the appropriate to the arbitrary or simply possible" (Hymes 1974a, p. 6). In defining his approach as functional, Hymes makes the point that in speaking of 'functions', "I do not intend to raise here the many issues that attach to the notion of functionalism in the social sciences and, more generally, in the philosophy of the sciences and humanistic disciplines" (Hymes, 1974a, p. 146). Hymes' functionalism is therefore not aligned with any larger functionalist movement within the social sciences, rather Hymes considers language as performing a range of communicative and societal functions. Hymes also makes the larger distinction between functional linguistics and what he calls structural linguistics.

Hymes sees his functionalism as part of a "long-term shift of emphasis in American linguistics...The shift can be loosely phrased as one from focus on structure to focus on function – from focus on linguistic form in isolation to linguistic form in human context" (Hymes, 1974a, p. 77). In comparing the structural approach (referred to in this book as received linguistic theory) with the functional approach, Hymes points out that with the former the emphasis is on universals and invariance and the context is "primarily a psychological one" but with the latter, the emphasis is on diversity and the context is "primarily sociological" (Hymes, 1974a, p. 78). Hymes provides a "comparison of foci in 'structural' and 'functional' linguistics":

"STRUCTURAL"	"FUNCTIONAL"
1. Structure of lg. (code) as grammar	Structure of speech (act, event) as ways of speaking
2. Use merely implements ...what is analyzed as code; analysis of code prior to analysis of use	Analysis of use prior to code; organization of use discloses additional features and relations; shows code and use in integral (dialectical) relation
3. Referential function...	Gamut of stylistic or social functions
4. Elements and structures as analytically arbitrary...or universal	Elements and structures as ethnographically appropriate
5. Functional equivalence of languages; languages essentially (potentially) equal	Functional differentiation of all languages; varieties, styles; these being existentially (actually) not necessarily equivalent
6. Single homogeneous code and community...	Speech community as matrix of code repertoires, or speech styles...
7. Fundamental concepts...taken for granted or arbitrarily postulated.	Fundamental concepts taken as problematic and to be investigated.

(Hymes, 1974a, p. 79).

Point One: the functionalist concern with the structure of speech rather than the structure of grammar. Primacy goes to *parole* rather than *langue* (Hymes, 1974a, p. 9). This is in contradiction to received linguistic theory from Saussure through Chomsky where the essential linguistic form is the grammar (whether conceived as social as in the case of Saussure or psychological as in the case of Chomsky) and where primacy goes to the independent supra-individual grammar (whether conceived of as *langue* or competence).

Point Two: Received linguistic theory either sees language use as irrelevant to the study of the independent linguistic system or sees use as some sort of simple correlation between code and actualization. The code (i.e the grammar) is the primary concern and therefore the analysis of code is prior to any analysis of use. The functional approach posits a systemic relationship between code and use, thus the code cannot be considered either prior to or separate from its use.

Point Three: Received linguistic theory considers the referential function of language to be its essential, most primitive function. The functional approach considers a range of functions, including social functions, as important.

Point Four: Received linguistic theory is based on the arbitrariness of linguistic form. The functional approach sees linguistic form often as less a matter of arbitrariness and more a matter of historical evolution and ethnographic appropriateness. Functionalists do not necessarily assume that there is no teleological relationship between linguistic form and function. (See Givón 1989 for a discussion of arbitrariness and functionalist linguistic theory. See Andresen 1987 for a related discussion of "modularity" versus "iconicity".)

Point Five: Received linguistic theory is based on the assumption that all languages are essentially the same, or, on the assumption that one can abstract away from individual differences. The functional approach is based on the relativistic notion that languages are not equivalent.

Point Six: The question of homogeneity of code versus what Hymes terms the "organization of diversity" is again part of the ongoing difference between an approach focused on universals and an approach focused on particulars.

Point Seven: Received linguistic theory postulates *a priori* categorization. In contrast, the functional approach considers categorization itself to be problematic. *A priori* categorization is problematic from the functional perspective because the actors who perform language are an integral part of the linguistic equation. What the actor herself feels or thinks about the linguistic actions she is performing is part of the definition of that performance. In this way, for example, Hymes considers the attitudes and beliefs of speakers to be an important component in defining linguistic boundaries: "what counts as a language boundary cannot be defined by only purely linguistic measure. Attitudes and social meanings enter in as well...Part of the creativity of users of language lies in the freedom to determine what and how much linguistic difference matters. The alternative view...conceals an unsuspected linguistic determinism" (Hymes, 1974a, p. 123). Attitudes and beliefs are excluded from received linguistic theory.

Hymes following this functional approach considers language a "device for categorizing experience" and "an instrument of communication" (Hymes, 1974a, p. 19). Following Jakobson, Hymes (1974a, p. 23) recognizes a number of distinct communicative functions which languages perform: "expressive, directive, contact [phatic], metalinguistic, contextual, poetic [stylistic], referential, and metacommunicative." According to Hymes these common functional categories can be used to focus on the addressor, on the addressee, on channels, on codes, on settings, on message-form, on topic, or on the event. For example, the expressive or emotive function is related to the addressor in that she is using language to express some aspect of herself, be it an emotion, or statement of identity. The directive function is related to the receiving participant of an interaction in that she is being persuaded, convinced, cajoled, etc, to perform a particular action, an action which is often desired by the person attempting to get her to perform it. The metalinguistic function is related to the code in that the code is being commented on, as in the case when one draws attention to a particular form or way of speaking in one's utterance. And the poetic function is related to the message form, as it is in the poetic function that attention to form is most evident. Nevertheless, though certain aspects of context are more often associated with certain functions, functions can be performed through a variety of ways and a number of functions can be performed at the same time.

Hymes' expansion of Jakobson's functional categories has a certain attractiveness in that one is able to talk about simultaneous layers of meaning in an utterance and relate different levels of speech to each other. In addition, one is sometimes able to relate form to function in an obvious way. For example, one can explain certain formulaic expressions and the role that they play in communication. The use of an expression such as "lovely day isn't it?" could be explained in terms of the phatic or contact functions, and an expression such as "can you pass the salt" could be explained in terms of the directive function. However, this functional model of Hymes is based on Jakobson's information theory which is a rather simplistic model of communication. It is a telecommunicational model of communication whereby an individual transmits a message to another individual. It is unidirectional and non-interactional. (See Anderson 1985, p. 134-139 for a discussion of Jakobson's information theory.) It is possible that a more complex interactional notion of communication would make Hymes' functional categories much less tidy.

Received linguistic theory gives priority to the referential function of language. This is partly because the primary function of language is considered to be thought rather than social interaction. Hymes does not deny the importance of the referential function but he stresses in addition the stylistic function: "languages have conventional features, elements and relations serving referential ('propositional', 'ideational' etc.) meaning, and they have conventional features, and elements and relations that are stylistic, serving social meaning" (Hymes, 1974a, p. 146). For Hymes the referential function is not prior to the social function of language: "Involvement with stylistic function, and social meaning, reveals that the foundations of language, if partly in the human mind, are equally in social life, and that the foundations of linguistics, if partly in logic and psychology, are equally in ethnography (ibid)."

Hymes' functional linguistic theory may be considered an attempt at redressing the unequal weight given to the referential function and ideational meaning over the stylistic function and social meaning. Hymes (1974a, p. 172) maintains that:

> When the reasons for excluding social factors are critically examined, and when one realizes that such factors cannot be consistently excluded, any attempt to deal with them in a principled way begins to makes formal grammar appear to be not the first, but the last step, in linguistic description and theory. The first step appears as ethnography of speaking, specifically, description of organization of linguistic means in

styles of speech in terms of the functional matrix of speaking in a community.

A further basic difference between received linguistic approaches and functional approaches are the units of analysis available to each approach. Received linguistic theory is sentence based and not focused on language beyond the sentence level, nor on the social functions of language, therefore received linguistic theory has not typically developed linguistic units which can account for language beyond the sentence or language in relation to social functions. Sociolinguists and other linguists such as those doing work in pragmatics and discourse have developed a variety of descriptive units and methods of analysis to counter this deficiency in received linguistic theory. (See Taylor and Cameron 1987; Schiffrin 1994, for a summary of various approaches.)

Hymes has suggested three bounded units for analyzing speech: the speech situation, speech event and speech act. The speech act is embedded in the speech event which in turn is embedded in the speech situation. The speech situation is the context within which the discourse takes place. It bounds the event and may be associated with a particular speech genre but is itself not governed by rules of speaking.

Hymes (1974a, p. 51) suggests that "ceremonies, fights, hunts, meals and lovemaking" would count as speech situations. The speech event is "restricted to activities, or aspects of activities, that are directly governed by rules or norms for the use of speech" (Hymes, 1974a, p. 52). The speech event therefore is delimited from other speech events by norms of behavior. If one knows the rules governing a certain type of speech event one can both name it and contrast it with other types of speech events.

The speech act is also a bounded unit whereby a particular social action is accomplished through speech. Hymes considers the speech act to be a minimal unit which "represents a level distinct from the sentence, and not identifiable with any single portion of other levels of grammar, nor with segments of any particular size defined in terms of other levels of grammar (ibid)." The example which Hymes gives of a situation, an event, and a speech act, is a party (speech situation) a conversation which takes place during the party (speech event) and a joke (speech act) which takes place during the conversation (ibid).

What do fights, hunts, meals or love making have in common? It would seem that a speech situation entails anything which people do. To have a meal does not require that one speak nor does a fishing venture but the great likelihood is that if one is having a meal or going fishing with other people one will at some point verbally or otherwise make some meaningful communication even if it is to go "oh wow" when someone catches a fish or pull away one's chair and rub one's stomach when the meal is over while making eye contact with someone else. Granted the speech situation is the general context surrounding the speech event, but why that might be important is not made explicit.

If all speech is normative, that is, it is learned under normative conditions and has social signification whenever it is used, then defining a speech event as something which is directly governed by rules or norms is not particularly helpful. Again what is it about a conversation and a lecture that make them speech events? It would seem that any speech governed by norms of behavior would be a speech event. The point of interest is not that they are speech events but the nature of the norms which supposedly govern them.

Hymes has pointed out that a speech act can actually be many things at once, for example a threat (referentially), a mock threat (expressively) and a summons (contact); that is, the message content is a threat, but the modality (key) is joking, but the norm of interaction is a summons (Hymes, 1973a, p. 53). He has also pointed out that, for example, the speech act of a joke may be embedded in any event and any event may be embedded in any situation (Hymes, 1973a, p. 52).

What is the point of all this embeddedness? How does one tell an act from an event from a situation? Suppose that a request is made during a conversation which occurs during a tennis match. This is a description of what actually happens, what does it add to our knowledge of what happens? Hymes has made the point that the ethnography of communication is more than description, that it is a theory (Hymes, 1967, p. 13). However, for these units to have any theoretical validity they have to be considered within the totality of Hymes' model. They cannot stand by themselves simply because they are context dependent. Furthermore, one is not provided with the means to recognize a situation event or act which one is not already familiar with. Situations, events and acts are defined in relation to each other and the other contextual components of Hymes' model. For example, the boundedness of an event, act, or situation can only be established in relation to the other embedded units. Despite Hymes' claims as to boundedness, these are not discrete units.

The speech act is not a grammatical unit. This is important because Hymes is attempting to find a genuinely functional unit. But it is not clear what type of unit it is. At times it seems similar to speech acts in the sense of Austin (1962) as an action, a reply, a request, a question, a command, etc., but at other times it seems to be a larger unit having to with a broader interaction, a joke, an exchange of greetings. (See Fasold 1990, p. 42-3,63 for this point and a discussion of speech acts, events and situations.) In this second sense of speech act, the emphasis appears to be on a social relationship. In the first sense, it appears to be more on an action being accomplished. Whether this is a correct representation or not, Hymes had reason to attempt to create functional units, but these units are undeveloped, too closely tied to ethnographic methodology, and need to be better integrated into his overall theory for them to have greater explanatory force.

Communicative Competence

> *In effect, Cartesian linguistics reduces 'competence' to knowledge of grammar, 'performance' to behavior, and 'creativity to novelty.'*
>
> Hymes, 1974a, p. 121

Hymes' most accomplished addition to theoretical discourse within received linguistics is his notion of communicative competence. It is partially Hymes' critique of Chomsky's initial formulation of the competence/performance distinction that led to the refinement of Chomsky's concept, to the point where current Chomskyian linguistic theory has developed a modular concept of competence which includes pragmatic competence in addition to grammatical competence.[7]

Chomsky devised the notion of competence to refer to the tacit knowledge that a native speaker has of her own language which allows her, for example, to recognize a sentence as belonging or not belonging to her language, and allows her to make a potentially infinite number of novel sentences in her language. This knowledge is of a grammatical sort, based in the language faculty of the brain and is independent of the speaker's ability to use the language or her actual use of the language. Competence here, in contrast for example to Saussure's *langue*, is a psychological construct anchored in biology and is unaffected by social concerns. Chomsky contrasts competence with performance which is behavior, the use of knowledge of language, or the actual use of language (Chomsky, 1965, p. 4).

Chomsky developed competence as part of his idealization of language. Competence is therefore posited in terms of the ideal speaker-hearer who has full knowledge of her language and who is part of a homogeneous speech community and therefore has a singular knowledge of her language as a pure object. In addition, competence as representative of ideal form is separated from the imperfection of performance. These imperfections which are based on physical, psychological and social limitations include such things as the limitations of physiological stamina, or memory constraints, or social mores of turn taking which would disallow, for example, the performance of an extremely long complex sentence though a person's grammatical competence may theoretically allow it.

This is the traditional platonic distinction between form and substance, or between the ideal universal and the real life imperfect actualization. Furthermore, there is no necessary relationship between the ideal form and the everyday actualization; hence Chomsky's position that studying language use (performance) will not reveal anything profound about our knowledge of grammar (competence). Here then is a sharp distinction between competence – that which is in the mind – and performance – that which may be witnessed as behavior. It is competence which is prior to performance and therefore it is competence which Chomsky proposes as the object of linguistic enquiry not performance.

In reacting to Chomsky, Hymes questions the reduction of competence to grammatical knowledge, the shift of competence as a concept away from ability, the reduction of performance to behavior, the sharp distinction between competence and performance, and the reduction of creativity to novelty. In discussing the contribution of folklore to sociolinguistics, Hymes makes the following observations about Chomsky's formulation of competence and his idealization of language:

> 1. Chomsky's attitude is rather neoplatonic. Competence is an ideal grammatical knowledge: performance, the use of language, is largely an imperfect falling away. Folklore recognizes the use of language as a positive accomplishment (...). Folklore, par excellence, understands the normal use of language as drawing on kinds of knowledge and organization that are parts of "competence" beyond the purely grammatical.
> 2. Chomsky's idealization of the "fluent speaker-user" in a homogeneous community makes the object of linguistics implicitly an abstract individual....In its analysis of performance, folklore recognizes the differentiation of knowledge and competence within a community with regard to speaking...
> 3. Chomsky's conception of the "creative aspect of language use" reduces "creativity" to novelty. This indeed is the focal point of his theoretical impact on linguistics – a conception of linguistics as concerned with explaining the use of language as an indefinitely large number of new sentences...Appropriateness is a relation between sentences and settings, and the setting must be analyzed as well. Moreover, creativity may consist in the use of an old sentence in a new setting just as much as in the use of a new sentence in an old setting (Hymes, 1974a, pp. 131,132).

For Chomsky competence is derived from an innate faculty which allows humans to acquire language (universal grammar). It is also, in terms of the acquisition of and knowledge of particular languages, the computational ability to accept or reject a piece of language (a sentence) as grammatical (belonging to the set) or ungrammatical (not belonging to the set). For Hymes however, competence is a much wider and more utilitarian use of the term. Competence here is not strictly a mental propensity, but an ability to act. Hymes distinguishes between four aspects of competence, which together encompass his use of the term. They are: systemic potential, appropriateness, occurrence and feasibility.

According to Hymes it is the first aspect of competence "systemic potential"; where Chomsky's notion of competence lies. The systemic potential is knowledge of the generative basis of a language, or universal grammar. Appropriateness is the knowledge of whether given a particular context certain behavior would be suitable. Occurrence is the knowledge of whether and to what extent something is done. And feasibility is the knowledge of whether and to what extent something is possible given available means (Hymes, 1974a, p. 95). Hymes' concept of competence incorporates all four.

For Chomskyian linguistic theory there is no theoretical necessity for establishing a relationship between language and language use. However, Hymes' functional approach is based on the systemic relationship between language and language use. It is not possible for Hymes to disregard language use or to posit a solely grammatical or autonomous linguistic faculty in formulating communicative competence.

Hymes argues therefore that there is another kind of competence other than grammatical competence which is equally important. Grammatical competence has been defined in terms of a person's ability "to produce, understand, and discriminate any and all of the grammatical sentences of a language" (Hymes, 1974a, p. 75). But Hymes points out that a person with only grammatical competence would be a "social monster" and that "a person who can produce all and any of the sentences of a language, and unpredictably does, is institutionalized" (Hymes, 1974a, p. 75,123). Hymes therefore suggests another type of competence, communicative competence – the ability to choose between a range of possible utterances the one which is appropriate to the situation. For Hymes communicative competence consists of a range of abilities including grammatical knowledge but not reducible to grammatical knowledge.

Chomskyian linguistic theory has recently reformulated the notion of competence developing a modular model whereby knowledge of language consists of grammatical competence, pragmatic competence and the conceptual system. Put succinctly "a speaker's grammatical competence is a knowledge of form and meaning; his pragmatic competence is a knowledge of conditions of appropriate use" (Botha, 1989, p. 75). According to Chomsky (1980, p. 59), grammatical competence is "the cognitive state that encompasses all those aspects of form and meaning and their relation, including underlying structures that enter into that relation, which are properly assigned to the specific subsystem of the human mind that relates representations of form and meaning." Pragmatic competence is "the system of rules and principles [that] determines how the tool [of language] can effectively be put to use....We might say that pragmatic competence places language in the institutional setting of its use, relating intentions and purposes to the linguistic means at hand" (Chomsky, 1980, p. 224-5). And the conceptual system "permits us to perceive, and categorize, and symbolize (....)." It "involves object reference...thematic structure, aitiational factors and the like" (Chomsky, 1980, p. 57-8). This is a model of knowledge of language (competence) which encompasses general cognitive processes such as perception, symbolization and memory functions; pragmatic processes which have to do with intentional language use; and grammatical knowledge which has to do with relationships between form and meaning. Hymes, though his was not a modular approach, anticipated this conception of competence by at least ten years.

Is competence an active ability or a passive capacity? Chomsky separates knowledge from use. Furthermore, language behavior is not evidence of language competence. It is not surprising therefore to find that competence in Chomsky's sense has nothing to do with an ability to perform. For example, if an aphasic has a period after injury and before recovery when she is no longer able to use the English language, Chomsky would argue that the aphasic nevertheless knows the English language. (See Chomsky 1980, Botha 1989, p. 47-59.) Chomsky would further contend that knowing a language is not like knowing how to ride a bicycle because the former is a matter of a specific mental structure (the language faculty) while the latter is a matter of a number of different mental and physical capacities. Hymes would probably hold that knowing how to ride a bicycle is actually somewhat like knowing a language; it requires a range of competencies, some people are more skilled at it than others, you learn it through doing it and one demonstrates one's knowledge of it by performing. This because for Hymes knowledge of a language also entails the ability to use it. Communicative competence is not simply a matter of passive knowledge but an ability to act: "One must recognize not only knowledge, but also ability to implement it (...). Especially, one must provide for motivation and value" (Hymes, 1974a, p. 96.)

The addition of motivation and value to a conception of competence is well outside the realm of Chomsky's definition of competence. It is important to the third aspect of Hymes' disagreement with Chomsky, the reduction of performance to behavior. Chomsky has made a distinction between I[nternalized]-languages and E[externalized]-languages. An I-language is a mental object, "some element of the mind of the person who knows the language (...)." An E-language is anything else, whether a set of objects such as sentences, or behaviors, or actions (Chomsky, 1986, p. 21-2). Chomsky argues that the study of I-language and grammars which correspond with I-language is more profound than the study of E-language or grammars which correspond with E-language. Consider the fact that the development of Chomsky's linguistic theory has to a great degree been motivated as an attack on behaviorism (and other anti-mentalist metatheories), that Chomsky conceives of competence as prior to and presupposing use, and that use is subservient to knowledge. These facts make clear that Chomsky's choice of "behavior" to define performance, relegates performance to an inferior status in his theory.

Hymes objects to this inferior status of performance in the competence-performance equation. As a functionalist Hymes sees performance as something more profound than mere behavior. And he does not accept "language use" as simply mechanistic actualization of competence. Hymes reformulates the term performance to correspond with folklorists and others who study verbal art to signify language use as a positive achievement and as something volitional and purposeful. Performance in this sense is a matter of value; for example this performance is more powerful than that, this performance more pleasing than that; because language is not simply a matter of mental objects, rather it is used within a communicative economy and has currency. Furthermore, language use is not simply behavior in any mechanistic sense of the term. It is intentional, motivated by a range of goals, needs, desires, interactional consequences, and so on. Performance is also important to the question of creativity.

In Chomskyian linguistics, in the attempt to get at the I-language, performance features are filtered out of the analysis. In Chomsky's (1965, p. 4) original formulation of the dichotomy, natural speech (i.e. performance) was said to demonstrate "numerous false starts, deviations from rules, changes of plan in mid-course, and so on." And these and other performance features such as "grammatically irrelevant conditions as memory limitations, distractions, shifts of attention and interest, and errors" needed to be filtered out (Chomsky, 1965, p. 3). Hymes points out that it is just these types of performance factors which received linguistic theory filters out – hesitations, interruptions, unfinished sentences, miscues, intonation and other prosodic features – which are meaningful in actual language use and important for our understanding of language. For Hymes a grammar should be able to account for these common occurrences:

> It is embarrassing at the very outset for a grammar, conceived as illuminating speaker's abilities, to be able to explain nicely mistakes that speakers almost never make [syntactic jumbles of the type "issue the us performance return let here"]...and to have nothing to say about "mistakes" that speakers make all the time – "mistakes", indeed, that are often the proper "mistake", so to speak, to make (Hymes, 1974a, p. 148).

To exclude language use (performance) from linguistic theory has another consequence: it excludes social meaning from linguistic theory. For Hymes, it is not that social meaning is something apart from language, so that one can simply in an *ad hoc* fashion attach social meaning to linguistic form, but rather social meaning is intricately connected to linguistic meaning. This is both in terms of understanding linguistic forms (because for Hymes form is emergent in relation to function), and in terms of understanding the metacommunication which envelopes linguistic form. Hymes maintains that "the interaction of language and social life must encompass the multiple relations between linguistic means and social meaning" (Hymes, 1974a, p. 31). For Hymes, then, performance is not extraneous to linguistic form or linguistic meaning, rather language is shaped by performance. In addition, one should not ignore performance factors because they are often important indicators of other levels of meaning which are taking place in an interaction.

Chomsky defines what he calls the creative aspect of language use as "the ability of normal persons to produce speech that is appropriate to situations though quite novel, and to understand when others do so" (Chomsky, 1975, p. 138). As Botha (1989) has pointed out, Chomsky excludes this area of concern from his linguistic theory because he considers the creative aspect of language use a "mystery"; i.e. something "beyond the domains of inquiry as we currently conceive them" (Botha, 1989, p. 51).

However, it is this very creativity of language use which is at the heart of Hymes' notion of communicative competence and his sociolinguistic theory. Hymes (1974a, p. 94) writes:

Chomsky's attempt to discuss the 'creative' aspect of language use (Chomsky 1966) suffers from the same difficulty as his treatment of competence. The main thrust is independent of situation. Chomsky specifies freedom from stimulus control, infinity of possible sentences, yet appropriateness of novel sentences to novel situations; but the first two properties, and the grammatical mechanisms he considers, can never account for appropriateness. A novel sentence might be wildly inappropriate. Appropriateness involves a positive relation to situations, not a negative one, and, indeed, a knowledge of a kind of competence regarding situations and relations of sentences to them.

For Hymes creativity is not a mystery which cannot be explained, instead it is an integral part of competence and performance, indeed, a necessary part of communicative competence. Creativity is evidence of the freedom and diversity of individuals and speech communities (Hymes, 1974a, p. 104). But creativity is not arbitrary or without constraints, hence it is explainable. If one considers the social nature of language use, if one focuses on "actual human beings and their abilities, and regard them as acquirers and shapers of culture, rather than merely as 'culture-bearers'" (Hymes, 1974a, p. 121) then one can describe and explain the "mystery" of creative language use.

Ethnography of Communication as Linguistic Theory

In short, linguists have abstracted from the content of speech, social scientists from its form, and both from the pattern of its use.

Hymes, 1974a, p. 126

The Speech Community

According to Hymes (1972, p. 43), "the natural unit of sociolinguistic taxonomy (and description)...is not the language but the speech community." The speech community is the "social matrix" which patterns language use. Hymes does not define what he means by "social matrix", but if one takes matrix to mean something within which something else develops, then the speech community is the source of language development.

Defining what is meant by speech community is problematic in two senses. First, it is problematic in that historically there has been a lack of scholarly consensus as to how to define a speech community. This is in great part because there is not a clear notion of what community is. (See Herrnstein Smith 1988 on the over-used and ill defined nature of "community".) To give adequate grounds for deciding whether someone belongs or does not belong to a particular community, as well as deciding what the boundaries of communities are, are ongoing sociological problems. Is communal identity a matter of shared rules of behavior, attitudes, beliefs, or knowledge? Are boundaries physical, material, psychological? (See Saville-Troike, 1982 for a brief discussion of these questions.)

Speech community as a concept is also built into Hymes' model to be problematic by the principle that descriptive constructs refer to emergent properties which cannot be established ahead of time. What a particular speech community is therefore a matter of ethnographic investigation and should not be presumed.

Differences in definitions of the speech community fall generally into whether the definition begins from a strictly linguistic basis, a sociocultural basis, or a basis of individual psychology. Simplistically put, speech communities have been defined in terms of sharing the same language (Bloomfield), sharing the same norms for language use (Hymes), sharing the same attitudes and values towards a language (Labov).

Hymes disagrees with Bloomfield's (1933) definition of speech community as a group of people who share the same language. According to Hymes (1972, p. 54), a speech community is "a community sharing rules for the conduct and interpretation of speech, and rules for the interpretation of at least one linguistic variety. Both conditions are necessary." Hymes stresses that "both conditions are necessary" because he rejects either a strictly linguistic or a strictly sociological definition of speech community. In stressing that a speech community cannot be defined by linguistic features alone, Hymes (1974a, p. 47) writes:

> The first confusion is between the notions of speech community and a language. Bloomfield (1933), and Chomsky (1965) and others have in effect reduced the notion of speech community to that of a language, by equating the two. The result is to make 'speech community' itself a redundant concept, having no part to play in research, beyond honoring its definitional foundations with its nominal presence.

Defining a speech community in terms of a language is inadequate because language boundaries are not strictly linguistic. Whether a variety counts as belonging to a particular language or not is a matter of historical and political considerations and not only linguistic criteria.[8]

The redundancy of the term speech community, which Hymes refers to above, is caused by community being defined in non-social terms and speech being defined in strictly linguistic terms. For Hymes, the speech community must be defined in social terms and speech must be considered as something more than grammar. Hymes (1974a, p. 47) writes:

> Speech community is a necessary, primary concept in that, if taken seriously, it postulates the unit of description as a social, rather than linguistic, entity. One starts with a social group and considers the entire organization of linguistic means within it, rather than start with some one partial, named organization of linguistic means, called a 'language.' And, "speech communities cannot be defined in terms of languages

alone in another respect. A person who is a member of a speech community knows not only a language but also what to say (Hymes, 1974a, p. 123).

In addition to claiming that sharing the same grammatical knowledge is insufficient, Hymes points out that sharing the same knowledge of rules of speaking is also insufficient. Speakers may belong to the same "sprechbund", meaning they share the same cultural norms of language behavior (politeness strategies, similar approximations for familiarity and distance, and so on), but they do not speak the same variety and are therefore not members of the same speech community. An example of this which Hymes gives is "a Czech who knows no German may belong to the same Sprechbund...but, not the same speech community, as an Austrian" (Hymes, 1974a, p. 49).

Hymes rejects the homogeneity of the speech community both as a theoretical idealization and as a description of reality. Instead, Hymes describes a speech community as an "organization of diversity" (Hymes, 1974b, p. 433). Diversity raises a number of questions for defining speech communities and the individual's relationship to them. Given both the diversity of the speech community and the diversity of the individual's participation in speech communities – people participate in a number of speech communities with varying degrees of membership – how can one know in particular cases whether someone is or isn't a member/participant in a speech community? For example, in what sense are two strangers on the street exchanging directions members of the same speech community? The fact that they share the "same" language would not be enough; what else would be required?

In attempting to deal with questions like these, Hymes distinguishes between a language field, a speech field, a speech network and a speech community (Hymes, 1974a, p. 49-51). He does not elaborate on the first three concepts. Hymes summarizes his account of the three concepts in this way: "In sum, a personal language field will be delimited by a repertoire of forms of speech; a personal speech field by a repertoire of patterns of speaking; and a personal speech network will be the effective union of these two. In virtue of such a union, one may be able to participate in more than one speech community" (Hymes, 1974a, p. 50).

Simplistically put, the first has to do with knowing the formal rules of languages (grammatical competence), and the second with knowing the normative rules of language use (communicative competence). A person may therefore have as their speech network a number of speech communities, that is, more than one combination of grammar and ways of speaking. A person may, for example, know how to speak a number of varieties of English as well as knowing how to behave appropriately across a range of geographical regions, contexts and situations.

Can a speech community be used to explain individual behavior? For example, can one explain an individual's linguistic behavior by claiming that she belongs to a particular speech community and persons who belong to that speech community behave in such a way? Hymes is against a correlational approach which would be a "mechanical amalgamation of standard linguistics and standard sociology" (Hymes, 1974a, p. 75). Following this reasoning, one would not be able to explain an individual's linguistic behavior by correlating it with a particular sociological unit such as gender, class, or ethnic group. Would a correlation with speech community be acceptable? If a speech community is an organization of diversity then the individual's relationship to any speech community is too fluid to allow for mechanical correlation. (See Hewitt 1988, for a discussion of membership and acceptance in speech communities.)

Nevertheless, Hymes' notion of "social matrix" makes the concept speech community useful as a normative concept: it is the speech community which enforces norms of behavior. It is in the speech community that one acquires and uses language. According to Hymes (1974a, p. 75):

> within the social matrix in which it acquires a system of grammar a child acquires also a system of use, regarding persons, places, purposes, other modes of communication, etc. – all components of communicative events, together with attitudes and beliefs regarding them. There also develop patterns of the sequential use of language in conversation, address, standard routines, and the like.

In this way there are normative rules of language use which are culturally based and which one learns in any social matrix within which one learns patterns of language use. Such a rule might be "children do not speak unless spoken to" or "children can speak whenever they want to". But, intervening in or interacting with these rules is "creativity". It is this creativity which disallows for determinism in the human condition. The normativity of the community is in a dialectic relation with individual freedom of the sort expressed by creativity. A speech community therefore does not determine the individual's behavior though it does influence it. (See Gal 1979 for a discussion of the relationship between the speech community and individual variation.)[9]

Though Hymes' concept of the speech community as the social matrix seems to capture the normative nature of language learning (see e.g. Bates 1976), and language use in general, his notion of community is too undeveloped (beyond the slogan of "organization of diversity") to adequately describe or explain the relationship between an individual and a community and the role that language plays in this relationship. Therefore, although the speech community has a central place in the ethnography of communication, it remains more as an abstraction. To contend with the actual context of utterance requires a closer look at interaction.

Context

Hymes uses the term context in its broadest sense to cover anything which could influence the production or interpretation of an utterance. Context is a complex system consisting of cognitive, sociocultural, discourse, psycho-biological, political and material factors (to mention an incomplete list). Based on what Hymes calls the culturally traditional "threefold division between speaker, hearer, and something spoken about" (Hymes, 1973a, p. 53), Hymes makes a list of components which make up the context of an utterance: message form, message content, setting, scene, speaker, or sender, addressor, hearer, or receiver or audience, addressee, purposes-outcome, purposes-goals, key, channels, forms of speech, norms of interaction, norms of interpretation, genres. Hymes also devised a mnemonic SPEAKING as a means of summarizing the components of this context. (Hymes' model can be found in a number of his writings in slightly differing forms. For a basic description of the model see Hymes, 1974a, p. 53-66.)

1. Setting and Scene: The setting places the utterance/discourse within a particular time and place. The scene Hymes refers to as the "psychological setting" (Hymes, 1972, p. 60), what Deborah Tannen (1979) has referred to as a frame. The frame sets up a set of expectations which allow for a specific interpretation of an interaction.

2. Participants: Hymes refers to participants as a universal, meaning that this is one element of the context that must always attain and will always be significant. Obviously one cannot have communication without any participants. Participants may include any combination of addressor, addressee, audience, speakers and hearers who may or may not be addressors and addressees. (See Schiffrin 1990a for a refinement of Goffman's model of participants to explain the possible relationships between speaker, hearer, audience, etc.) Certain speech events require a particular number of participants or particular types of participants. Given the interactive nature of communication, who the participants are will greatly influence the interaction.

3. Ends: Communication is purposeful in nature, one wants to persuade someone, get something done, express a particular sentiment or identify with a particular group or point of view. The goals (what one hopes to achieve) and outcomes (the typical culturally defined purposes) of an interaction will frame how the interaction is conceived as well as one's evaluation of it.

4. Act Sequence: The act sequence consists of what is said and how it is said, what Hymes refers to as the message form and message content. One way to distinguish between form and content is in the reporting of what someone said. If one says "She shouted, get the hell out of here" then one is reporting the form and the content. If one says "She told someone to leave" then one would be reporting the content only.[10]

5. Key: The key is the modality of the speech act, the "tone, manner or spirit in which the act is done" (Hymes, 1972, p. 62). The signalling of the key, whether we should act or interpret something as serious, joking, etc, is often done non-verbally as with a wink or gesture, which can convey the message "I'm only joking", or "Take me very seriously!"

6. Instrumentalities: This has to do with the way the "message" is transmitted, is it face to face, over the telephone, is it oral, written, chanted, whistled, sung? There are definite constraints and freedoms associated with certain instrumentalities. For example, you cannot see the reactions of your interlocutor if you are communicating over the telephone or by letter or telegram. This can make this type of interaction quite different from face to face interaction.

7. Norms of Interaction and Interpretation: Rules in the ethnography of communication are normative in nature. There are norms as to turn taking, pitch and loudness of voice, degree of friendliness or distance that one may approximate, and so on. The way one knows whether one has behaved in consort with the norms, or interpreted an event or interaction normatively, is by the reaction that one receives from others, verbally and non-verbally; that is, by the consequences of one's actions.

8. Genres: There are certain types of language use that can be categorized as typically belonging to poetry, advertisement, riddles, fairy tales, proverbs, lectures, and so on. Delimiting particular genres is done through attention to form and the typical correspondence between a particular form and a particular context. For example, in American academic culture lectures usually take place in an academic setting such as a university or some similar institution which have demarcated spaces such as auditoriums, and the form usually follows that of spoken literary writing with a sequencing which includes obviously segmented openings and closings.

In considering this description of context, one starts with the participants. With participants one must consider the intentions of the participants (ends), the attitudes of the participants (key), the positioning of the participants (key and scene). There is the material aspect of the context: the setting and the instrumentalities. The form of the discourse (genre and act sequence). And the social norms which direct interaction and interpretation. Context is therefore a matter of textual properties, mental properties, social properties and material properties.

The relationship between these properties is ultimately what defines the utterance. A different combination of components or different types of relationships between components would be a possible indication of different types of utterances, speech acts, events and situations. A switch in setting might, for example, change the definition of a lecture to a talk or discussion; or a switch in scene might change a joke into a threat.

Metalinguistic knowledge of terms such as lecture, talk, joke, threat, etc. is part of the context of defining a joke, a threat etc. Could one recognize a "joke", a "threat" or a "lecture" without knowing ahead of time what they were. How, for example, would someone who had never attended a lecture or anything like it know without being told that they were attending a lecture? Therefore, how does Hymes' model of context relate to communicative competence.

It is an etic grid. It allows an observer of an event to describe in etic terms the event as it is going on or after the event, to describe the context of a text. But how etic is it really? Could someone describe all the components of Hymes' context without prior knowledge? The answer is no. One would have to know already a range of things about settings, about participants, about modalities, about instrumentalities, etc. The question then remains, how would one be able to describe something one had never experienced before? The answer is that one would describe it in terms of frames of prior experience.

Say, for example, one had never been to a feminist consciousness raising group and one did not know the norms of interaction (for example, everyone gets to speak in turn without interruption). One could nevertheless describe aspects of it which were familiar – it takes place at someone's home, all the participants are female – but how would one know, for example that the ends were some sort of solidarity or personal catharsis? How long would it take as an observer to come up with the norms of interaction and interpretation and what means would one use to arrive at one's conclusions? How would one know what was actually important to other participants as opposed to what was important to oneself? In other words, is this model of context more than a descriptive tool? For example, is it what participants in an interaction might choose as their experience, as the context of their interaction? Is Hymes' notion of context simply a heuristic construct or does it make some further claim, such as that context is part of communicative competence?

Context entails a whole range of attributes (physical, social, cognitive, etc.), but how much of context is part of communicative competence? Communicative competence allows one to know when an utterance would be appropriate or not based on one's experience with speech routines. Now, is this knowledge the context for one's behavior, based on the components of context which Hymes has listed; or, is this knowledge separate from context, that is, is any knowledge independent of context? This is of course not a question which Hymes asks so he does not provide an answer. However, given his relativism it would be hard to imagine that he would accept context free knowledge. Nevertheless it is not clear exactly how context is related to communicative competence in his model. If context is simultaneously everything and everywhere – in the minds of the participants, in the text, in the society, in the physical world, in the metaphysical world; then it is not clear just what is the relationship between individual mind and all encompassing context.

Context is a fundamental feature of Hymes' theory because of the reasons already discussed, i.e. its relativism and its concentration on *parole* which is always situated language. Context is therefore the construct which can situate speech and which can explain why utterances are different, yet also be able to relate utterances together. Context is important to Hymes' theory because of the functionalist basis of his theory and because of his belief in the emergent properties of language whereby form and meaning emerge in contexts.

Hymes' model of context may also be understood in terms of ethnographic description. His typology is designed to be a tool of ethnographic description of the sort which could be used by a participant observer. The fact that it is of a typological form with broad etic categories which have to be filled in case by case is typical of traditional ethnography.

Given the centrality of context in Hymes' theory, a more developed notion of context is needed, one that is better integrated with the other aspects of the theory, such as communicative competence and the emergence of knowledge. Instead, context for Hymes seems to be a sort of holistic check-off sheet. When approaching language use there are a wide range of variables which interact with each other to make the instance what it is. Context seems to be all the variables that Hymes could think of which would be potentially part of the particularities of an utterance.

In this way, it is not clear what context is. Context seems at times to be something apart from form and content, and at other times not. For example, Hymes (1974a, p. 157) maintains that in order to understand the relationship between context and language use, and in order to understand whether a particular case of language use is appropriate or not, an ethnography must account for "(1) a set of alternative linguistic forms; (2) a set of contexts (specified in terms of participants, etc.); (3) unmarked values (social meanings) of forms and contexts; (4) a set of relations between forms and contexts." The first is the linguistic pool from which one chooses to use a particular form, the second is the context which frames or defines one's choice, the third is the social meanings which might apply to the choices one may make and the contexts one might find oneself in, and the forth is the normal relation between a form and a context.

Suppose for example that one may insult someone by using a number of different forms. Suppose one didn't want to insult someone, one instead wanted to show intimacy and solidarity through mock insult. One knows the value of certain forms and the contexts in which those forms are usually used. Given one's additional knowledge of the particular context, a friendly gathering with an intimate, one is able to choose an insulting form, and the relation between context and form will mediate in such a way that our "insult" is not taken as an insult but as a token of affection and comradery. (For studies of social argumentation, ritual insult and other types of playful forms of competition, see Bateson 1970; Labov 1972b; Schiffrin 1984.) Context in this case would seem therefore something apart from linguistic form. However, form is actually part of the context in Hymes' Speaking grid because he includes message form and message content within the context. There is therefore some lack of clarity in such basic issues as the relationship between text and context. (For a discussion of different perspectives on the text-context relationship, see Schiffrin, 1994.)

Ways of Speaking

Hymes attempts to develop functional linguistic units which are not wedded to discrete formal categories such as a language or a code. Hymes (1973a, p. 67) suggests repertoires, routines, patterns of use, ways of speaking, as alternatives to such received categories. He writes:

> Empirical and theoretical work has begun to provide a way of seeing the subject 'steadily as a whole.' It suggests that one think of a community (or any group, or person) in terms, not of a single language, but of a *repertoire*. A repertoire comprises a set of *ways of speaking*. Ways of speaking, in turn comprise speech styles, on the one hand, and contexts of discourse, on the other, together with the relations of appropriateness obtaining between styles and contexts. (Emphasis in original.)

Insisting on diversity Hymes argues that, "No normal person, and no normal community, is limited in repertoire to a single variety or code, to an unchanging monotony which would preclude the possibility of indicating respect, insolence, mock-seriousness, humor, role-distance, etc. by switching from one code variety to another" (Hymes, 1967, p. 9).

A repertoire is the resources available to an individual with which to express a wide range of meanings. This repertoire may include a number of languages and language varieties, or just one language but with a knowledge of the situational variations of that language. To borrow Herrnstein Smith's economic analogy, a repertoire is part of a person's economy and "a subject's experience of an entity is always a function of his or her personal economy" (Herrnstein Smith, 1988, p. 31). This personal economy is "multiply and differently configurable in terms of different roles, relationships, and in effect identities (citizen, parent, woman, property owner, teacher, terrestrial organism, mortal being, etc) in relation to which different needs and interests acquire priority (and, as may happen, come into conflict) under different conditions (ibid)."

Depending upon the contingencies of the situation (i.e. the context) an individual will choose elements of their repertoire in relation to their personal economy and the needs of the moment to express themselves in a meaningful way. Now the choices which are conventionally available to them to, for example, express their anger as a property owner, or express their concern as a teacher, will be part of the ways of speaking which are available to them. It is important to note here that a repertoire is not equivalent to a discrete language, grouping of languages or codes; it is not a discrete entity.

Hymes defines ways of speaking as a "primitive." He also defines it as "the speech economy of a community" (Hymes, 1972, p. 57-8). It is "the heuristic, or regulative, idea, that communicative conduct within a community comprises determinate patterns of speech activity, such that the communicative competence of persons comprises knowledge with regard to such patterns." Ways of speaking "can be taken to refer to the relationships among speech events, acts, and styles, on the one hand, and personal abilities and roles, contexts and institutions, and beliefs, values, and attitudes, on the other" (Hymes, 1974a, p. 45).

Ways of speaking is the relationship between personal economy and the community's speech economy, between what Hymes calls speech events, acts and styles, personal economy and social normativity. Ways of speaking are patterned behaviors (routines) learned within a social matrix which are applied in particular situations depending on personal economy and consequences of action. It is a person's communicative competence which allows her to judge the consequences of her actions, to plan strategies, to have expectations as to what is supposed to happen or what may happen or what is expected of her, in short, to make sense of the situation and act accordingly.

Hymes has described style as a way of speaking. One speaks relatively fast or slow, loud or soft, with or without much pausing, and so on. But how one speaks will carry meaning over and above referential meaning. How one speaks will carry social meaning as to one's attitude towards what one is saying (irony, anger, humor, etc.), our position relative to the other participants in the speech event (more or less intimate, more or less powerful, more or less responsible), and so on.

Another way to look at this is to consider Halliday's division of language use into the ideational, interpersonal and textual functions. (See Halliday, 1973, 1978.) When one speaks one conveys a certain amount of ideational information, social information and textual information. One conveys something about ideas, attitudes, things, identities, emotions, the genre and structure of the discourse (these are mine and not Halliday's terms). And one conveys all of this "information" simultaneously. One may by the choice of a lexical item in one's utterance refer to an object in the world and at the same time index oneself as a particular type of person. It is possible, however, that certain features of a language system are more frequently used, or more likely to be used to convey separately ideational, interpersonal, or textual meaning.

In this way Hymes, suggests that such things as intonation, pitch, and tempo are strictly stylistic, they carry non-referential meaning – they are not referring to things in the world or expressing ideas, but are expressing social relations, social meaning.

Conclusion

Hymes has made a call for revolutionary change, not only in the way linguistics is perceived and performed, but in the way academic disciplines are conceived and practiced, and he has provided a framework for this change. He defines sociolinguistics as a restructuring not only of linguistics but science. The restructuring of science entails the end to a fragmentary approach to human life and is multidisciplinary in scope. The restructuring of linguistics entails a new form of description which is based on an ethnographic approach, and a new emphasis on language use rather than abstract grammar. Hymes calls for a method which is holistic and emergent in nature – one which is contextualized both in reference to the sociopolitical context in which the scholar is working, and the context which envelopes the specific language use she is studying.

This is the framework that Hymes has provided but his work is peculiarly unfinished, strong in metatheory but weak in detail.[11] His methodology, which is directly borrowed from anthropology (ethnography) seems capable of describing and accounting for highly structured, or highly symbolic and ritualistic events, but seems incapable of adequately describing and accounting for the more individual aspects of language use. The non-ethnographic aspects of his methodology, those which come from ethnomethodology, speech act theory, discourse analysis and pragmatics, are poorly integrated into his theory because they were being developed at the same time as, or many years after, he had laid his foundations.

Hymes has provided us with a particularistic linguistic theory which has anticipated the metatheoretical issues with which such a theory must grapple with, but which does not have the technology with which to accomplish its task. Whether the technology which now exists – more complex theories of communication, more interactive approaches to language performance – could revise Hymes' work such that his strength of metatheory can be met with strength of detail is a question which remains.

Notes

[1] See Bauman and Sherzer 1975, and Philipsen and Carbaugh 1986, for bibliographies of the ethnography of communication. Names associated with the early development of the field include John Gumperz, Charles Frake, Joel Sherzer, Richard Bauman, Regna Darnell, and Susan Ervin-Tripp. More recent applications of the ethnography of communication have been in the field of education. See for example Heath 1983. In addition to the influences on the development of his thinking that Hymes cites such as Malinowski, Firth, Jakobson, Sapir, a close reading of his work will reveal additional influences from Goffman, Austin, Halliday, Bernstein, and the ethnomethodologists in particular Garfinkel, Sacks and Schegloff.

[2] Hymes is of course not singular in this approach. Sociolinguistics in its early years was known for the activism of its practitioners. (See, Shuy 1988 for a personal account.) A similar position to the one stated by Hymes, for example, has also been maintained by Labov. See, for example, Labov 1982.

[3] By speech Hymes does not literally mean speech but uses the word to include all uses of language "including writing, song and speech-derived whistling, drumming, horn calling, and the like" (Hymes, 1972, p. 53).

[4] When Hymes makes reference to Chomsky (and therefore when I make reference to Chomsky unless otherwise stated) he is referring to early Chomskyian theory, probably that of Chomsky's 1965 *Aspects of the Theory of Syntax*, as well as his 1966 *Cartesian Linguistics* and 1968 *Language and Mind*. The aspects of this theory which he is most strongly responding to are the notions of the ideal speaker/hearer, competence, and language universals.

[5] For a discussion of the difference between Chomsky-type and Greenberg-type universals see Botha, 1989. Botha refers to Greenberg-type universals as "cross-linguistic generalizations" (Botha, 1989, p. 133). For work done from both perspectives see Shopen, 1985, 2 vols.

[6] For a collection of Whorf's writings, see Carroll (Ed.) 1957.

[7] See Botha 1989 for a discussion on Chomsky's reaction to Hymes' communicative competence. I have no direct evidence that Chomsky was influenced by Hymes (that is, I have not read Chomsky acknowledging such an influence) but Chomsky does cite Hymes (see, for example, Chomsky 1986) and I think it telling that Chomsky chose to use the word appropriate as in the following definition of the creative aspect of language use: "the ability of normal persons to produce speech that is appropriate to situations (...)" (Chomsky, 1980, p. 76).

[8] Hymes takes into account the beliefs and attitudes of speakers in definitions of language, and he maintains that definitions of language are political. For example, even such tests of language boundaries as mutual intelligibility are political. Common examples of this are Chinese varieties which are mutually unintelligible but considered the same language, while there are mutually intelligible varieties such as Hindi and Urdu in north India which are considered different languages (Gumperz 1972, p. 228).

[9] Hymes does not define what he means by creativity though he gives examples of it: "the freedom to determine what and how much linguistic difference matters"; the use of "an old sentence in a new setting...the use of a new sentence in an old setting" (Hymes, 1974a, p. 123,132). Nevertheless, creativity would seem to be related to the intentional basis of language use (that communicative means are used towards ends), that language use is volitional, and that language is exemplary of the Romantic notion of the creative nature of the human spirit. (See for example, Hymes comparison of Herdian linguistics and Cartesian linguistics, 1974a, p. 120-124.)

[10] Since Hymes maintains: "It is precisely the failure to unite form and content in the scope of a single focus of study that has retarded understanding of the human ability to speak, and that vitiates many attempts to analyze the significance of behavior" (Hymes, 1973a, p. 54). I am not sure why he makes this form/content dichotomy or why he uses the term act sequence which has to do with the sequencing of speech acts in a discourse.

[11] In defense of Hymes, he has referred to his theoretical model as "toward a theory" (Hymes, 1972a, p. 52). He seems to have left the detailed workings of the system to emerge through observation of particulars in actual occurrences, that is, concrete language use. In a sense, Hymes has created a theoretical framework which is open-ended, and which others should add details to depending on the findings of specific work. In this way one may see Gumperz's development of interactional sociolinguistics as filling in many of the holes in Hymes' model. It might be unfair to criticize Hymes for a theory which is weak on the exemplar level and therefore "unfinished" if one grants that his theory is meant from an ideological perspective to be "unfinished"; i.e. emergent and contextualized. Nevertheless, theories which are meant to be emergent and contextualized (rather than abstract and static) can produce well defined constructs.

4

William Labov and Sociolinguistic Realism

> *...more than anything else, I benefitted from Weinreich's calm conviction that we are moving in the direction that a rational and realistic linguistics must inevitably follow.*
>
> Labov, 1972a, p. xv

Sociolinguistics According to William Labov

> *I have resisted the term* sociolinguistics *for many years, since it implies that there can be a successful linguistic theory or practice which is not social.*
>
> Labov, 1972a, p. xiii

> *In spite of a considerable amount of sociolinguistic activity, a socially realistic linguistics seemed a remote prospect in the 1960's. The great majority of linguists had resolutely turned to the contemplation of their own idiolects.*
>
> Ibid.

William Labov laid a foundation for sociolinguistics, a point of view and a method, which has had an immense influence over the development of sociolinguists. Labovian linguistics has become synonymous with sociolinguistics in many linguistic circles and though this trend has weakened, the influence of Labov over the development of modern sociolinguistics should not be underestimated.[1]

A review of Labov's work starting with his early work on Martha's Vineyard (1963), continuing with his work on New York City (1966), his work on the Black English Vernacular (1972b), and his recent work on Philadelphia (1980b, 1986, 1987b, 1989) reveals metatheoretical consistency over more than twenty years.

For Labov sociolinguistics "is a somewhat misleading use of an oddly redundant term" (Labov, 1972a, p. 183). It is "misleading" because it somehow implies that sociolinguistics is something other than linguistics, and it is "oddly redundant" because it implies that there can be a linguistics which does not consider language socially. For Labov, sociolinguistics is linguistics proper: "the general study of the structure of language" (Labov, 1975, p. 77). He therefore resists the implication that sociolinguistics is something other than, or less than, linguistics. However, for Labov the study of language structure must take place within the social context of the speech community.

Thus his resistance to the term sociolinguistics with its implication that linguistics proper does not need to consider language as a social phenomenon.

In keeping with his insistence on sociolinguistics as linguistics proper, Labov from as early as 1966 rejected the suggestion that sociolinguistics needed to be an interdisciplinary field (a view advocated by Hymes). Labov defining this type of sociolinguistics as "the comprehensive description of the relations of a language and society", called it "an unfortunate notion foreshadowing a long series of purely descriptive studies with little bearing on the central theoretical problems of linguistics or of sociology" (Labov, 1966/82, p. vii).

It is not that Labov denies the useful or even necessary contribution to the study of linguistics from other fields; rather he has suggested that narrow formalism is detrimental and that linguistics can be enhanced with knowledge of physiology, the social use of language and cognitive processes (Labov, 1975, p. 130); but his concern is ultimately with the linguistic system from a strictly linguistic perspective. Explanation for linguistic phenomena such as language change may be social, but this does not then require the sociological study of language change. Labov's focus remains with linguistic facts. These linguistic facts are sometimes but not always related to specific social facts.

Labov has distinguished between sociolinguistics as the sociology of language, the ethnography of speech, and his own approach. The sociology of language "deals with large-scale social factors, and their mutual interaction with languages and dialects...The linguistic input for such studies is primarily that a given person or group uses language X in a social context or domain Y" (Labov, 1972a, p. 183). The ethnography of speech studies "... the patterns of use of languages and dialects within a specific culture (...). This functional study is conceived as complementary with the study of linguistic structure (ibid)". And the sociolinguistics which Labov proposes: "the study of language structure and evolution within the social context of the speech community. The linguistic topics to be considered here cover the area usually named 'general linguistics,' dealing with phonology, morphology, syntax, semantics" (Labov, 1972a, p. 184).

Given Labov's distinction between these different approaches to sociolinguistics it is clear that he places his work squarely within received linguistics in terms of its topics of concern (phonology, morphology, syntax and semantics), and that he leaves the questions of culturally patterned language use and socially or situationally constrained language to other types of sociolinguistics. Extrapolating from these distinctions, it would seem that Labovian sociolinguistics is not centrally concerned with large-scale socio-political issues which guide language choice and language behavior, nor is it centrally concerned with cultural aspects of language use. Instead, it would seem to be a type of micro-linguistics (cf. Lyons 1977a,b), one which unlike most received approaches to linguistics places the locus of language in some sort of social order (the speech community) rather than the individual.

Labovian sociolinguistics is the study of language in its social context (cf. Labov 1972a), but this is not to be misinterpreted as a functionalist study of language use, nor should social context be confused with cultural, socio-cognitive, interactive or phenomenological notions of social context. Labovian sociolinguistics is not a theory of *parole*, nor is it a study of language use for descriptive purposes, but a study of language use for what it reveals about linguistic structure (*langue*). For Labov language and social context are two separate entities and sociolinguistics correlates linguistic facts (phonology, morphology and syntax) with social facts (class, gender, age).

Labov's formulation of sociolinguistics is metatheoretically guided by three types of realism: metaphysical realism, scientific realism and mundane realism. Mundane realism, unlike the former two types of realism which are historically related to a particular philosophical tradition, is the label here given to Labov's contention that a realistic linguistics must be concerned with the secular everyday world that "real" people live in, that linguistics must some how realistically reflect the linguistic facts of these lives. The object of linguistics should therefore be, in Labov's words: "(...) language as it is used in everyday life by members of the social order, that vehicle of communication in which they argue with their wives, joke with their friends, and deceive their enemies" (Labov, 1972a, p. xiii).

What is often termed metaphysical realism is "the belief that the world exists independently of our knowledge of it. What this means is that for any proposition p, to the question 'Is p true or false?' the world has a determinate answer irrespective of our ability to calculate the answer" (Luntley, 1988, p. 1). The realist position that things exist, truths exist etc, independent of our ability to cognize them – that there is a "mind-independent physical world" (Vision, 1988, p. 14) – is in contrast to such anti-realist or irrealist positions as nominalism and conceptualism.

According to Rescher (1987, p. xi), nominalism holds that: "Abstracta have no independent existences as such. They only 'exist' in and through the objects that exhibit them. Only particular (individual substances) exist. Abstract 'objects' are existents in name only, mere thought-fictions by whose means we address concrete particular things". And conceptualism holds that "While abstracta do not exist independently as such, they have a quasi-existence that does not wholly depend on the objects that exhibit them. This quasi-existence takes a *conceptual* form. They 'exist' through their being conceived in the minds of people who are naturally disposed to group together various items that roughly answer to these conceptions (...)(ibid)". (Emphasis in original.)

Scientific realism is the application of metaphysical realism to science. It maintains that "science describes the real world: that the world actually is as science takes it to be and that its furnishings are as science envisions them to be" (Rescher, 1987, p. 4). Scientific realism maintains that the real world exists independent of the cognitive abilities of humans, yet there is a correspondence between the real world and the scientist's theories about the real world. This is in contrast to instrumentalism which holds that the theoretical entities of science "do not exist at all; they are merely useful thought-fictions that we invoke in providing explanations for observable phenomena" (Rescher, 1987, p. xii). And it is in contrast to what Rescher calls approximationism, the tenet that scientific theoretical entities do not really exist, but there is some approximate correspondence between "scientific ideas and reality itself (ibid)".

Labov is a philosophical realist, holding both the metaphysical and scientific realist positions. As mentioned, social context for Labov is not to be confused with the views of context taken in an interactional, phenomenological, or socio-cognitive approach. These are all irrealistic approaches which hold that reality is constructed to some extent by interaction between the individual and the world, and through the cognitive schemas with which the individual orders the world. In contrast, Labov holds the realist position that social context is made up of social facts which act upon the individual but which are not created by the individual. A social fact is "a *form of behavior*, which is (1) *general* throughout a society, and (2) that exercises *constraint over individuals*; (3) but this constraint is peculiar in that it is generally *unconscious*, and so cannot *directly coerce*: it merely leaves *no options* for acceptable behavior (emphasis in original)" (Dinneen, 1989, p. 34). A social fact thus has an independent existence and is therefore an abstract object in the realist sense.

Given Labov's definition of his approach to sociolinguistics, he is concerned with the abstract linguistic system (*langue*). This system is made up of linguistic facts, linguistic objects which are the theoretical entities of the scientist (i.e. the linguist) and which following scientific realism correspond with the real world independent of individual's abilities to recognize them. In this way Labov makes a distinction between the scientific object *langue*, which is the object of linguistic enquiry, and language as a "symbolism", which is the non-scientific way people experience and speak about language. According to Labov (1987, p. 128,134) there are:

> (...) two conceptions of language. One is the set of socially significant symbols: the words and sounds that are perceived and recognized by most members of society as identifying a particular language variety (...). The other is the linguistic system, as the linguist describes it(...). These two types of language show radically different patterns of transmission and learning(...). The small number of stereotypes available to members of the community provide the concrete materials for discussions of the community's 'language'. They almost always refer to surface features of the linguistic system. The ideas conveyed are vague, overparticular, misleading and very often dead wrong, if they are taken as referring to the linguistic system that people actually use (...).

Labov places the locus of language in the community and issues of grammar are settled at the level of the community. For example, if there is a question of whether X variable belongs to Y or Z grammar this question will be settled in terms of an entire group of speakers rather than an individual speaker. What are valid criteria for deciding whether someone does or does not belong to a particular speech community? The realist criteria are objective linguistic facts which are independent of the subjective beliefs or perceptions of language users. In this way, given conflicting criteria for membership in a speech community, Labov chooses what he considers to be essential features of the linguistic system over what he considers to be inessential features of the socio-semiotic system.

Labov (1980a) discusses the case of "Carla", a non-Black woman who was able to create "the effective social impression that she was speaking the Black English Vernacular and the impression of black identity" (Labov, 1980b, p. 379). Carla relies on a range of formulaic strategies related to discourse style, such as the use of certain lexical items, negative inversion, adverb placement, and effective use of stress, pitch and tempo. In this way Carla is able to convince others that she is speaking BEV. That is, Blacks given her speech in voice samples and asked to judge her speech uniformly judged her to be speaking BEV (ibid). Labov, however claims that Carla is not really a member of the BEV speech community because she has not learnt the defining rules of BEV grammar: the BEV tense and aspect system (ibid). To be able to acquire or manipulate social symbols is therefore not sufficient, one must have acquired the essential rules of the grammar.

There are two interesting points to note here. First, the rules of the grammar which define one's membership are not subject to conscious acquisition or manipulation, they are part of the independent abstract grammatical system. Second, as Labov has noted above, the acquisition of the grammatical system and the acquisition of the socio-semiotic system are different, one can consciously acquire a number of different discourse styles; however, one cannot consciously acquire a number of different grammars.[2]

Sociolinguistic Theory and Linguistic Theory

> *It seems natural enough that the basic data for any form of general linguistics would be language as it is used by native speakers communicating with each other in everyday life.*
>
> Labov, 1972a, p. 184

> *The data that we need cannot be collected from the closet or from any library, public or private; fortunately for us, there is no shortage of native speakers of most languages if we care to listen to them speak. Without such empirical data, we are now in the process of producing a great many well-formed theories with nothing to stand on: beautiful constructions with ugly feet.*
>
> Labov, 1972b, p. 124,125

> *... the aim here is not necessarily to provide linguistics with a new theory of language, but rather to provide a new method of work.*
>
> Labov, 1972a, p. 207

Labovian Sociolinguistics as Received Linguistics

Labov (1975, p. 78) in his review of 50 years of American linguistics divides the history into two periods: 1925-1955 when American linguists "were concerned with the description of language on the basis of objective facts", and 1955-1975 when American linguists became "increasingly concerned with the explanation of the language faculty through the study of intuitions". Labov suggests that "we can build directly upon the achievements of both periods of American linguistics, recognizing the defects of their empirical base, without losing the glimpse of formal structure that we have obtained" (Labov, 1975, p. 128,129).

Labov may be seen as attempting a synthesis between these rival factions in received linguistics. It is a synthesis which is seen as building upon past accomplishments, making improvements where necessary but not fundamentally challenging basic tenets. This is a positivist notion of science, that science progresses in a cumulative fashion with an ever increasing body of correct knowledge. Labov therefore rejects anti-positivist notions of the development of science such as Kuhn (1962).

In advocating an eventual convergence ("realistic linguistics") between these rival factions in linguistics (those practicing linguistics based on introspection versus those practicing linguistics based on observable data), Labov rejects the anti-realist point of view that there is no single linguistic reality and that therefore such a convergence is impossible. Labov's rejection of the Kuhnian perspective is vehement:

> It is suggested that we have two incommensurable 'paradigms'. This is a fashionable view, and the construction of such paradigms is a favorite occupation of those who would prefer to discuss the limits of knowledge rather than add to it. There is a tendency to see linguistics as a kind of debating society, where the winner is awarded the privilege of not reading the papers of the losers, and re-writes the history of the field in favor of some more remote progenitor (Labov, 1975, p. 128).

The issue for Labov is therefore not what is linguistics – "(...) it no longer seems necessary to argue about what is or is not linguistics" (Labov, 1972, p. xiii) – but what method leads to the most realistic description and explanation of the object of linguistic enquiry. One therefore does not find, for example, any theoretical discussion of the received rules or units approach to linguistics (see, for example, Taylor and Cameron 1987 for a critical discussion of this received approach), though one does find Labov disagreeing with particular rules or formulations of rules. One does however find much discussion of method and data as they relate to theory. Labov was not attempting to create a new paradigm by developing sociolinguistics, but viewed sociolinguistics as an improved version of received linguistics.

Labovian Linguistics and Saussurian Linguistics

What type of linguistics is Labovian linguistics? It can be viewed as an attempted synthesis between individual and social approaches to linguistics. (In a similar vein it could be even viewed as an attempted synthesis between formal and functional approaches to linguistics.) Another way of describing this synthesis is to do so in terms of Saussurian linguistics.

Labov's sociolinguistics may be defined as conforming strongly to a particular reading of Saussure. Labov uses Saussurian terminology (for example, *langue* and *parole*), cites Saussure, criticizes Saussure, and develops what he calls the Saussurian Paradox to explain an apparent irony in linguistic methodology[3], but he does not discuss Saussure in a general theoretical way or in any depth. The times when Labov does discuss Saussure's theory is when he disagrees with Saussure. (For example, Saussure's synchronic/diachronic distinction and the claim that one cannot study language change in process.) It is therefore somewhat of a leap to present Labov as a Saussurian when he does not explicitly do so himself. Nevertheless, Labov claims that linguistics is the study of *langue* and therefore there cannot be a linguistics which is not social in nature. Furthermore, Labov claims that the locus of language is in the community and that *langue* is a social fact which determines/constrains language behavior. These are basic tenets of a particular reading of Saussurian linguistics.[4]

There have developed from different readings of Saussure's writings a number of distinct and sometimes competing schools of thought. (See Joseph, 1990a for an interesting discussion of the role of ideologically selective readings of Saussure in the history of linguistics.) There is for example the continental and primarily French development of structuralism which is not solely linguistic in nature, and similarly the post-structuralists who, despite their name, include much of Saussure's semiotic notions in their work. And there is more generally the field of semiotics. In terms of linguistics, there is less focus on Saussurian semiotics and more a focus on such constructs as the *langue/parole* dichotomy, the synchrony/diachrony dichotomy, and the structuralist notion of language being a system of relations.[5] It is this last reading of Saussure that is of concern here.

Saussure made a distinction between "*la langue*", "*la parole*" and "*le langage*." This three-way distinction, despite continuing difficulties in interpreting what Saussure meant, became immensely influential in modern linguistics in the form of the *langue/parole* dichotomy and the claim that the object of linguistic inquiry is *langue* rather than *parole* or *langage*. *Langue* is the real object or pure form, the abstract supra-individual grammatical system which all speakers of a particular language share to some extent but which no one speaker commands in full. This is not to say that *langue* is the sum total of the competencies of all speakers of a language; *langue* is independent of any individual or group of individual's abilities. *Langue* is therefore a universal.

Parole on the other hand is actual utterance and as such is individual, particularistic, context bound, "never the same, often completely novel and unrepeatable in its concrete detail" (Dinneen, 1989, p. 37). *Langage,* the most difficult of the three terms, may be read as the combination of *langue* (the abstract system) and *parole* (the concrete system). In this way it combines both the universal aspects of *langue* and the particularities of *parole.* (See Joseph, 1989 for a different reading of *langage* by Piero Bottari who holds that *langage* is most close to Chomsky's notion of competence.)

Saussure, in attempting to establish linguistics as a science held that both *parole* and *langage* were too unstable and particularistic to be the object of scientific enquiry. According to Dinneen (ibid), "If there were to be a Science of Language [as Saussure was proposing], its object should be stable, uniform, identical in all instances, and not subject to reformulation upon renewed examination. That means that it cannot be something concrete. And that is why de Saussure defines *la langue* as a pure form". This explains the received linguistic focus on the abstract system.

Saussure was not only attempting to establish linguistics as a science; he was also attempting to establish linguistics as an autonomous field. That is, linguistic facts would be explained by other linguistic facts rather than for example psychological factors. As Joseph 1990b, p. 1 quotes "(...) linguistics has as its true and unique object *langue* envisaged in itself and for itself." In attempting to establish linguistics as autonomous, Saussure held that one should not consider all aspects of language because then "a number of sciences (psychology, physiology, anthropology, grammar, philology, etc.) will be able to claim language as their object (ibid)".

Saussure objected to the notion of using individual psychology as explanation for linguistic phenomena, and he objected to the individual as the locus of language or the focus of inquiry since he considered the individual level of language to be too chaotic for scientific study. Saussure maintained that "(...) *langue* is an eminently social thing, no fact exists linguistically until the moment it becomes everybody's fact, whatever its starting point may be." And, "*Langue* is absolutely social. Every individual fact has value only when it becomes social." (Quoted in Joseph, 1990b, p. 1.)

Dinneen (1989, p. 37) has argued that though there is no direct proof that Saussure read or was influenced by Durkheim, one can nevertheless argue that language for Saussure "can be taken as implied in conditions for identifying what Durkheim called a 'social fact'." This chapter will assume Saussure's conception of *langue* as a social fact as a valid (though not exclusive) reading of Saussure. In addition, for the analysis at hand, it is known that Labov is familiar with Durkheim, that he uses the term social fact, that he accepts language to be a social fact, and most importantly that he accepts the above reading of Saussure. In Labov's words: "Now we are coming to see that the social contract that lies behind Saussure's conception of *langue* is a linguistic reality. The set of forms and meanings that is transmitted to the language learner rests on a fundamentally homogeneous structure, which like other social facts is binding on every individual" (Labov, 1987, p. 129).

Earlier a social fact was defined as being general throughout society (note Saussure above that no fact exists linguistically until the moment it becomes everybody's fact), as exercising constraints over individuals and that these constraints are generally unconscious rather than directly coercive. Labov, similar to Saussure, rejects the individualist psychological description or explanation of language and instead locates language in the community.

In writing about the community as educator, Labov explicitly rejects "the individual psyche, molded by the innate capacity and particular make-up of the language learner", and instead begins with "language as a social fact the system of communication used in everyday life and controlled by the social compact to assign certain meanings to certain forms and their arrangements" (Labov, 1987, p. 129). Language, as in the case of other social facts (for example marriage customs), is therefore not the property of the individual but the property of the community, and the individual simply inherits the constraints by virtue of being a member of the community. The notion of language as social fact therefore allows Saussure and Labov to remove the individual or individual instances of behavior from their theory in favor of the social order.

This question of social facts and their coercive nature has led to criticism against both Saussure and Labov that their linguistic theories are deterministic. (See for example, Cameron 1987, 1990 for criticism of Labov, and Mayzor 1989 for criticism of Saussure.) What does it mean for example when Labov (1989, p. 130) refers to the linguistic system of the (non-Black) Philadelphia speech community as governing "the speech of Philadelphia with an iron hand?" Is the claim that language is always social then less a matter of language being used in social interaction between individuals, and rather that language is a social contract which systematically determines individual behavior?

The corner-stone of Saussurian linguistic theory is the arbitrary nature of the linguistic sign. By arbitrariness is meant that there is no natural or necessary correspondence between a word and what it refers to. For example, there is no natural or necessary reason why a cat should be called "cat" or "gato" and so forth. The arbitrariness of language is used to support both the autonomy of linguistics and the supra-individual social nature of language. If language is arbitrary then it cannot be studied as a natural kind or psychological object because its arbitrariness, it is argued, requires that it be considered in terms of itself. In addition, the arbitrariness of language requires that there be some social convention by means of which correspondence between the linguistic sign and its referent can be established. It is therefore through the social conventions of the group that language is a meaningful system.

There is an ongoing tension in Labov's work between the claim that the object of linguistic enquiry is orderly, systematic and non-particularistic (if studied properly), and Labov's disagreement with Saussure, Chomsky and others who insist upon the necessary homogeneity of the linguistic object. On the one hand we have Labov agreeing with Saussure that *langue* is fundamentally homogeneous on the level of the community (see, for example Labov 1989), but disagreeing with Saussure that the scientific study of language needs to ignore real heterogeneity, as well as disagreeing with Saussure's contention that *parole* is chaotic and unmotivated.

Weinreich, Labov and Herzog (1968, p. 121) criticize Saussure for not adequately accounting for language as a social fact and for his "precondition of dealing with language as a social phenomenon [which] was still its complete homogeneity." They go on to argue for the motivated and orderly nature of variation by maintaining that "deviations from a homogeneous system are not all error-like vagaries of performance, but are to a high degree coded and part of a realistic description of the competence of a member of a speech community" (op cit, p. 125). They argue that "nativelike command of heterogeneous structures is not a matter of multidialectalism or 'mere' performance, but is part of unilingual linguistic competence" (op cit, p. 101). And they offer a traditional functionalist explanation for this fact: "(...) in a language serving a complex (i.e. real) community, it is *absence* of structured heterogeneity that would be dysfunctional (ibid)". (Emphasis in original.)

Labov therefore argues for an approach which takes into account the functional need for variation within a speech community. Labov however is not interested in those "differences [which] don't make a difference" (Labov, 1975, p. 79). He is not interested in variation which cannot be systematically explained in terms of the linguistic system. For Labov, then, "(...) the fundamental postulate of linguistics set out by Bloomfield at the beginning of our development still stands without question: that some utterances are the same (ibid)". Systematic variation is a matter of alternative ways of saying the same thing. However, the signification of "saying the same thing" is restricted to linguistic meaning:

> We may want to give great attention to differences in intonation contour, nasalization, or foregrounding of linguistic elements: but these will be studies of expressive style or interactive force which must rest on the perception that these variants are alternative ways of saying 'the same thing' in a linguistic sense. The linguist interested in more complex structure should feel free to proceed further on the basis of these facts about sameness" (Labov, 1975, p. 81).

One can therefore ignore the non-linguistic significance of this variation, (for example the expressive or interactive aspects of the utterance), simply assuming that for linguistic purposes they are not important. This can be justified because the linguistic system and non-linguistic system are not integrated but are considered as separate entities. Labov, therefore despite his expressed differences with Saussure over the homogeneous nature of *langue*, seems to have no real difference with him on this score.

As suggested earlier, Labov may be seen as attempting some kind of synthesis between disparate schools within the study of language structure. This synthesis may also be seen as an attempt to relate *parole* to *langue* in a more synthetic way, showing a systematic relationship between *parole*, the observable phenomena, and the abstract system, *langue*.

If Labov is viewed as a participant in normal science, and normal science is concerned with orderly, replicable, and generalizable entities, there is a metatheoretical motivation for Labov's focus on the orderliness of *parole* rather than on the unique particularities of *parole*. If the realistic object of enquiry is the observable language that people actually perform (and one is studying this mundane object as a means of studying the abstract object), in order to make scientifically verifiable statements one must be able to show a motivated and orderly correspondence between the mundane object and the abstract object.

In this way Labov disagrees with the contention that *parole* is to a large extent ungrammatical, instead maintaining that: "In the various empirical studies that we have conducted, the great majority of utterances about 75 percent – are well-formed sentences by any criterion" (Labov, 1972a, p. 203). And he goes on to add that when editing rules are applied "the proportion of truly ungrammatical and ill-formed sentences falls to less than two percent (ibid)". If *parole* is to a great extent grammatical, and if variation can be shown to be correlatable in a replicable and theoretically motivated fashion, then it follows that *parole* can indeed be studied scientifically.

By expanding the scientific study of language to include both *langue* and *parole*, Labov may be seen as either fulfilling the Saussurian premise that a Science of Language would eventually include the study of *langage* (both *langue* and *parole*) or, if one reads Saussure differently, as expanding Saussurian linguistics beyond the scientific study of *langue* to include the scientific study of *parole* (in relation to *langue*).

Saussure in attempting to establish linguistics as a science distanced himself from much of the work on language which had been previously done, much of which was historical in its emphasis. Saussure stressed that to be able to study a language structurally one needed to do so in a static sense; that is, study a language in only one state at a time. Saussure did not believe that language change could be observed in progress and suggested that the study of language structure and the study of language change be done separately. This is where Labov clearly differs with Saussure. Labov's work, which has been predominantly concerned with language evolution and change, is fundamentally opposed to this view of language change. His work has demonstrated that linguists are able to show language change in progress. (See for example 1972a, 1980b.)

Labov, Chomsky and the Empirical Foundations of Linguistics

Explicit metatheoretical argument in Labov's work may be understood as a sustained call for empirical foundations for linguistics. (See, for example, Weinreich, Labov and Herzog 1966, Labov 1972a, 1975, 1989.) The overriding nature of this concern in Labov's work cannot be over emphasized. In writing on "the study of language in social context" for example, there is almost no theoretical discussion or definition of social context. Instead there is extended argument for Labov's empirical program for linguistics with data taken from sociolinguistic studies (hence the term social context) as providing support for his call for an empirically based linguistics. This argument, coupled with Labov's rejection of individual psychology as a frame of reference for linguistics, as well as rejection of the "idiolect" or individual grammar as the correct object of linguistic enquiry, places Labov at odds with Chomsky and Chomskyian linguistics.[6]

Labov's argument against Chomskyian linguistics is against the individual as the source of linguistic data. It is against the use of intuition as valid data or the basis for valid explanation. It is an argument over where the locus of language is, what the object of linguistic enquiry is, and the nature of empirical explanation.

Labov's disagreement with Chomsky is not formal. Labov accepts much of generative grammar's formalism. In addition, Labov is in apparent agreement with Chomsky over the purpose of linguistics. Labov accepts the received linguistic position that "we are engaged in the general study of the structure of language, not gathering particular facts about languages; our aim is to understand the human capacity to construct a language system and not just collect the output of that system" (Labov, 1975, p. 77). Labov's disagreement with the Chomskyian approach is over how one goes about doing linguistics and how one proves which approach is correct: "(...) we all want our explanations and analyses to be right; very few linguists are interested in grammar which is universal but wrong (ibid)".

Labov's chief concern is therefore methodological: what means will best garner the facts which can prove that one is right rather than wrong. In Labov's words, "I do not believe we need at this point a new 'theory of language'; rather, we need a new way of doing linguistics that will yield decisive solutions" (Labov, 1972a, p. 259). For Labov the "new way of doing linguistics" is empirical studies of speech communities, with solutions to be found in data gathered from the speech community. The rationale for this position is that by this method "we encounter the possibility of being right: of finding answers that are supported by an unlimited number of reproducible measurements, in which the inevitable bias of the observer is canceled out by the convergence of many approaches (ibid)". In contrast to Chomsky, the solution for Labov is not to be found in intuition, in the use of introspective data, or the study of grammar at the level of individual psychology.

In this chapter Labov is defined as a realist. Chomsky is also a realist (see Chomsky 1986, Botha 1989, Pateman 1987.) How then do two competing realists decide who has the most realistic theory, description, or explanation? Labov appeals to mundane realism, that his data corresponds with what people actually do, and Chomsky appeals to psychological realism, that his data corresponds with the actual workings of the brain. Not surprisingly, Chomsky's linguistic theory is not a theory of what people do but a theory of the structure of the mental language faculty, and Labov's linguistic theory is not a theory of the mind but a theory of language structure as it is embedded in social structure.[7] Labov and Chomsky therefore place the locus of language in two different places, and thus their object of enquiry is not the same.

Given Labov's fundamental belief that language is social – that language is a social fact – it follows that Labov would object to linguistic enquiry which did not proceed from this basic assumption. In earlier works, Labov frequently objects to what he calls the idiolect as being the object of linguistic description. According to Bloch, as cited by Labov (1972a, p. 192), the idiolect is "the speech of one person talking on one subject to the same person for a short period of time." This actually corresponds with certain definitions of utterance and may be seen as a unit of discourse rather than as referring to individual grammar. It is possible that Labov might have been objecting to the utterance as the correct object of linguistic description but he does not say so directly. He does goes on to point out that "it must be noted that the very existence of the concept 'idiolect' as a proper object of linguistic description represents a defeat of the Saussurian notion of *langue* as an object of uniform social understanding (ibid)". Though this statement would preclude the study of utterance, which is not uniform, Labov is also objecting to a more generalized sense of the idiolect, the study of the individual grammar rather that the social grammar; the focus of language in the individual rather than the social group.

The questions of where language is located and what the object of linguistic enquiry should be are closely related. For Labov the locus of language is not in the individual but in the community – "Language is not a property of the individual, but of the community" (Labov, 1989, p. 52). It is not that Labov denies a biological basis for language – "There is general agreement that language is an instrument of communication that depends jointly on an underlying physiological system and a system of social control" (Labov, 1989, p. 1). However for Labov the answer to his question of "where to find the most systematic view of the linguistic system – in the individual who carries the genetic mechanism or in the community that exerts the stimulus and control (ibid.)", is in the community. The object of linguistic enquiry for Labov is therefore the community and not the individual.

Labov considers language to be a social fact and locates language in the community-at-large rather than in the individual. Chomsky on the other hand considers language to be a mental property and locates language in the species rather than in any social group. Chomsky's general theory of linguistic structure is concerned with the language faculty, "a particular component of the human mind" (Chomsky, 1986, p. 3) which is species endowed. In addition, Chomsky states that the standpoint of generative grammar "is that of individual psychology (ibid)". Because the language faculty is species specific, one can assume that any (normal) member of the species will be endowed with such a faculty and therefore any (normal) individual member of the species is acceptable as a specimen. If one adds to this the Cartesian notion that knowledge is attained most immediately and completely through intuition, one arrives at the conclusion that the individual and individual intuitions are acceptable means of approaching reality.

However for Labov this is unacceptable. It is unacceptable both in terms of the individual as the locus of language and object of enquiry and intuition as an acceptable form of knowledge. Labov objects to individual psychology as the standpoint of grammar. Since Labov accepts the social definition of the linguistic system (*langue*), no one individual is able to represent this overall system. Only individuals in relation to other individuals may show systematic behavior.

For Labov intuition is not an acceptable means of approaching reality because it is internal, subjective and there are no grounds for comparing intuitions. The problem Labov has with intuition is three-fold: 1.) intuitions cannot be replicated, 2.) with intuition as data there is no principled way to decide between different linguistic theories and, 3.) the intuitions of the linguist are unreliable.

Point one is the contention that intuitions cannot be replicated. Given the important standing the replication of findings has in normal science, one can understand why this would be an important issue for Labov. Since the act of intuiting is a mental process which cannot be observed there is no way to know whether your intuitive processes at two separate instances are the same. Furthermore since they are your intuitions (or someone else's) there is no way that someone else can replicate them. This means that introspective data cannot meet Labov's positivist requirement that the body of replicable data expand so that there be an increasing number of converging evaluations of the data.

Point two is the contention that intuitive data cannot decide between contending linguistic theories. For Labov the use of intuition to decide differences is not effective because there is no principled way to choose between different intuitions; one could simply say "well that is my intuition" as a means of final argumentation. In Labov's words: "The study of introspective judgments is thus effectively isolated from any contradiction from competing data. But frequent retreats to the idiolect have the bad consequence that each student of the general structure of language will then be confined to a different body of facts" (Labov, 1975, p. 86).

The third problem Labov has with intuitions is their apparent unreliability. In Labov's words: "There are no findings as yet that support the hope that the introspective judgments of linguists are reliable, reproducible, or general in their application to the speech community" (Labov, 1975, p. 88). In addition, though Labov is not consistent on this point and sometimes accepts the intuitions of native speakers to be valid (see, for example, Labov 1972b), native speakers' intuitions on grammaticality and acceptability also are not reliable in that there is often widespread disagreement.

Labov also points out that one should not rely on linguist's intuitions since they often depart from the intuitions of ordinary people. Labov fears that this discrepancy will lead to rarified problems and solutions which do not reflect reality. Labov (1972a, p. 199) cautions that "as linguists become more deeply involved in...theoretical issues, it is likely that their intuitions will drift further and further from those of ordinary people and the reality of language as it is used in everyday life...linguists cannot continue to produce theory and data at the same time."

For Labov, then, the means for comparing theories, descriptions, explanations, and so on, and in deciding which one is right, is to be found in data gathered from an ever expanding number of members of social groups: "(...) through the direct study of language in its social context, the amount of data expands enormously, and offers us ways and means for deciding which of the many possible analyses is right" (Labov, 1972a, p. 202).

Part of Labov's disagreement with Chomsky may be traced to a difference in conception of what a theory is and the role that a theory plays in scientific enquiry. Chomsky (1986, p. 19) has defined a grammar as "a description or theory of a language, an object constructed by a linguist." The object which is constructed by the Chomskyian linguist follows certain explicit principles of idealization which ignore any aspects of real language use which are considered extraneous to the purpose at hand, (i.e. the study of universal grammar or the study of a specific grammar). In this way real life variation is idealized away. (See Chomsky 1986 for an explanation and justification of this approach.)

This approach to theory by Chomsky is typical of and accepted within the tenets of scientific realism. Suppe, for example, (1989, p. 65) explains it in the following way:

> A science does not deal with phenomena in all of their complexity; rather, it is concerned with certain kinds of phenomena only insofar as their behavior is determined by, or characteristic of, a small number of parameters abstracted from these phenomena. Thus in characterizing falling bodies, classical particle mechanics is concerned with only those aspects of falling-body behavior which depends upon mass, velocity, distance traveled over time, and so on. The color of the object and such are aspects of the phenomena that are ignored; but the process of abstraction from the phenomena goes one step further: We are not concerned with, say, actual velocities, but with velocity under idealized conditions (...).

In this way Chomsky is concerned with the idealized conditions of species homogeneity (for universal grammar) and idealized speech communities (for the study of specific grammars). Theory building for Chomsky is therefore neither driven by a need to correspond to mundane reality nor necessarily derived from data found in real life situations, because the object of enquiry is not realistic in this sense. Furthermore, it is the theory which drives the data; that is, data is deduced from the theory rather than the theory induced from the data.

Labov's approach to theory may be seen as quite different to that outlined above. It is not that Labov does not abstract away from phenomena or idealize, but that he has a more positivist notion of what a theory is. Labov's realism is of the sort that the objects he claims to exist do in fact exist. In other words, for Labov a grammar should not be a construct of the linguist which corresponds to some idealized reality but should instead correspond to particular observable facts. Labov would be in accordance with the supposition of realism which Suppe states as (in his view mistakenly) holding "that all theoretical entities are particulars and that if a realistic theory is to be empirically true, the theoretical entities must exist" (Suppe, 1989, p. 100).

Labov proposes that the means by which one can choose between disparate analyses is to choose the one which best corresponds with the data; the one which best demonstrates the existence of the theoretical entities generated by the linguist's theory. Labov follows the positivist position that "observation yields factual knowledge which can be used inductively to confirm or disconfirm laws or theories and provides a neutral factual basis for assessing the relative merits of competing theories" (Suppe, 1989, p. 301). Labov has stated that the intuitive approach "offers us no means of discovering whether our model is right or wrong" (Labov, 1972a, p. 200). Labov therefore argues against the position he suggests Chomsky holds, that "there will always be many possible analyses for each body of data, and we will need internal evaluation measures to choose among them" (Labov, 1972a, p. 202). Instead Labov maintains that there is indeed only one correct analysis, that its correctness can be established externally, and that correctness can be established in a theory independent way. Labov's positivism is demonstrated through his objection to the Kuhnian claim that there is no neutral basis for choosing between theories, and his objection to the theory driven (thus un-neutral) nature of Chomsky's explanation. Labov and Chomsky may be seen therefore as fundamentally disagreeing over the nature of theory and data.

Labovian Sociolinguistics as Linguistic Theory

The Speech Community

Labov considers language as a social fact to be the property of the community rather than the individual, and he considers the object of linguistic description to be the language of the community rather than the individual. Given that Labov locates language in society, there are a number of interesting questions: How does one go about locating language in society when our evidence is from individuals? What are the criteria for deciding on membership in a particular social order such as a speech community? Why and how does language as a social fact affect the behavior of individuals? What is the nature of the social order that requires or allows language to act as a social fact? And how do members of a social order participate in that order through language? These are questions having to do with the relationship between the individual and society, and the role that the acquisition and use of language plays in this relationship.

As was discussed previously in the chapter on Dell Hymes, the speech community is not an easy entity to define in a non-trivial way. This is something which Labov acknowledges: "It must be admitted that there is no agreement as to how to define a speech community, and it may be asked whether the speech community exists as a definable object" (Labov, 1980a, p. 368). Nevertheless Labov (1972a, p. 158) suggests the following definition: "a speech community cannot be conceived as a group of speakers who all use the same forms; it is best defined as a group who share the same norms in regard to language." These norms are not so much norms of use as norms of interpretation, or more accurately, shared attitudes towards stigmatized forms (Labov, 1972a, p. 146). In addition, members of the speech community share a set of interpretive norms in terms of "patterns of social stratification, style shifting, and subjective evaluations" (Labov, 1989, p. 2).

Note that Labov is placing language in the public domain and the speech community is defined in terms of normativity. It is not that members of a speech community use the same forms or share the same norms of usage, but that they share the same normative system of values. In discussing the normative nature of language, Taylor (1992, p.13) makes the following observations:

> It is thus typical of human language that its speakers treat it as a normative activity, as is manifested in such remarks as "you *should* answer when you are spoken to", "'You is' is *wrong*: "'You are' is *correct*,"(...)". In other words, metalinguistic remarks such as these are not characteristically treated (talked about: evaluated, explained, corrected, etc.) as empirical hypotheses, describing how some person or group does in fact behave. Rather they are treated as having a normative function: that of telling our interlocutors how they *should* behave. One consequence of the pervasive normative use of such reflexive phenomena is that the language acts of those in our community can be brought into the kind of conformity that is required to make those acts useful in the accomplishment of social activity. From this perspective, therefore, language appears not as an autonomous system of formal regularities but as a normative practice, the regularity of which we ourselves create, police, and reward in the very performance of that practice, and to which we attribute what amounts to a moral value...(emphasis in original).

Though Taylor does not use the term social fact (and may not accept it as a valid concept) his observations on the normativity of language can be used to demonstrate more clearly what Labov seems to be saying above. If this normativity is framed in Labov's terms of language as a social fact, then it is the publicness of language and its integrated role in the social order that constrains both individual use of language – ways individuals think and talk about language – and which leads to the types of shared norms of a speech community to which Labov refers to above.

Despite the normative nature of the general definition of the speech community, definitions of individual speech communities have typically been made by Labov primarily (or solely) on the basis of formal properties. A trend in Labov's work seems to be a move away from normativity, such as the subjective reports in his New York study (1966), to more formalist definitions of speech communities, for example the use or non-use of the short "a" pattern in Philadelphia (Labov, 1989). From this perspective the linguistic "orderly heterogeneity" that Labov claims exists in a speech community "normally rests on a uniform structural bases: the underlying phrase structure, the grammatical categories, the inventory of phonemes, and the distribution of that inventory in that lexicon" (Labov, 1989, p. 2).

Thus despite Labov's objection to the speech community defined as "a group of speakers who all use the same forms", in actuality he defines speech communities in terms of formal properties. This problem may be related to Labov's apparent desire to keep sociolinguistics within received linguistics and away from the ethnography of communication and the sociology of language.

Such formal definitions of the speech community apparently lead Labov to claim that New York City is a speech community (1966, 1972a), and more recently the non-Black population of Philadelphia (1989).[8] But even more broadly, Labov (1989, p. 2) claims that "the English language is the property of the English speech community, which is in turn composed of many nested subcommunities. There is no doubt that Philadelphian speakers of English are members of the larger community of American English speakers, and the even larger community of all speakers of English." The entire world population of speakers of English therefore comprise a speech community.

If a speech community is defined as a group of speakers speaking the same language (a definition used by John Lyons, 1977) then if not terribly meaningful it is at least not illogical to refer to all speakers of English as a speech community. However, following Labov's own stricture that interpretive norms and not use define a community, it is not possible that all speakers of English in the world are members of the same speech community. If one wants to claim that all speakers of English on the level of *langue* share the same language (i.e. share the same fundamental grammar) then why use the term community at all? Suffice to say what is trivially true, all speakers of English speak English. This is a linguistic fact and not a sociological fact, as there is no particular sociological factor which can define English given that speakers of English belong to a wide range of conflicting sociological categories and institutions. The word "community" adds nothing to entities defined solely by formal linguistic properties, given that whether one follows Chomsky's psychological universals (competence), or Labov's sociological universals (*langue*), the individuals in such a community seem to have no choice but to have the grammars that they do indeed have.

The question of community cannot be dismissed and remains a problem for Labov because unlike those who consider language a property of the individual, or the property of the species, Labov considers language a property of the community. Labov cannot therefore simply rely on formal definitions of speech communities which are based on grammatical properties and at the same time conform to his own theoretical tenet of normativity. Of course one could claim that grammatical properties are also social and subject to normativity, but Labov makes a distinction between language as a linguistic system and as a social semiotic system, and it is only the latter which is subject to value. Labov is therefore caught somewhat in a bind of maintaining received linguistic theory's autonomy of the linguistic system while at the same time arguing for the societal embeddedness of the linguistic system. There is then the problem of a speech community where speech becomes the basis of definition rather than community. At the same time Labov provides only meager social theory to help us delineate one community from another or explain an individual's membership in one or more communities.

In the case of "Carla", the young White woman who was disallowed membership in the Black speech community by Labov because she did not control the tense-aspect system of Black Vernacular English (Labov, 1980), what if Carla shared the same normativity (i.e. values towards language) as speakers of Black Vernacular English, yet didn't control the tense-aspect system, would she be considered a member of the speech community then? Following Labov's general definition of speech community the answer would be "yes", but based on his definitions of specific speech communities, the answer would be "no".

In a recent article entitled "The exact description of a speech community", Labov defines non-Black Philadelphia speakers ("roughly one million persons" Labov, 1989, p. 53) as a speech community in terms of the patterns of use of the short "a". It is this one feature which distinguishes White Philadelphian speakers from other speakers of American English. That it is actual use of a linguistic form that is the distinguishing factor and not normative interpretation can be easily seen, as Labov himself states that his description of the Philadelphia short "a" pattern "is accurate enough to serve as a guide for someone who wants to talk like a Philadelphian" (Labov, 1989, p. 51).

Can the use of a short "a" be traced to normative interpretations? That is, do White Philadelphians use the short "a" because this is the correct thing to do? Or put more broadly, since formal linguistic criteria as observed through language use is the basis for membership in a linguistic community is there a relationship between use and normativity?

Labov distinguishes between the linguistic system which one acquires simply by growing up in a community and the socio-symbolic system which one may acquire in other ways, or which one may manipulate for symbolic reasons. The uniform grammatical structure (Labov, 1989, p. 2) upon which use is based is not something the individual has any control over, therefore a White Philadelphian does not choose to use the short "a"; she can't help but use it.

According to Labov the linguistic system is supra-individual. In addition, language as a social fact is general in its reach and constraints over the individual, but in an unconscious manner which does not directly coerce. According to Labov (1987, p. 129), in learning a language members of a group are socialized into the "social contract" which is binding. If the short "a" in

Philadelphia is a part of *langue* for White Philadelphians then this is binding upon the individual.

As in Taylor's description of the normative nature of language, normativity is created, policed and rewarded by language users through the reflective use of language. In this way there are such statements as "Oh she speaks very well", or "Don't speak that way, we don't speak like that", and so on. One could then observe metalinguistic language behavior as indicative of the normative notions of a particular community. But this is not the type of language use which is being used to define a speech community. Instead they are formal linguistic features, the tense-aspect system, the short "a". One could claim that these linguistic forms are in use as evidence of the normativity of language, but one could only draw an equation between form and normativity if one had a completely deterministic notion of language. If one maintained that people have no choices in the way they perform language, a claim no one would make.

The question nevertheless arises as to how much control the individual does have over language choices and how these choices are related to other choices such as social identity. Labov would seem to maintain that the individual has little choice. According to Labov "language is no less determinate than other forms of social behavior. (In fact,...it is more highly determined than all other forms)" (Labov, 1966/82, p. 37).

Explicating the relationship between the individual and the group (or individuals and universals) is difficult and not easily resolved. Labov in a sense inherits Saussure's problem of explaining how *langue* which is supra-individual becomes part of the individual. (See, R. Harris 1987b for a discussion of this issue.) How does one go from social facts to individual psychology? The answer is apparently in the social construction of the individual.

According to Labov, the way *langue* becomes part of the individual psyche is in the following way. The child is exposed first to her mother's language, then to an increasing number of other adults, and then from the age of four or so the child is exposed to the language of her peers. It is the peers who most affect the child's language growth. According to Labov all of this is unconscious learning. The unconscious influence of exposure to others' language, however does not end with childhood or adolescence; "speakers continue to analyze the linguistic patterns of their language as they grow older developing a more abstract grammar over time" (Labov, 1987, p. 131).

Despite the ability for adults to alter phonological output and to acquire new lexical items etc, it is the grammar one first learns from one's mother (or similar care-giver) which Labov claims to be most fundamental. He writes:

> We can conclude that the peer group can transmit rules of the sound system, primarily additive rules of the output, with simple phonetic conditioning, and under this influence, speakers can remold their local accents to conform with the peer group patterns that are socially significant. But no amount of peer group influence can alter consistently

the original dictionary entries that determine the categories of the phonological system: these are acquired in their most consistent form from the original care-givers when language is first learned (Labov, 1984 , p. 136).[9]

This is rather confusing. On the one hand there seems to be grammar which is acquired at a very early age and which stays with one for the entirety of one's life, and on the other hand a grammar which continues to develop throughout the entirety of one's life. It would seem to be the first grammar that Labov deems to be most important for membership in a particular speech community.

In considering language as a social fact, Labov is correct to point to the normativity of language as a defining principle of language and a means of talking about speech communities. However, because he ignores the individual and relies on an overly deterministic social model, he provides a very weak notion of how the individual is socialized into the group, how language is learned, what a community is and how individuals belong to communities.

Given that to study the linguistic system, one must study how individuals use it, there must be a relationship drawn between the individual and the system. By making the individual subordinate to the community, and by having language behavior determined by the community and not by the individual, one is not given a very good sense of how language behavior actually works.

How can one maintain that language is located in the community when the language behavior being studied is taken from individuals? Labov's answer to this would seem to be that the particularity of the individual should be ignored, and instead the individual is defined in terms of supra-individual categories such as class and gender. The individual is therefore a token of a type and an individual's speech is analyzed as tokens of types. Once the individual is identified with a type then she is related to the larger group strictly in terms of that type. The multiplicity of the individual is factored out and the language behavior of the individual is abstracted to the community. But this is circular since individuals are to be considered in relational terms with the overall system, in order to make relations between the individuals there must be some *a priori* notion of the system. Defining an individual in terms of the community, therefore requires some *a priori* notion of the community.

What is criteria for membership in the community? Although Labov defines criteria in terms of normativity, that is values towards language use, he also disregards the stated values of individuals if their judgements do not correspond to formalistic linguistic criteria. For example with the case of "Carla", though members of the Black community might accept someone as speaking enough like their normative notion of what it means to speak like a Black person, this is not criteria for belonging to the speech community, since the deficiency on the part of the speaker in terms of the Black vernacular grammar will preclude her membership. The complex issues of identity, particularly those issues of self definition, are therefore not considered by Labov in defining speech community. (For an insightful discussion of identity and language behavior see Hewitt 1986.)

The answer to the question of why and how language as a social fact affects individual behavior would seem to lie in the notion that one is affected by social facts irrespective of one's abilities to notice their coerciveness. Why this is so is not at all clear, but how it is so seems to have something to do with the arbitrary and public nature of language and the way in which language is acquired. The answer would seem to lie therefore in socialization, but Labov provides a very undeveloped model of socialization. (See Schieffelin and Ochs, 1986 for a discussion of language and socialization.)

Related to this question of socialization is the larger issue of the relationship between language and society; what is the nature of the social order such that language is an integral part of it? And how is it that language defines one's participation in that social order? It is not clear how Labov sees the relationship between language and society. Cameron (1990, p. 81) suggests that it is a 'language reflects society' account and that such an account "implies that social structures somehow exist before language, which simply 'reflects' or 'expresses' the more fundamental categories of the social." Cameron, who sees the relationship between language and society as much more complex, suggests that Labovian sociolinguistics does not provide a satisfactory explanation of why people behave linguistically the way that they do (ibid). Without a clear social theory, one which explicates the relationship between the social order and language, explaining linguistic behavior in terms of a social order will most likely be lacking.

Realism, Data, Style and the Vernacular

Labov believes that theoretical problems or differences between vying analyses may be solved through empirical evidence. This evidence is in the form of data collected from speakers identified as belonging to a speech community. It is interesting to note that Labov's concern with "social context", or the intersection of "linguistic structure" and "social structure" (cf. Labov 1972a), is thus subordinated to the empirical basis of linguistic explanation that collecting realistic language data represents. In other words, the focus on social context is not an attempt to build a theory about the role social context plays in language; but rather, social context is the place where data is collected.

According to Labov data should come from everyday speech in natural settings. The reasoning being that the more everyday and natural the speech, the more realistic. However, there is a problem in that the act of observing speech makes it uneveryday and unnatural (it is not a normal past time to have ones speech observed for linguistic analysis). This is what Labov has called the observer's paradox: "our goal is to observe the way people use language when they are not being observed" (Labov, 1972a, p. 61).

The various ingenious ways of collecting data which Labov devised may be seen as an attempt to minimize the observer's paradox. These various elicitation techniques will not be discussed here (see Labov 1984 for ample discussion) except for mention of the most paradigmatic form of elicitation, the sociolinguistic interview.

Labov has maintained that "no matter what other methods may be used to obtain samples of speech (group sessions, anonymous observation), the only way to obtain sufficient good data on the speech of any one person is through an individual, tape-recorded interview: that is through the most obvious kind of systematic observation" (Labov, 1972a, p. 209). Labov then went on to claim that it is speech in "natural groups", rather than the speech of one individual, which is "the best possible solution to the observer's paradox (...)" (Labov, 1972b, p. 256). Nevertheless, whether individual or multi-person interviews, the sociolinguistic interview has remained as the paradigm means of gathering speech data.

The sociolinguistic interview was designed by Labov to meet a number of goals. In addition to counteracting or avoiding the observers paradox, the sociolinguistic interview was designed to elicit a large body of systematic and representative data, including what Labov calls socially realistic data – necessary social and demographic information about the informant – and linguistic data subject to both internal (one can compare different styles or topic shifts, for example, within the speech of the same person) and external comparison (one can compare the speech of two different individuals within, for example, similar textual contexts such as narratives).[10]

Though the sociolinguistic interview is designed to elicit a wide range of data, not all of it is equally interesting to Labov. To understand this consider Labov's notion of what represents the most realistic data. Labov is concerned with the most systematic linguistic data; speech which is most reflective of the underlying uniform structure (the community grammar). But according to Labov certain types of speech are less systematic than others and therefore more representative of the idiolect than the sociolect. For Labov the linguistic system is below the level of consciousness and social facts also exist below the level of consciousness. It is Labov's position therefore that the more unconscious speech is, the more it will be systematic and representative of the speakers underlying linguistic competence. Other types of speech will produce data which show high degrees of hyper-correction, and other forms of self correction and self consciousness, which according to Labov lead to unsystematic variation (Labov 1972a, 1972b).

The previous chapter on Dell Hymes discussed the importance of style to the ethnography of communication. Style is also important in Labov's linguistic theory. Labov recognizes two different senses of the word style. There is style as previously discussed in the chapter on Dell Hymes – a "way of speaking", means by which a speaker transmits a multilayered message including emotive and indexical information about herself. And there is Labov's notion of style – greater or lesser conscious attention paid to speech.

Labov accepts the first sense of style as being of interest to linguists, but sees it as being too unsystematic and context bound to be useful in linguistic analysis. He maintains instead that style in the second sense is useful since it is systematic, being "ranged along a single dimension, measured by the amount of attention paid to speech" (Labov, 1972a, p. 208). It is this second sense of style which is of concern here.

Labov is looking for the most realistic data; the purist data which most closely approximates the underlying essential linguistic system. Labov divides style along the dimension of most attention paid to speech (the most formal style) and least attention paid to speech (the most casual style). It is the casual style which is most realistic because it exhibits the least interference between the underlying system and behavior. Or put another way, the relationship between the universal system (*langue*) and the particular actualization (*parole*) is most systematic. Casual speech would be for example "the everyday speech used in informal situations, where no attention is directed to language" (Labov, 1972a, p. 86). But what does Labov mean by "attention paid to speech"?

If language is normative as Labov has claimed, and if members of a speech community participate in shared normativity, are there not norms for all types of public language behavior? All public (i.e. involving more than one person) language games, whether formal or informal, intimate or unintimate, have normative constraints and these constraints include constraints on form. It is not true therefore that there ever is a situation where "no attention is directed to language". There is no situation where speech simply pours forth in a completely automatic and unmonitored form except in certain types of pathologies resulting from brain damage and other sorts of neurological trauma. What Labov seems to be getting at is a relaxed type of speech, in a relaxed type of situation where someone might be able to express their level of comfort by saying something such as "I really feel like I can be myself and not worry about how I talk." Because Labov's realism requires essentials, Labov is required to find an essential self (a person at her most self-like), an essential community (a person who most represents the essence of the community) and essential language behavior (a style which most represents the essence of the linguistic system).

These essential elements come together within Labov's construction of the vernacular: the most casual speech style in Labov's style continuum. Labov uses the term vernacular in two senses. The first is when "the minimum of attention is given to the monitoring of speech" (Labov, 1972a, p. 208). The second is the speech of inner city "street-wise" young Black males (Labov, 1972b). At first glance these two senses of vernacular may seem unrelated, but they are in fact closely related. They are related in Labov's work, a good portion of which developed out of work done on the Black Vernacular, and they are related theoretically, both being motivated by Labov's fundamental belief that only unconscious unreflective speech will give the linguist unadulterated data.

Labov does not consider all styles to be of equal interest to linguistics. Some styles "show irregular phonological and grammatical patterns, with a great deal of 'hypercorrection'" (Labov, 1972a, p. 208). But the vernacular is "more systematic speech, where the fundamental relations which determine the course of linguistic evolution can be seen most clearly." Therefore "observation of the vernacular gives us the most systematic data for our analysis of linguistic structure (ibid)".

In terms of unreflective speech, though Labov does not make this correlation directly, he seems to be suggesting that reflective speech (attention paid to language) leads to irregularity because it somehow interferes with the natural unconscious processing from *langue* to *parole*. Keeping in mind Labov's argument against introspection and the idiolect as the object of linguistic description, again Labov exhibits his contention that conscious language processes are untrustworthy: "it is no exaggeration to say that the more people introspect about their language the more confused they become" (Labov, 1989, p. 51). The important point to note here is that not all language use is appropriate for linguistic study. Furthermore, realistic data does not include all uses of language. Are all members of a speech community therefore not of equal interest to the linguist either?

Labov's second use of the term vernacular is nearly equivalent to "dialect", and is therefore more like the traditional meaning of vernacular, the non-official or non-standard language or variety spoken by natives of a particular place. The vernacular of concern here is Black English Vernacular. (Labov 1972b.)

In terms of the speech community that speaks this dialect (and Labov refers to it as a dialect, see e.g. Labov 1972b; 1989), in sharp contrast to all non-Black residents of Philadelphia, or all speakers of English in the world, it is a rather specialized speech community: the speech of urban lower class pre-adolescent and adolescent Black males (Labov, 1972b).

Labov in introducing his study *Language in the Inner City* clearly states that he is not studying Black English. The term Black English would be used more appropriately "for the whole range of language forms used by black people in the United States" (Labov, 1972b, p. xiii). But Labov does claim that he is representing "the relatively uniform dialect spoken by the majority of black youth in most parts of the United States today, especially in the inner city areas of New York, Boston, Detroit, Philadelphia, San Francisco, Los Angeles, and other urban Centers. It is also spoken in most rural areas and used in the casual, intimate speech of many adults. (ibid)." This is rather a large geographic area (both urban and rural, East, West and Mid-West) and if adult casual speech is included it pertains to a large number of people. In fact, despite Labov's above mentioned caveat to the contrary, his work has been seen as pertaining to Black people in general, and much of his later claims about the grammar of Black English is based on this original corpus. (See Faye Vaughn-Cook 1987 for a critical view of Labov's claims about Black English.)

In what way can the above mentioned speech community (lower class young Black males) be representative of such a large group of people?

To answer this consider the earlier question of the essentialist basis of realism – who best represents a community? And whose linguistic behavior is best representative of the underlying community grammar? If one accepts that certain members of the group speak the most realistic form of the language, the most unconscious attention-free pure form, then one could assert that this rather specialized speech community (young lower-class Black males) is ideally representative of the larger speech community.

How is it that these young men might be candidates for the best representatives of the vernacular in both Labov's first sense of the term – casual speech, free from attention paid to language – and his second sense of the term – Black English as a dialect?

First consider the relationship between the dialect and the standard and relate this to the choice of informants. Labov acknowledges that there are genuine bi-linguals and allows that a linguist can in a preliminary way rely on a bilingual informant. However, he strongly doubts that bi-dialectals exist. Hence he stresses the difficulty of finding an untainted informant who knows both the standard and the vernacular. This is because "speakers who have had extensive contact with the superordinate form no longer have clear intuitions about their vernacular available for inspection" (Labov, 1972a, p. 214).

Labov seems to hold that one can control two separate languages without interference because they are completely separate systems, but that one cannot control two or more dialects without interference because dialects are not separate systems. The reason he gives for this is:

> Dialect differences depend upon low-level rules which appear as minor adjustments and extensions of contextual conditions, etc. It appears that such conditions inevitably interact, and although the speaker may indeed appear to be speaking the vernacular, close examination of his speech shows that his grammar has been heavily influenced by the standard. He may succeed in convincing his listeners that he is speaking the vernacular, but this impression seems to depend upon a number of unsystematic and heavily marked signals (Labov, 1972a, p. 215).[11]

Earlier we discussed why Labov excluded "Carla" from being a member of the Black speech community. Her exclusion relates to the above quote where Labov suggests that a person "may succeed in convincing his listeners that he is speaking the vernacular, but this impression seems to depend upon a number of unsystematic and heavily marked signals." Though this quote was some ten years earlier, it is the same argument which Labov later uses against Carla's membership in the Black community. It is an argument also used against the Black middle-class, or educated Black's generally including Black community leaders. (See Labov 1972b). Can one assume that Labov's young male informants have limited exposure to the superordinate dialect and that therefore they would not have the types of problems that Labov alludes to above?

Consider this question in terms of age, class and gender. Labov has suggested that in "some sharply differentiated subsystems, a consistent vernacular can be obtained only from children and adolescents: the grammars of adults seem to be permanently changed by their use of standard rules" (Labov, 1972b, p. 257). Labov maintains that this is the case for the Black vernacular as well as Hawaiian Creole (ibid). Apparently:

> as the young adult is detached from the teenage hang-out group he inevitably acquires a greater ability to shift towards the standard language and more occasions to do so. (...) In general, working adults will use a sharper degree of style shifting than adolescents in their careful speech with outside observers, and only under the most favorable circumstances will their vernacular system emerge (Labov, 1972b, p. 257-8).

Adults are therefore suspect vernacular informants; the fact that these informants are pre-adolescent and adolescent would then be defended in that only they can truly represent the vernacular. But this would lead to a rather odd notion of a speech community since if the vernacular is only spoken by children and adolescents then adults could not be members of the Black vernacular speech community. This would make the Black vernacular an age-graded variety which one would then grow out of.

Labov's young men are all lower class. Labov in his chapter "The Logic of Nonstandard English" (1972b) argues for the purity and directness of working class speech:

> Our work in the speech community makes it painfully obvious that in many ways working-class speakers are more effective narrators, reasoners, and debaters than many middle-class speakers who temporize, qualify and lose their argument in a mass of irrelevant detail. Many academic writers try to rid themselves of that part of middle-class style that is empty pretension and keep that part that is needed for precision. But the average middle-class speaker that we encounter makes no such effort; he is enmeshed in verbiage, the victim of sociolinguistic factors beyond his control (Labov, 1972b, p. 214).

Labov, who self-described this chapter as a polemic (Labov, 1972b, p. xvi), is of course attempting to counter the deficit notion in education that Blacks are non-verbal and that only what may be called middle-class norms are acceptable. However, if one relates this quote back to the question of grammatical interference from the standard to the vernacular, the notion that there are only a few ideal informants who have intuitions which can be trusted (see below), and the question of membership in the speech community, it becomes problematic as to whether educated Blacks may be members of the vernacular speech community.

Support for this concern over whether the educated Black middle-class might not find themselves excluded from genuine membership in the vernacular speech community can be found in Labov's concern with speakers who claim membership in the speech community when membership is not due: "The ways in which such speakers convince their listeners that they are speaking the vernacular is an important problem for sociolinguistics study. Educated leaders of the black community in the United States provide many examples of this phenomenon" (Labov, 1972b, p. 215).[12] Adults may be excluded from the vernacular community, it would also seem that educated Blacks due to their involvement with the standard may also be excluded.

Labov has said that the vernacular "is the property of the group, not the individual. Its consistency and well-formed, systematic character is the result of a vast number of interactions; the group exerts its control over the vernacular in a supervision so close that a single slip may be condemned and remembered for years" (Labov, 1972b, pp. 256,257). Labov seems to have a rather monolithic conception of normativity with an all powerful (undefined) group exerting control over the individual. One wonders if such close supervision is possible anywhere except maybe in military academies. This question of group supervision of the vernacular is of interest to us generally in our attempt to understand how the group commands the individual, but here it may also shed some light on the question of gender, male grouping norms and Labov's vernacular informants.

Labov (1972b, p. 256) proposed natural groups as the best possible solution to the observer's paradox because the "natural interaction of peers can overshadow the effect of observation and helps us approach the goal of capturing the vernacular of everyday life in which the minimum amount of attention is paid to speech (...)" (Labov, 1972b, p. 256). Actually it is in group situations when the type of control Labov mentions above might be exerted (an individual by herself might feel less socially constrained than with a group of her peers to whom she feels in various ways obligated). It is possible that all male groups, especially the age group pre to adolescent, expect and exert controlling behavior of the sort of which Labov gives examples (Labov 1972b). All-male groups would therefore best exhibit the type of behavior that Labov wants to claim exists on an essential level for social groups generally.

Another reason for Labov's informants being male is because according to Labov generally speaking women hypercorrect towards the prestige forms (Labov 1972a). (For a discussion of the gender pattern see Cameron, 1986; Fasold 1990.) Cameron (1986) has argued against this portrayal of women as perpetual "lames", that is outsiders to the core values of the vernacular community. Nevertheless in Labov's view like the middle-class, women tend not to be most representative of the vernacular linguistic norms. These young men are therefore ideal representatives of the vernacular because they are young, uneducated and male.

Labov does not trust the intuitions of linguists, nor indeed does he trust the intuitions of most ordinary citizens. However, "once in a great while we encounter an informant who seems almost immune to 'correction' of this sort – who seems to have direct access to his intuition, despite his knowledge of the standard dialect. An important task for psycholinguists is to identify other traits which accompany or determine this behavior, so that we will be able to search a given population for 'ideal' informants" (Labov, 1972b, p. 214). There are therefore people who truly have direct access to the grammatical system through their intuitions. (In fact Labov (ibid.) suggests here that the linguist with the aid of psychologists track these people down.) As just outlined above, Labov's informants seem to fit the description.

But how well do these informants compare with other individuals in the community in terms of speech style, do they or don't they pay attention to their speech? Even the most simplistic and cursory studies of African American speech behavior have noted the importance of speech performance in the African American community. Attention to language is an everyday occurrence and one is evaluated in terms of one's ability to use language consciously and effectively. Given this cultural emphasis, and given that young Black men place a particularly strong emphasis on speech performance in groups, and indeed that hierarchical relationships within young Black male groups is based importantly on speech performance, Labov in his search for the ideal unreflective informant might instead have stumbled upon an extremely (possibly the most) self aware group of individuals. Milroy (1987) supports this point:

> It is clear that speakers can 'perform' in the vernacular under appropriate circumstances, demonstrating, for example, a wide range of vernacular phonological features in much the same way as they might, in different sets of circumstances, demonstrate their control over a set of features closer to the standard. (...) Moreover, many of the vernacular verbal arts described by Labov...such as 'toasting' or 'sounding' inevitably involve rather self-conscious performance and so can hardly be described as unmonitored speech styles. Yet, they constituted an important source of information on the structure of Black English Vernacular (Milroy, 1987, p. 58).

Wolfson similarly criticizes Labov's treatment of style, pointing out that speakers of the vernacular are careful and conscious of their speech performance (Wolfson, 1982).

If one rejects the notion that attention paid to language is self correction only in the direction of the superordinate (so-called standard) norm, then it is simple to see that these young men could be paying great attention to language, and actually self-correcting in the direction of the so-called vernacular norm. Labov's notion of what counts as least attention paid to speech is thus circularly based on preconceived cultural notions of vernacular speech. Taking into account the notion of performance (see e.g. Bauman 1974), one can realize that there can be great attention paid to speech, attention to form, attention to delivery, attention to the impact on one's audience, in the most casual of circumstances. Milroy (1987, p. 179) points out that if one takes into consideration audience design, (and here she quotes Bell: "at all levels of language variability people are responding primarily to other people. Speakers are designing their style for their audience"), then the question of style and performance cannot be ignored. The adolescents who might have been impressing Labov with what he seems to see as their free ways were probably extremely aware of their affect on their peer group and extremely conscious of whether they were performing at their peak or not. Obviously this did not lead to correcting towards the standard and instead led to consistent vernacular speech. Therefore, Labov's findings would reflect consistency as they would not reveal what was not taking place, correction towards the standard.[13]

Given Labov's notion of best data, and given his essentialist notion of the make up of the vernacular, a rather curious group of individuals, young lower-class urban Black males, came to represent the Black speech community. It is interesting to note how similar this search for the ideal informant is to traditional dialectology, except in the case of dialectology an older rural male rather than a young urban male was considered the ideal.

Labov's notion of the speech community includes a number of embedded speech communities, so that one starts with all speakers of English, then one arrives at the sub-group of speakers of American English, then the sub-group of speakers of Black English, then the sub-group of speakers of Black Vernacular English. Although Labov starts off with lower-class urban Black young males, he broadens Black Vernacular English to include Black people generally, irrespective of age group, gender or geographical region. Given that the concept of the speech community is flexible enough to allow for small homogeneous groups such as same-class, same-gender, same-age groupings, in what way is this vernacular speech community related to the larger speech community of speakers of Black Vernacular English who are not homogeneous as to class, gender or age?

That broadly speaking there is a speech variety identifiable with a large number of Black people in the United States is uncontroversial. However, this speech variety is much more complex and is based on a more complex grouping of people than the youth that Labov initially used in his study. Typically speech from such a specialized group would be considered an argot rather than a dialect pertaining to a general community of some millions of people. A variety it is, but a variety too restricted to be used as indicative of the speech of a general population. It is therefore important to make clear how this variety is representative of the larger language varieties that Black people may use. In addition, considering the question of whether this group of informants is ideally suited to represent the vernacular as casual speech, based on the competitive and self conscious nature of the speech of lower-class urban Black males in groups, the answer is no.

Variation, the Sociolinguistic Variable and Variable Rules

Labovian linguistics quickly became synonymous with the study of linguistic variation and change. As Fasold (1990) has pointed out: "Many of the concepts and methods that were to influence linguistic studies of change and variation originated with Labov's classic *The Social Stratification of English in New York City*" (Fasold, 1990, p. 223). The study of variation itself has developed a number of different approaches or different areas of contention which will not be dealt with here. (See Fasold 1990; Romaine 1982.) Though there have been many attempts at changing or improving the Labovian model, here the concern is only with variation as it applies to Labov's linguistic theory.[14]

Labov's work on variation and language change may be seen as motivated from two fronts: a dissatisfaction with the lack of an empirical basis and the trivialization of linguistic variation in received linguistics, and a dissatisfaction with the state of dialectology. Many aspects of Labov's work on linguistic variation and change may be viewed as continuing the tradition of dialectology. Labov has surveyed large areas, for example New York City and Philadelphia, which represent large numbers of people. His work has relied on information from previous dialectal studies. He has referred to the varieties spoken by the various groups he has studied, be they local residents of Martha's Vineyard, or Black inner city youth, as dialects. And he has acknowledged that his early studies were modifications of techniques used in dialectology (Labov, 1984, p. 28). This is partly reflective of his early training in dialectology under Weinreich. But under Weinreich he also developed his emphasis on empiricism and it is here that he made his departure from traditional dialectology.

For Labov dialectology's reliance on intuition, asking people how they spoke rather than observing them speaking, was mistaken. (This is a position he holds against Chomskyian linguistics as well: "When we study what people do rather than what they think they do, we get a simpler and more understandable view of the linguistic system " Labov, 1989, p. 53.) Labov's dissatisfaction with dialectology is related to theoretical issues which have already been discussed in this chapter: introspection and the role of the idiolect in linguistic description. By eliciting a response, through the use of a word list for example, the dialectologist was relying on the introspection of the informant, therefore moving the informant from an unreflective state to a conscious state. Labov believes that it is only in the unreflective state that one will get systematic data.

Labov also noted that dialectologists typically studied isolated idiolects as if they had no systematic connection to the community dialect (the sociolect): "Before systematic means of studying the speech community were developed, linguists tended to believe that a language was nothing but a conglomerate of individual systems or idiolects" (Labov, 1984, p. 129). The use of introspection therefore led to unsystematic variation, but variation, systematic or unsystematic, could not be accounted for anyway because of the practice of studying isolated idiolects. Labov therefore set out to show that variation is systematic and motivated, not random (free variation) or the individualism of the idiolect.

Nevertheless, there is an unresolved tension in Labov's work on variation between his quarrel with received linguistic theory and its claim to the homogeneous nature of language, or its abstraction away from diversity, and his own claims as to the systematic nature of language variation, the homogeneous basis of language structure, and the orderly nature of the speech community. On the one hand, there is his claim that language behavior is heterogeneous, and on the other hand, his emphasis on the orderliness of this heterogeneity; that variation is neither rampant nor unmotivated, and that though there may be great variation on the individual level, on the group level there is great uniformity.

Labov has defined a sociolinguistic variable as "one which is correlated with some nonlinguistic variable of the social context: of the speaker, the addressee, the audience, the setting, etc" (Labov, 1972a, p. 237). Actually the type of social context that Labov lists here is more typical of that suggested in the ethnography of communication that what is used in variation analysis (social context is class, gender, age, race, or ethnic group identity of the speaker and stratification based on these social categories.) It is therefore odd that Labov uses this concept of social context in his definition of sociolinguistic variables as he does not employ it in his own work.

Here consider a brief example – studies of the alternate use of the velar nasal or apico-nasal in words ending in "ing". The proportionate use or non-use is plotted in a graph from formal to casual style and in terms of social variables such as gender and class. On the whole the apico-nasal form is found more frequently in casual style and is used more frequently across all styles by working class men as compared with working class or middle class women. [15]

The sociolinguistic variable is based on the linguistic variable: an optional formal means of saying the same thing. Labov maintains that not all variation is meaningful to linguistics. For example, two different forms may mean the same thing linguistically but not socially or emotively. If this is the case then it is only the linguistic meaning which is important for the purposes if variation analysis. (For controversy over the linguistic variable see Lavandera 1978; Romaine 1981; Huspek 1986.) The linguistic variable is therefore independent of social factors, and the sociolinguistic variable is therefore the independent linguistic variable correlated with some independent social variable.

A problem then arises in explaining the sociolinguistic patterns of variation which are found. Why do men use the nasal form of "ing" more and the apico-nasal form less? In other words, what is the relationship between linguistic variation and social variation? Cameron, in pointing out weaknesses in the explanation of variation, makes the point that "Concepts like 'norm', 'identity' and so on, and sociological models of structures/divisions like class, ethnicity and gender are used as a 'bottom line' though they stand in need of explication themselves" (Cameron, 1990, p. 81). In other words, the sociolinguistic variable is founded on unexplicated notions of social variables.

The initial development of the variable rule was very important for Labovian sociolinguistics, as it attempted to show that sociolinguistics could make an important contribution to received linguistics (generative phonology in particular). In addition, it was meant to buttress Labov's claim that sociolinguistics was simply part of received linguistic theory rather than in competition with it. (See for example 1972b, p. 127 where Labov supports Chomsky's claims with his data on BEV.)

Labov developed variable rules as an extension of generative rules. He introduced the variable rule formalization in 1969 in a paper on the ordering of contraction and deletion rules of the copula in BEV. Labov objected to the fact that in generative grammar one had only the choice of categorical rules, which would always apply, and which would therefore not be able to account for variation, or the choice of optional rules which would not capture the systematic nature of the variation (Labov, 1969, p. 737). Labov therefore proposed a rule which could more or less apply depending on the linguistic environment or the linguistic environment and the social context.

This was at the time the most important development in Labovian sociolinguistics. It provided sociolinguistics for the first time with formalism comparable with received linguistic theory. And it made the ambitious claim that "it will be possible to enlarge our current notion of the 'linguistic competence' of a native speaker" (Labov 1969, p. 736). It gave sociolinguistics a chance at legitimacy within received linguistic theory, a chance to be embraced by Chomskyian linguistics.

Fasold has noted the non-sociolinguistic nature of the initial study of variation: "Empirical studies of linguistic variation (such as Labov...1969 ...) were conceived fundamentally as a better way to find out how language works. They were sociolinguistic only out of necessity" (Fasold, 1985, p. 515). As Fasold has pointed out, this was not sociolinguistics in the sense of following from a sociolinguistic theory, but was generative theory (except with actual corpora rather than invented sentences and introspection). But was this really generative theory or was this something else?

If one defines generative grammar to be something more than a formalism (a way of writing grammatical rules for example) but to be a theory based on the psychological reality of rules (see Chomsky, 1980), it is hard to see how variable rules as a theory and not just a formalism can be considered a legitimate part of generative theory. This is because of the fundamental difference between Chomskyian and Labovian linguistics over the locus of grammar. It is also because generative grammar studies types without reference to tokens, but Labovian variation is based on tokens.

Chomsky has referred to the incorporation of probabilistic rules into the grammar as leading to "absurdity" (Chomsky, 1966, p. 36). Despite at least a decade of work on fine-tuning the variable rule concept and providing empirical support for its validity, the notion of variable rules has never been incorporated into Chomskyian linguistic theory. Even keeping in mind possible politics surrounding Chomsky's negative position, this historical fact would seem to point to the strong possibility that generativist linguists did not consider variable rules as a valid extension of generative theory. One reason for this is related to the fact that the sentence not the utterance is the linguistic object in generative grammar. As Kay and McDaniel noted:

> grammar deals only with types, never with tokens. In the generative framework, an optional rule is just one that adds a new class of sentences (seen as linguistic types) to the set of sentences that is generated by the grammar. ('Generate' here has, of course, nothing to do with the real time production of actual utterances (= sentence tokens) by real people.)...The frequency with which a sentence is produced as an utterance (token) is simply irrelevant (Kay and McDaniel, 1979, p. 153).

By not perceiving the difference between the utterance based nature of his work (or simply disregarding this fact) and the sentence base of generative theory, Labov was unable or unwilling to see the fundamental incompatibility between variable rules and generative theory. It is not that Labov was in fact incorporating utterances into his linguistic theory; he was abstracting away from utterances, but this was a type-token relationship which did not address the more fundamental question of the nature of sentence grammar.

Labov for example apparently didn't address the question of how one gets from the contextualized utterance to the decontextualized sentence, or what the relationship between the individual entity and the statistical generality is (a problem which generative grammarians didn't have since their grammar was based on deductive rather than inductive principles.) Labov's solution was to simply assume that one could recognize that X variable was a token of Y type and categorize it as such, then count it and compare its frequency in A population with its frequency in B population. In this way a corpus would be scanned for variants of the variable (for example, apico-nasal versus nasal "ing") and a judgement made as to which of the two phonological possibilities a particular phonetic realization fit. The environment of the variable would then be noted, and then one would go on to the next token.

Apparently the more tokens in a corpus the better. Though Labov has maintained that one can get an adequate sample from a fairly small number of tokens, the greater the number of tokens seems to be taken as support for an analysis being correct. In this way Labov (1989, p. 51) supports his contention that "we have worked out a reasonably accurate description of the Philadelphia short a pattern" by noting that the analysis was based on 6,233 tokens. In addition, elicitation procedures have always been used to maximize the number of tokens of the variable that the analyst is looking for. (Reading sections of the sociolinguistic interview, for example, are written with specific variables in mind.) But no matter how many tokens Labov might amass as evidence that his analysis is correct, a generativist would not be persuaded since an accumulation of tokens is not criterion for deciding any theoretical issue in generative grammar.

Labov considered variable rules to be part of a speakers' competence. Generative theory considers rules to be psychologically real and that the locus of the grammar is in the individual as a biological endowment. Labov follows the Saussurian position that the locus of the grammar is not in the individual but in the community. Now, if rules are categorical then both the psychological and social approach are fine; in the former case, the rule is biologically determined and in the latter, it is socially determined. Now what if rules are variable, but systematically variable rather than randomly variable: how will this be represented in the speaker's mind?

Fasold (1978), in a discussion of language variation and linguistic competence isolates six different hypotheses as to what the speaker "knows":

1. speakers know "the precise frequency percentage they should have as the output of a variable rule in some environment."
2. probability values are "part of a speakers linguistic competence."
3. speakers have knowledge of environmental factors affecting variability but neither probability values nor the exact frequency of output are "directly part of...linguistic knowledge."
4. "linguistic competence should include (a) knowledge of what environmental factors contribute to application of the rule, and (b) knowledge of the relative weight of each."
5. "speakers know what features in the environment of a variable rule favor application of the rule, but their competence does not include knowledge of which ones favor application more than others."
6. speakers "know that there is variation at certain points of syntax and phonology, but...environmental factors influencing frequency of application of an optional rule are not subject matter for linguistic theory" (Fasold, 1978, p. 85-87).

The first and most powerful hypothesis would require that speakers constantly monitor their speech so that their speech would always reach the precise percentage reflected in the group average. There is some argument as to the precise nature of probabilistic mental processing, but whatever the exact nature of probability capabilities we have as humans, the above hypothesis seems humanly impossible. It would require constant adjustment of one's output based on some group norm, but it is not clear how the individual would know precisely what this group norm is. In addition, the group norm does not remain constant (if it did there would be no language change) so the individual would be adjusting to a fluctuating unknown.

The hypotheses which Fasold favored were numbers three and four, whereby fixed probabilities are not part of linguistic competence, but the speaker would have knowledge of environmental factors contributing to application of the rule. It seems to me that this knowledge of environmental factors, however, would only be able to explain so-called internal linguistic variation and not sociolinguistic variation. It could not account for stylistic or contextual variation. This is because the linguistic environment is usually quite simple (for example, a matter of plus or minus a vowel) while the sociological environment is very complex. The issue therefore becomes more broadly not simply a matter of linguistic competence but a matter of communicative competence.

Hypothesis six, the weakest hypothesis, is the most attractive. Whether one chooses to speak in a particular way is not simply a matter of linguistic environments. Certainly the phenomenon of so-called hypercorrection is an example of disregard for the relative weight of linguistic environments. But even if this is considered an anomaly, the fact remains that a linguistic environment cannot force a person to speak in a particular way. As long as a rule is optional and not categorical, one has a choice in terms of rule application. Why a person will use a particular form in a particular way is based not only on the relative weight of a linguistic environment but importantly on the context: who one is talking with, what is the prior text, what one is trying to accomplish, etc. It is not possible that social context could be incorporated into a linguistic theory solely concerned with linguistic competence. Hence, the correct generative position that frequencies of applications of optional rules would not belong to a generative linguistic theory.

Fasold, in describing the sixth hypothesis above, makes the observation that it "is the one implicit in all generative theories which do not include variable rules" (Fasold, 1975, p. 87). This disagreement over the position of variable rules in a speakers "knowledge", with variationists adopting some version of two through five, and generativists adopting six, again demonstrates the basic differences between generative theory and Labovian variation theory.

Baker and Hacker (1984) have suggested that rules in the Chomskyian sense are not rules in any usual sense of the term: because they are not rules which one follows, rather they are a description of one's supposed biological programming. One therefore has no choice, for example but to have the principle of subjacency in one's grammar. It seems that a variable rule is also not a rule in the usual sense of the term since one cannot follow a statistical probability. It is instead a formal description, or as Fasold has recently put it "a display device" (Fasold, 1989, p. 18). But what are variable rules a display of? A display of what people know? What people do? What people are likely to do?

To answer this question one has to consider the role of idealization in Labov's work on variation. As Milroy has pointed out:

> Although the models produced by sociolinguists are often felt in some sense to be closer to the data base than those of other types of linguist, it is important to remember that a representation such as Labov's famous graph of the variable realization of /r/ in New York City is actually an idealized model of *sociolinguistic structure*; the figures upon which it is based are the product of a long process of sociological, mathematical and linguistic abstraction (Milroy, 1987, p. 1). (Emphasis in original.)

A variable rule is not a display of what people know. It is also not a display of what people actually do since it is so abstracted from actual individual behavior, but it is possibly a display of what people are likely to do if they follow certain principles of linguistic structure and certain principles of prescribed social behavior.

Conclusion

In this chapter, the following arguments have been presented: 1) that Labov can be seen as a scientific realist who separates the linguistic system from the conceptions that ordinary people have about language and their symbolic language behavior. 2) that Labov may be seen as a positivist whose agenda has been the building of empirical foundations for linguistics. 3) that Labov positioned himself as a participant of normal science and received linguistics and that in this way he may be seen as continuing certain aspects of Saussurian linguistics.

There has recently been a flurry of interest in Saussure. (See for example Culler 1986; Harris 1987.) John Joseph has argued that Saussure is extremely relevant to linguistics at this time and that only a social redefinition of linguistics will rescue the autonomy of linguistics from the cognitive and computational sciences. (Joseph 1990b). The call for a social redefinition of linguistics, however, is not necessarily to be confused with functionalist approaches to linguistics nor especially with discourse approaches which do not concentrate on sentence level grammar. It is a call to place grammar (*langue*) more definitively in the social order while at the same time studying linguistic structure as an autonomous entity.

This call for some sort of reconsideration of the social aspect of the linguistic system has also recently come out of the generative camp. Pateman (1987), for example defends generativism on grounds of its realism, but also suggests it needs to expand into the social world. Pateman suggests a definition of language which he calls "dualism": language defined as a social fact but that social fact is not a linguistic fact; that is, some linguistic facts are social facts and some are not. Here both the autonomy of the linguistic system and the social nature of language are retained. How this works in generativism at the moment is apparently through the modular approach, which includes a pragmatic module in the general theory of linguistic competence. (See Newmeyer, 1983; Botha, 1989.)

It is not clear whether the neo-Saussurians and the neo-generativists are calling for the same thing or not, or even if what they are calling for is possible, but it does shed some interesting light on Labov.

Labov has attempted to readdress what he perceives to be two misapplications of Saussurian linguistics: the ignoring of the social nature of Saussure's conception of *langue*, and the dismissal of *parole* in the complete linguistic equation of *langage, langue* and *parole*. By reasserting not only the social nature of language (that language is used for communication), but its particular social nature (that it is a social fact and therefore a supra-individual system), and by developing proof of the systematic nature of *parole*, Labov can be seen to have attempted to do just the sort of thing that Pateman and others have been calling for, a autonomous (i.e. realist) linguistic approach which is socially based.

However, one is still left with the problem of explicating the social nature of language and it is here that Labov's attempt at a synthesis fails. He does not incorporate the social dimensions of language into his linguistic theory. Joseph (personal communication) supports this positions: "[Labovian sociolinguistics] tries to engulf the social within the standard model of individual competence. 'Variable rules' seem to me to be an attempt to 'adjust' the notion of *langue* just enough to take account of the existence of variation, but not so such as to make it irreconcilable with the *langue* concept of 'mainstream' linguistics. No doubt, if this attempt had succeeded...at least the linguistic world of the last quarter-century would have been far less polarized and fragmented."

Notes

[1] The influence of Labovian sociolinguistics over the development of sociolinguistics could be documented through a historical analysis of papers published, positions held in linguistic departments and other institutions by those trained within the disciplinary matrix, and so forth. That Labovian sociolinguistics has dominated sociolinguistics is an impression shared by others, for example Cameron (1990) equates sociolinguistics with the "Labovian quantitative paradigm". Despite admitting the existence of other approaches "such as ethnography of speaking, discourse analysis, sociology of language", Cameron defends her position in the following way: "To the criticism of narrowness and bias, however, I would respond by asserting that my definition of sociolinguistics reflects a historical (and academic-political) reality; over the last fifteen years the quantitative paradigm has so successfully pressed its claims to the central and dominant position in language and society studies, that for most people in the field (and especially most *linguists* in the field) 'sociolinguistics' does indeed mean primarily if not exclusively 'Labovian quantitative sociolinguistics' (emphasis in original)" (Cameron, 1990, p. 82). With the advent of discourse analysis and interactional sociolinguistics the dominance of Labovian sociolinguistics is lessening. Hudson's (1989) review of Newmeyer's fourth volume of his Cambridge series *Language: The socio-cultural context* is possible evidence of this trend. Hudson here complains that the volume is lacking in good Labovian sociolinguistics. (Hudson; 1989, p. 816) The volume actually contains a number of either Labov's students or fellow practitioners in the variationist paradigm, nevertheless Hudson feels a certain lack. This lack which is not empirically demonstrated is likely Hudson reacting to a possible realignment away from Labovian sociolinguistics which is very slowly taking place, or possibly a schism within the field of sociolinguistics between those who want sociolinguistics to be more like received linguistics and those who don't.

[2] Labov does not state what theory of language acquisition he adheres to, but he seems to be following the received position that acquisition of grammar takes place automatically and unconsciously. It would therefore be impossible to consciously acquire a language. In contrast the acquisition of style and semiotic systems such as dress can be consciously pursued. It would seem that the aspect of language which Labov maintains is a social semiotic system and which is differently acquired from grammar would seem to have (at least potentially) a conscious and volitional aspect to its acquisition.

[3] The Saussurian Paradox: Labov has used the Saussurian Paradox to explain what he sees as the unfortunate development and dominance of nonempirical approaches in received linguistics: the fact that the grammar of the individual may be studied as representing the grammar of the group. Labov argues that because *langue* is a property of the group and therefore all members of the group have access to the same linguistic system (*langue*), linguists are able to

study *langue* simply by studying one individual. In contrast, Labov claims that in order to study the language behavior of the individual (*parole*) one must study language in "its social context" (Labov, 1972a, p. 186). Individual behavior must be seen in comparison with the overall behavior of the group. Hence, Labov claims that individual differences between speakers "can be examined only in the field by a kind of sociological survey" (Labov, 1972a, p. 267). The individual therefore must be compared to some sort of group norm or group ideal. However, the opposite is also possible. If *parole* is individual and particularistic one need only look at individual instances of *parole*, yet Labov maintains that this paradox suggests that the study of parole "requires a social survey." (Labov; 1975, p. 81) Likewise one could equally argue that if *langue* is a social fact imposed on the level of the general community, one needs to study *langue* on a large scale social level rather than by considering the speech of only one individual (*langue* which is social is not the same as Chomsky's notion of competence which is species universal and therefore theoretically allows one to consider the competence of any one individual.) Labov's Saussurian Paradox is therefore not logically necessary.

[4] I am not a Saussurian scholar and am therefore relying on interpretations of Saussure by others, in particular Dinneen 1989; Harris 1987, 1988a and Joseph; 1989, 1990a,b. There is controversy over the influence of Durkheim in Saussure's work; however, Saussure did consider *langue* to be a "social fact", whether this was following Durkheim or not. A social fact according to Durkheim is: "every way of acting, fixed or not, capable of exercising on the individual an external constraint; or again, every way of acting which is general throughout a given society, while at the same time existing in its own right independent of its individual manifestations"(Durkheim, 1938, p. 13). Labov, (though he does not cite Durkheim) may be seen as following a position which unifies Saussure and Durkheim whether they were unified in Saussure's life or not.

[5] See, for example, Parret 1983, Harris 1987, Joseph 1989.

[6] Labov has consistently made reference to the term idiolect from as early as 1966 to as late as 1989. By idiolect he seems to mean the individual properties of the speech of one person, what one might call the individual grammar. The individual grammar considered in these terms is considered by Labov to be the least social, most unsystematic and unrepresentative of the over all system. Labov uses the term idiolect to refer to a number of different things including Chomsky's notion of grammar, the role of introspection is generative grammar, and the idiolect as utterance (the speech of one individual at one moment in time). The term seems therefore to be used as a sort of catch-all pejorative.

[7] Chomsky (1980) has claimed that language is the mirror of the mind and therefore one is able to get at the workings of the mind through studying

language. Labov has been less explicit, but it is possible that Labov believes that language is reflective of society, or embedded in society, and, therefore, the study of language will say something about society or the study of society will say something about language. Thus, for example, Labov is able to claim that the reason Black Vernacular English is growing more unlike White English varieties is because Blacks and Whites are segregated (Labov and Harris, 1986).

8 Labov does include normativity in his definition of New York city as a speech community in that he assumes a certain amount of shared values as to stigmatized speech, likewise he includes normativity in his definition of Philadelphia in that he assumes that White Philadelphians share the same speech values. However, despite the statement of normativity as the basis upon which these communities are defined, if you actually look at his work and what he is focusing on it is not normativity but linguistic behavior. There is therefore an inconsistency between his theoretical claims and his methodology.

9 This is a rather odd statement given all the evidence that children don't speak like their parents but instead speak more like their peers. Also given the fact that people often completely forget the first language they learn when they are removed from it and learn another, and that people are able to completely change their accents, and to have many different accents at the same type. For our purposes it shows the inadequacy of explanation as to how the individual learns the sociolect, and exposes the deterministic nature of Labovian linguistics.

10 For discussion of the sociolinguistic interview see Milroy 1987, Wolfson 1976. The traditional sociolinguistic interview consists of a module of questions and reading tests aimed at getting demographic information, style shifting, narratives, language attitudes, and specific sociolinguistic variables. The interviewer attempts to engage the interviewee in as many different speech styles as possible, but preferably as casual as possible.

11 Labov's contention that the standard interferes with the vernacular is interesting given that his study on the relationship between the vernacular and performance in school in reading and writing concludes that it is not structural interference from the vernacular that leads to poor performance but functional problems having to do with a clash of values and norms (Labov, 1972b). If structural interference from the vernacular to the standard exists, but not as a serious problem, why would the opposite, interference from the standard to the vernacular, not also be a minor problem, one that simply requires a few surface adjustments? Somehow the standard must be a more powerful dialect than the vernacular, but why this would be so is not explained. One could assume that this is so for socio-political reasons but if we follow the hallowed modern linguistic tradition that all varieties are equal in

the strictly linguistic sense, then the superiority of the standard language should not be a matter of linguistic superiority. Interference would therefore be an example of socio-political factors influencing the linguistic system. One could also make the claim that the vernacular is somehow derived from the standard and is therefore subsumed by it, but whether this is the actual historical development of the vernacular or not is open to question.

[12] If one considers this pronouncement within the socio-political context of a White linguist writing about the Black community, it is truly startling. The feelings of community members whether linguistically correct or not are real, and therefore it is mistaken to not grant credence to the feelings of ordinary people who accept someone as a member of their own group for whatever reasons. A strictly linguistic definition of a speech community will not be able to capture how membership is actually negotiated.

[13] There is also the added question of informants performing in ways that are fraudulent in the sense of knowingly performed for the benefit of the ethnographer. This has been an ongoing problem in anthropology; see for example, the controversy over Freedman's claims that Margaret Mead's informants told her what she wanted to hear about sexual practices in Samoa; and is a problem for sociolinguists collecting data. Labov presents the fact that he uses "natives", men from the actual community as facilitators with informants, as if being native is criterion enough.

[14] Labov's work on variation has spawned many attempts at refining the paradigm. See for example Ammon et al 1988; Milroy 1986 on networks; Romaine 1982 on speech community; Cheshire 1982 on vernacular norms.

[15] The study of "ing" as a sociolinguistic variable has become an exemplar (in the Kuhnian sense) in the Labovian paradigm following studies on "ing" by Labov, 1966; Trudgill, 1974.

5

John Gumperz and Interactional Sociolinguistics—Intentionality, Interpretation and Social Meaning

> *The question can be put as follows: what does an interactive approach to communication in which problems of understanding are studied not in terms of meanings inhering in a given text or stretch of discourse, but rather as outcomes of inferential judgements made in the course of situated processes of conversational exchange, imply for our theories of communication and language use?*
>
> *John Gumperz, 1984, p. 1*

Sociolinguistics According to John Gumperz

> *There is a need for a sociolinguistic theory which accounts for the communicative function of linguistic variability and for its relation to speakers goals without reference to untestable functionalist assumptions about conformity or nonconformance to closed systems of norms. Since speaking is interacting, such a theory must ultimately draw its basic postulates from what we know about interaction.*
>
> *John Gumperz, 1982a, p. 29*

Interactional sociolinguistics is a relatively later development in the history of 20th Century sociolinguistics, coming into maturity somewhat after the sociology of language, the ethnography of communication, and Labovian sociolinguistics. Interactional sociolinguistics has its foundations in interactional sociology, in particular the work of Goffman and Garfinkel, most importantly the development of conversation analysis.[1] It also has its foundations in the so called ordinary language philosophers, Strawson, Austin and most importantly Grice, and the ensuing development of pragmatics which evolved from the ordinary language movement. Interactional sociolinguistics also evolved out of the ethnography of communication, in particular Hymes' notions of context and communicative competence. And, in terms of linguistic analysis, interactional sociolinguistics follows closely the London School tradition began by Firth, continued by such scholars as Halliday, which stresses the importance of supra-segmental linguistics, in particular prosody and discourse coherence.[2]

Interactional sociolinguistics is an interdisciplinary field with a diverse heritage, and unlike the ethnography of communication developed by Hymes, or early sociolinguistic variation theory developed by Labov, is too diffuse to have one particular paradigm leader. This being acknowledged, Gumperz may be seen as having developed and defined a particular type of interactional sociolinguistics, (one which acknowledges the traditions stated

111

above), one which not only has influenced important work done by others (Deborah Tannen for example) but more significantly, states a general theory of sociolinguistics which goes beyond the particular concerns of Gumperz's own work and creates a distinctive paradigm.[3]

Gumperz distinguishes interactional sociolinguistics from its predecessors, ethnographic sociolinguistics and Labovian sociolinguistics, by pointing out their explanatory inadequacy in accounting for individual behavior – the actual behavior of actual language users in face to face communication.

Gumperz says of the results of surveys of the type typical of Labovian sociolinguistics: "Valid as they are as statements about behavioral trends, such observations tell us relatively little about what is being communicated in the situation at hand" (Gumperz, 1982a, p. 31). And again:

> Yet, important as quantitative sociolinguistics is, its applicability to the analysis of actual processes of face to face communication...is nevertheless limited...The fact remains that linguistic variable counts, no matter how sophisticated, are statistical generalizations based on data collected by survey methods rather than on findings validated through in depth analyses of linguistic competence. Such measures apply to behavioral trends in population aggregates and necessarily rely on *a priori* assumptions of what is shared, how it is distributed and how significant and generalizable it is. The relationship of social survey data to individual behavior is a matter of social theory that for many years has stood at the core of the debate between order theorists who argue that social norms and categories pre-exist, and individual behavior and conflict or action theorists, who see human interaction as constitutive of social reality (...) (Gumperz, 1982a, p. 26).

This quote contains a number of important points which are fundamental to Gumperz's theory of sociolinguistics and which separate him sharply from Labov. First is Gumperz's choice of face to face communication as the level of linguistic analysis rather than "population aggregates", a level of analysis which he sees leading only to "statistical generalizations". Second is Gumperz's concern with knowledge, knowledge which he takes to be problematic in terms of "what is shared, how it is distributed and how significant and generalizable it is." The sociolinguistic knowledge which Gumperz is concerned with is at the level of the individual, not at the level of the speech community. Third, Gumperz follows the "individual behavior and conflict or action theorists, who see interaction as constitutive of social reality", rejecting the position Labov holds, and Gumperz claims order theorists hold, that "social norms and categories pre-exist" (Gumperz, 1982a, p. 26).

Gumperz's early work was ethnographic in nature,[4] and his sociolinguistic theory is in many ways grounded within the ethnographic tradition. Nevertheless, Gumperz disagrees with what he perceives to be the seemingly non-interactive nature of sociolinguistics within the ethnography of communication:

...they tend to see speech events as bounded units functioning somewhat like miniature social systems where norms and values constitute independent variables, separate from language proper (...) The question of how group boundaries can be determined, is not dealt with, nor are the issues of how members themselves identify events, how social input varies in the course of an interaction and how social knowledge effects the interpretation of messages (Gumperz, 1982a, p. 155).

Gumperz's sociological theory is grounded in human interaction whereby meaning, order, structures, etc. are not pre-determined but evolve within interaction based on a complex range of material, experiential and psychological factors. Gumperz's linguistic theory is aimed at the level of the individual rather than the group (unlike Labovian linguistics which is a linguistic theory of speech communities) but it is not individualistic or asocial. Rather, it is based on a social theory of language which rejects the separation of language from social context. In addition, it is a sociolinguistic theory which is concerned primarily with knowledge – how linguistic behavior creates interpretation, how intention leads to linguistic behavior, how successful communication is related to sociolinguistic knowledge.

Gumperz's approach "focuses directly on the strategies that govern the actor's use of lexical, grammatical, sociolinguistic and other knowledge in the production and interpretation of messages in context" (Gumperz, 1982a, p. 35). To do this he focuses on a number of "contextualization cues" – "any feature of linguistic form that contributes to the signalling of contextual presuppositions" (Gumperz, 1982a, p. 131), signalling to the participants in the actual interaction, and later to the analyst, whether communication is proceeding smoothly and how intentionality is being communicated and interpreted.

The method for doing interactional sociolinguistics which Gumperz advocates is a form of microanalysis. He starts with "the basic socially significant unit of interaction in terms of which meaning is assessed": the activity type or activity (Gumperz, 1982a, p. 131). The speech activity is "a set of social relationships enacted about a set of schemata in relation to some communicative goal" (Gumperz, 1982a, p. 166). (See Levinson 1979 for a detailed discussion of speech activities.)

Speech activities are of the type that are commonly referred to in a given culture by such expressions as "discussing politics", "telling a story to someone", "chatting about the weather (ibid)". An activity type, however "does not determine meaning but simply constrains interpretations by channelling inferences so as to *foreground* [in original] or make relevant certain aspects of background knowledge and to underplay others" (Gumperz, 1982a, p. 130). Gumperz stresses that "although we are dealing with a structured ordering of message elements that represents the speaker's expectations about what will happen next, yet it is not a static structure but rather it reflects a dynamic process which develops and changes as the participants interact, moreover, its basis in meaning reflects something being done some purpose or goal being pursued" (Gumperz, 1982a, p. 131).

A speech activity is a means by which one orders one's expectations as to what sort of interaction one is participating in, but this initial ordering of expectations undergoes reevaluation, development and change over the course of the interaction. Interpretation of meaning is therefore a dynamic process which emerges through interaction.

A speech activity is also something which is grounded in intentionality, as Gumperz suggests above "its basis in meaning reflects something being done some purpose or goal being pursued." The interpretation of meaning in interaction is therefore to a great extent an interpretation of intent. In asking what is this activity? one is asking what is the purpose of this activity. What are participants trying to accomplish? The dynamic and intentional nature of interaction are two fundamental principles in Gumperz's theory.

Since the first step in analysis is some hypothesis as to what the speech activity is, one has to have knowledge of a possible range of speech activities with their attendant expectations. When doing work in a culture with which one is not familiar, it is necessary therefore to do ethnographic investigation to find out how speech activities are defined in that culture. Much of Gumperz's work is based on the assumption that participants in different cultures have different expectations about what comprises a specific speech activity. (See Gumperz 1982b for descriptions of cross-cultural interactions.)

Gumperz maintains that conversational exchanges have dialogic properties which allow the analyst to get at inferential processes. Two such dialogic properties are: "(a) that interpretations are jointly negotiated by speaker and hearer and judgements either confirmed or changed by the reactions they evoke – they need not be inferred from a single utterance, and (b) that conversation in themselves often contain internal evidence of what the outcome is, i.e. of whether or not participants share interpretive conventions or succeed in achieving theory communicative ends" (Gumperz 1982a, p. 5). Following the dialogic properties of conversation Gumperz suggests that "by careful examination of the signalling mechanisms that conversationalists react to, one can isolate cues and symbolic convention through which distance is maintained or frames of interpretation are created" (Gumperz 1982a, p. 7).

In his own work, Gumperz has looked at code switching, prosody, formulaicity, and contextualization conventions as signalling mechanisms. In terms of conversational coordination, Gumperz suggests that "examination of participants success in establishing common themes, maintaining thematic continuity or negotiating topic change at the level of content yields empirical evidence about what is achieved. The timing of speakership moves and listenership response can be examined through rhythmic or nonverbal cues, to check for evidence of breakdown on conversational coordination" (Gumperz, 1982a, p. 6).

The aim of the analysis is not to make claims about psychological reality – what an individual really has in her mind. Rather, "insights about participants' ultimate aims and personal motives cannot be recovered. But the aim of sociolinguistic analysis is to specify the conditions of possible communication not to determine ultimate meanings" (Gumperz, 1982a, p. 208).

Sociolinguistic Theory and Linguistic Theory

> *When linguists speak of language structure they generally refer to abstract features derived by decontextualizing procedures which take into account only a portion of the totality of communicative signs that may enter into the interpretation of communicative acts.*
>
> *John Gumperz, 1982a, p. 16*

> *Interpretation always depends on information conveyed through multiple levels or channels of signalling and involves inferences based on linguistic features that from the perspective of text based analysis count as marginal, or semantically insignificant.*
>
> *John Gumperz, 1982a, p. 207*

As should be clear from reviewing the list of foundational influences on the development of the field of interactional sociolinguistics cited at the beginning of the section above, Gumperz's theory of interactional sociolinguistics is not centrally grounded in received linguistic theory. It is discourse rather than sentence based, and it is concerned with the communication of intent not grammaticality. The units of analysis are either not traditionally linguistic (such as speech activities) or are based on aspects of linguistics (such as prosody) which are considered peripheral in received linguistic theory.

Gumperz has pointed out that Saussure drew a "basic distinction between what he called core and marginal features of language" (Gumperz, 1982a, p. 16). The core features are related to referential information and include: "segmental phonemes, grammatical markers or affixes, basic syntactic categories and certain elements of tone or stress in languages (ibid)". Marginal features, on the other hand, are related to the expressive function of language, "the expressive quality of a message but not its basic meaning (ibid)". These features include "intonation, speech rhythm, and choice among lexical, phonetic and syntactic options ..." (ibid). Gumperz goes on to add that Saussure's basic distinction "continues to be observed by most modern linguistics (ibid)".

As Gumperz noted received linguistic theory considers the core to be composed primarily of segmental features. The core includes only those aspects of language which are considered part of the grammar, whether the grammar is a system like Saussure's *langue*, or Chomsky's "grammatical competence." The core is concerned only with sentence level grammar and formal features are decontextualized and idealized. In contrast, in Gumperz's theory not only is his concentration on what received linguistics considers marginal aspects of language, but his analysis is always based on contextualized language. The reason why Gumperz includes these marginalized features is that his theory of language is not simply a theory of grammar but a theory of language as communication. The communication of feelings, of intentions, of identities, of social meanings are signalled in these "marginal" aspects of language.

The form of microanalysis which is used in Gumperz's method is similar to conversation and discourse analysis generally in that actual interaction is recorded, transcribed and then analyzed. The emphasis of Gumperz's analysis is on the success of conversational coordination between participants. Within the evolution of 20th Century sociolinguistics, microanalysis of discourse data was first and most influentially fueled by the work of ethnomethodologists doing conversation analysis. The work done in conversation analysis was done initially within the context of a particular internal theoretical and methodological argument within the discipline of sociology. Whatever linguistic experience the individuals practicing conversation analysis in its initial stages may have had, the rules and units of analysis being used were *not* those of received linguistics.

In developing conversation analysis ethnomethodologists were concerned with sequencing, how one act was constrained by a previous act, or how one act systematically followed another act. They developed units of analyses such as turns, adjacency pairs, topics, repairs, presequences. (See Atkinson and Heritage 1984 for examples of work done in conversation analysis as well as discussion of ethnomethodology.) From this incomplete list it should be obvious that these are not the segmental features of received linguistics: there are no phonemes, no phrase structures, no syntactic transformations.

Though Gumperz went on to emphasize something different from conversation analysts (such as the interpretation of conversational intent rather than the structural analysis of social order, and suprasegmental features such as intonation which conversational analysts often ignore), his tools of analysis and his methodology (gathering of conversation and then micro analyzing it) to an important extent is grounded in conversation analysis. His work abounds with reference to and examples from Sacks, as well as Schegloff.[5]

In contrast to the Cartesian nature of received linguistic categories which are discrete, follow the law of the excluded middle, and are universal, Gumperz says of the linguistic phenomena which he analyzes:

> The linguistic character of contextualization cues is such that they are uninterpretable apart from concrete situations. In contrast to words or segmental morphemes which although ultimately also context-bound, can at least be discussed in isolation, listed in dictionaries and explained in grammars, contextualization phenomena are impossible to describe in abstract terms. The same sign may indicate normal information now under some conditions and carry contrastive or expressive meanings under others (Gumperz 1982a, p. 170).

The particularity of Gumperz's theory therefore puts him at odds with the normal scientific construction of received linguistic theory. His suggestion that contextualization phenomena are impossible to describe in abstract terms has very profound implications for theoretical construction generally, and specifically for linguistics concerned with particularity.

Interactional Sociolinguistics as Linguistic Theory

> *... member's situated interpretations take the forms of judgement of intent. All such interpretations presuppose shared social knowledge yet this knowledge is not usually overtly verbalized. Rather it serves as the input for judgements of what the speakers want to achieve.*
>
> John Gumperz, 1982a, p. 36

Intentionality and the Rational Actor

Within Gumperz's formulation of interactional sociolinguistics we come across such terms as strategies, goals, motives, intent, means, ends. Though according to Gumperz what we do as communicators is based on tacit knowledge, "the objects of study are automatic, context and time bound inferential processes not readily subject to conscious recall", it is knowledge that can be made conscious. (See for example Garfinkel's 1967 experiments.) Despite the automatic nature of much of linguistic behavior, communication is intentional.

Intentionality is based on the principle that "there is an intuitive distinction between what people do and what happens to them" (Brand, 1984, p. 3). Intentionality is often defined in terms of goals, planning, purpose, future action. It belongs to the voluntary realm of mental processes and therefore has played a central role in philosophical discourse on such questions of free will and causation.

Intentionality has also been defined in terms of reference and signification and therefore is also central to questions of meaning and in particular the interpretation of meaning in interaction. For example one prominent view of meaning, which (according to Searle) derives from Grice, is that "for a speaker to mean something by an utterance is for him to make that utterance with the intention of producing certain effects on his audience" (Searle, 1983, p. 161). (For a discussion of intentionality see Searle 1983; Brand 1984; Addis 1989.)

For Searle (ibid) the fundamental question pertaining to intentionality is "What are the characteristics of speakers' intention that make them meaning conferring?" That is, how does one get from specific noises or movements or marks on paper to the interpretation of a specific meaning? When a person raises her hand in a particular way, how does one decide that she is greeting one rather than performing an involuntary act such as the product of a muscle spasm? How when a person performs a particular intonational contour does one decide that she is being friendly rather than hostile? For Gumperz these are matters of convention based on the social nature of language. Or in Searle's words, "language is essentially a social phenomenon and that the forms of Intentionality underlying are social forms" (Searle, 1983, p. viii).

Why is intentionality important for Gumperz's theory? Gumperz is concerned with conversational inference which he defines as "the situated or context bound process of interpretation by means of which participants in an exchange assess others' intentions, and on which they base their responses" (Gumperz, 1982a, p. 153). Intentionality is of fundamental concern for Gumperz because Gumperz's theory of interaction is based on the notion that participants in communication make inferences about the meanings of the actions of their fellow participants. Interaction is a form of action and actions are intentional. The understanding of inference in relation to action therefore requires a theory of intentionality.

Intentionality is a form of rationality; that is intentionality is a mental state. Though Gumperz does not make this point explicitly, rationality is assumed in his theory of interactional sociolinguistics. (See Garfinkel 1967 for an extensive discussion of "rationalities" – different ways of defining "rational.") It is not however a mechanistic rationality (for example, reduced to involuntary brain functions), but a rationality informed by moral choices in that language behavior is normative: "all verbal behavior is governed by social norms specifying participant roles, rights and duties vis-a-vis each other, permissible topics, appropriate ways of speaking and ways of introducing information" (Gumperz, 1982a, p. 164).

As Taylor and Cameron (1987) have noted rationality is also a basic principle for both ethnomethodology and Gricean pragmatics. Gumperz may be seen as sharing certain notions of rationality with both Gricean pragmatics and ethnomethodology, yet also differing in some important ways.

Gricean Pragmatics

The "ordinary language school" of language philosophers has had a great influence on the development of interactional sociolinguistics because it greatly influenced the development of discourse pragmatics. H. Paul Grice in his recent collection of works discusses the ordinary language school to which he reportedly belonged. He argues that in reality there was no such homogeneous a group and he points out the differences between such members as Strawson, Austin and himself. He does however agree that they all held certain principles in common. One was the belief that they needed to "uphold in one form or another the rights of the ordinary man or of common sense in the face of attacks which proceed from champions of specialist philosophical or scientific theory. (...) specialist theory has to start from some basis in ordinary thought of an informal character" (Grice, 1989, p. 345).

Grice disagreed with the notion that ordinary thought should be simply dismissed either at the beginning of theoretical development or "ignored, like a ladder to be kicked once the specialist has gotten going (ibid.)." The ordinary thought that goes into ordinary linguistic behavior was therefore of importance to Grice, a point of view also shared by Gumperz.

Grice in developing his notion that communication is to an important degree cooperative (Grice's Cooperative Principle), stresses the rational basis of this cooperation. He states: "Our talk exchanges do not normally consist of a succession of disconnected remarks, and would not be rational if they did" (Grice, 1989, p. 26). One of Grice's "avowed aims is to see talking as a special case or variety of purposive, indeed rational behavior ..." (Grice, 1989, p. 28). This purposive rational behavior is analogous to other purposive and rational behavior "in the sphere of transactions that are not talk exchanges (ibid)." Grice stresses that it is not that we all must in fact follow his Cooperative Principle (defined below) but that it is something "that is *reasonable* for us to follow, that we *should not* abandon (emphasis in original)" (Grice, 1989, p. 29).

Grice devised a "... rough general principle which participants will be expected (*ceteris paribus*) to observe, namely: Make your conversational contribution such as is required, at the stage at which it occurs, by the accepted purpose or direction of the talk exchange in which you are engaged" (Grice, 1989, p. 26). This is the Cooperative Principle to which Grice added four maxims: the maxims of Quantity, Quality, Relation, and Manner. Grice also considered the possibility that there may be many other maxims as well "aesthetic, social, or moral in character, such as 'Be polite'..." (Grice, 1989, p. 28).[6]

Though this is not the way Grice presents the Cooperative Principle, one may consider it as a sort of prescriptive guideline to behavior or indeed as a reflection of a specific cultural notion of what is rational and orderly behavior. What counts as a "succession of disconnected remarks" is after all a culture specific notion. Gumperz who stresses the cultural nature of interpretation makes this point:

> ultimately, of course, anything that is said is subject to being evaluated in terms of social norms and established criteria of truthfulness and rationality. But the contextual criteria in terms of which these judgements are made are often quite different from those applying to conversation inference and thus has important implication for our understanding of culture and communication (Gumperz, 1982a, p. 171).

Gumperz thus distinguishes between the sorts of criteria of truthfulness and rationality of the sort Grice has suggested above, and the sort of inferencing which takes place in conversation. Cultural assumptions as to truth and rationality are therefore not universally applicable. The important point here is that unlike Grice, Gumperz is making a distinction between conversational inference and other forms of inferencing. Gumperz, unlike Grice, is therefore not reducing conversational inference to universal logical properties.

Grice and Gumperz both stress cooperation as the basic principle underlying communication. For Grice the Cooperative Principle is a matter of relevance. Participants will work to make an utterance relevant because they assume that unless someone is completely irrational their contribution will be somehow relevant to some context at hand. (See Sperber and Wilson, 1986 for this discussion.) Particular sorts of meanings are generated (implicatures) when participants stray from the norms of interaction which Grice codifies in his maxims. For example, an abrupt change of topic in an otherwise unremarkable conversation might make you wonder if you might have inadvertently stumbled on a taboo subject.

Grice's notion of implicature and the generation of inference from the Cooperative Principle is fundamental to Gumperz's own work. For example Gumperz (1982a, p. 94) explains code switching in terms of the Cooperative Principle. However there is an added dimension to the role of cooperation in Gumperz's theory which goes beyond the maxims and implicatures. For Gumperz there is the added dimension of cooperation as involvement. In Gumperz's words, "what is to be interpreted must first be created through interaction, before interpretation can begin, and to that end speakers must enlist others' cooperation and actively seek to create conversational involvement" (Gumperz, 1982a, p. 206). For Grice the assumption of cooperation (i.e. relevance) allows for the generation of contextualized meaning, but for Gumperz cooperation is a pre-condition for contextualized meaning. That is, Grice assumes that presuppositions (such as those codified in his maxims) as to what is rational, normal, etc, are shared and that participants can therefore simply proceed. For Gumperz part of interaction is the negotiation of what is and isn't shared presuppositions, and successful communication is not possible without some agreement as to what is going on.

In developing the Cooperative Principle Grice defines it in terms of all-things-being-equal ("ceteris paribus") – if all things are equal then nothing in particular is implicated by one's actions. For Grice it is only transgressions from the norm which generate implicatures. Gumperz also sees inferencing as occurring in terms of something more or less like what a participant expects as normal, but Gumperz does not start from the universal neutrality of all-things-being-equal whereby there is some sort of fixed meaning or ideal standard with which one judges others' actions. The generation of implicatures is therefore much broader for Gumperz than for Grice, because anything in the context at a given time can generate implicatures.

What is the process of implicature for Gumperz? How does an action, such as suddenly raising one's voice, implicate some meaning? According to Gumperz the first step in interpretation is a general framing of the situation. He points out that we are "exposed to a multitude of signals, many more than we could possibly have time to react to", therefore "before even deciding to take part in an interaction we need to be able to infer, if only in the most general terms what the interaction is about and what is expected of us" (Gumperz, 1982a, p. 1). After this initial framing, what follows is a series of interpretations which take place throughout the interaction as knowledge shifts and emerges through the evolving conversation: "... interpretations are jointly negotiated by speaker and hearer and judgements either confirmed or changed by the reactions they evoke" (Gumperz, 1982a, p. 5). How do Grice's implicatures relate to the joint negotiation of meaning?

One is able to interpret an utterance within a sequence of utterances because of rational capabilities. As Taylor and Cameron (1987, p. 85) have noted, "... the conversationalist follows the CP [Cooperative Principle], and may justifiably be assumed by his audience to follow the CP (ceteris paribus), because it conforms to principles of human rationality." A person signals or may be interpreted as signalling a particular meaning. For example in Gricean terms some manipulation of a Maxim such as failing to follow the Maxim of Quantity – "Say as much as is required" – by evasively saying nothing,[7] or in Gumperz's terms through some manipulation of social identity such as code switching. These types of meanings will be arrived at through rational means. The implicature that is generated by saying nothing or by code-switching will depend on the context. Whatever the interpretation made on the part of the participant or analyst, for example a sudden rise in loudness interpreted as anger, clearly some implicature will have been created. Conversational cooperation is therefore not possible without rational abilities, what the neo-Griceans Sperber and Wilson (1987, p. 65) have described as a type of guessing.

Sperber and Wilson reduce Grice's Cooperative Principle to a principle of relevance which works in terms of a specific application of the more general mental process of deduction. The logical process by which one arrives at a definition of a discourse routine or the meaning of an utterance is a type of deductive process similar to guessing. One sees that a person is behaving in a certain manner, that she is saying certain things and that there are a range of other contextual considerations, such as what has taken place previously, and one deduces that all these things together (most of which one may not be conscious of) mean something: she is happy to see you and she is inviting you to lunch with her tomorrow. (This example is not Sperber and Wilson's.)

Despite the fact that both Gumperz and Sperber and Wilson's theories of the communication of intent are based on rationality, they are based on two separate theories of knowledge. For Gumperz the knowledge involved in the interpretation of intent is social knowledge. Gumperz's rationality is based on the social nature of mind. In distinguishing their approach to the study of intentionality from that of Gricean pragmatics, Gumperz and Cook-Gumperz (1982, p. 17) write, "When we talk about intent therefore, we mean the socially recognized communicative intent that is implied in particular kinds of social activities signalled in discourse." And they also note: "In dealing with conversational exchanges we do not and need not treat the psychological issue of what an individual has in mind, but rather we focus on how intent is interpreted by ordinary listeners in a particular context (ibid)."

Sperber and Wilson in contrast subscribe to the individual nature of mind. In addition, they maintain that the primary purpose of language is nor communication but information processing. For Sperber and Wilson the interpretation of meaning is reducible to innate deductive processes which are part of the brain's biological functioning and which one cannot help but perform: "Communicators do not 'follow' the principle of relevance; and they could not violate it even if they wanted to" (Sperber and Wilson, 1986, p. 167). For Gumperz inferencing processes are derived from socio-cultural frames learned over time through interaction with others and are not reducible to biology.

The work of Sperber and Wilson highlights the differences between Gumperz and Gricean pragmatics because they represent a clear extreme which easily demonstrates these differences. But the differences between Gumperz and Grice are not as easily drawn since Grice is not as clearly an adherent of individualist psychology.

Both Gumperz and Sperber and Wilson reject the logical basis of Grice's theory of inferencing. In the case of Sperber and Wilson they reject the logical basis of relevance (that one follows logical rules of inferencing such as following the maxims) in preference for a global deductive principle. In the case of Gumperz, conversational inferencing cannot be reduced to logical processes because conversational inferencing is a mental process which involves much more than logical principles. This is because social interaction involves too wide an array of mental processes and states (sensory perceptions, the emotions, decoding of symbolism) to be governed solely by principles of logic.

Ultimately these are different notions of language. For Gumperz language is broadly defined and communication is placed centrally within the functions of language. For Sperber and Wilson language is narrowly defined in terms of information processing and communication is seen as a sort of unessential bi-product. For Grice language is less narrowly defined than for Sperber and Wilson in that communication is considered essential, but communication is seen more in terms of logical reasoning than social interaction.

Ethnomethodology

The importance of the work of conversation analysts to the development of interactional sociolinguistic theory is not simply at the level of micro-analytic methods and constructs, it is also at the metatheoretical level, at the level of ethnomethodology. The work of Harold Garfinkel, in particular those aspects which incorporate the work of Alfred Schutz, defines ethnomethodology as strongly based on a particular type of rationality, one which may be called common-sense. In Garfinkel's words: "I use the term 'ethnomethodology' to refer to the investigation of the rational properties of indexical expressions and other practical actions as contingent ongoing accomplishments of organized artful practices of everyday life" (Garfinkel, 1967, p. 11).

Schutz in developing his theory of sociology strongly opposed the positivist position that the scientist has superior knowledge, comprehension and explanatory power regarding ordinary phenomenon over the common person. Similarly Garfinkel dismisses the notion that "the objective reality of social facts is sociology's fundamental principle" (Garfinkel, 1967, p. vii). Instead he holds that "the objective reality of social facts *as* [in original] an ongoing accomplishment of the concerted activities of daily life, with the ordinary, artful ways of that accomplishment being by members known, used, and taken for granted, is, for members doing sociology, a fundamental phenomenon (ibid)."

The question here for interactional sociolinguistics is whether the objective reality of linguistic/sociolinguistic facts is a fundamental principle (as it is in Labovian linguistics), or whether the ongoing accomplishments of users of language, along with their common sense knowledge and behavior, is a fundamental phenomenon upon which sociolinguistic theory builds?

Gumperz makes the point that "we cannot assume...that the linguist's notion of grammatical system is equivalent to the folk notion of language. The two concepts reflect different ways of abstracting from communicative behavior and the relationship between them must be established empirically: it cannot be taken for granted" (Gumperz, 1982a, p. 21). Though Gumperz does not discount the scientific notion of language, and in fact accepts it as a valid part of his concept of communicative competence, he also does not discount the folk notion of language.

Ordinary language knowledge is an intrinsic part of Gumperz's sociolinguistic theory. Therefore given the choice between what a linguist has *a priori* decided is the linguistic system, or has decided is the most crucial part of the system, and what actual users of the language find most salient, Gumperz would place greater import on the ordinary rather than the scientific.

One aspect of practical knowledge which is important to Gumperz's theory of communication is the common sense accountability of participants. Accountability (what Gumperz sometimes calls "evaluation")[8] is an important concept in ethnomethodology. It is a particular type of reflexivity which allows for the "visibly-rational-and-reportable-for-all-practical-purposes" (Garfinkel, 1967, p. vii) ability of ordinary people to produce "practical sociological reasoning (ibid)." In interactional sociolinguistics it is this reflexive ability which makes communicators accountable in their actions, which makes them able to explain their and others behavior, as well as adjust to unfolding situations.

This type of rationality is assumed in the analysis of intent and interpretation in Gumperz's sociolinguistic theory. The common sense reasoning of participants in conversations under analysis is actively sought out in Gumperz's method of interactional sociolinguistics. In this way Tannen (1984) for example, asks participants in a Thanksgiving dinner what they thought was going on, how they felt during particular moments, how they analyzed particular exchanges, and so on. That participants insights, experiences, etc. were considered valid is evidenced by Tannen then going back and reconsidering her own analysis of what had happened in the light of what she had been told. Gumperz and Tannen therefore consider the interpretations of the participants as data. Interactional sociolinguistics rejects the notion that only the scientific definition of language is the level at which valid analysis can take place.

Gumperz in agreement with ethnomethodology over the importance of ordinary knowledge and the role of reflexivity is in strong disagreement with ethnomethodology over the role of culture in the analysis of conversation. Gumperz states: "Conversational inference is best seen not as a simple unitary evaluation of intent but as involving a complex series of chain of judgements focusing on both content and on relational assessments of how utterance strings are to be integrated into what we know about our culture and about the immediate situation" (Gumperz, 1982a, p. 207). Gumperz stresses cultural knowledge, but ethnomethodological conversational analysis is concerned with conversation as an autonomous system. From their perspective one need not go outside of the text (outside of what people say) to search for answers to what takes place within a conversation. In fact one should not, therefore constructs such as culture, class, gender, ethnicity, etc, are not considered as having explanatory validity in analyzing an exchange. (For example, see Roark 1986 for Schegloff's objections to the use of sex, occupation or status as means of explaining conversational phenomena such as overlapping interpreted as interruption.) Yet this internal order is supposed to say something profound about social order generally. In this way, Sacks (1984, p. 24), in defense of studying such talk as "I had a good breakfast this morning" and "How are you" writes; "It is possible that detailed study of small phenomena may give an enormous understanding of the way humans do things and the kinds of objects they use to construct and order their affairs."

It is paradoxical that conversation in ethnomethodological conversational analysis is considered a form of social order, yet is not related to other social orders. The autonomy of conversation in conversational analysis is something which bothers Gumperz. For example, Gumperz criticizes conversational analysts for not showing "how strategies of conversational management are integrated into other aspects of speaker's linguistic knowledge" (Gumperz, 1982a, p. 160).

For Gumperz, culture is the social order which informs conversational order. He advocates his cultural stance in the following way:

> In order to account for inter-speaker differences in background knowledge, a sociolinguist needs to know how speakers use verbal skills to create contextual conditions that reflect particular culturally realistic scenes. How are speakers' grammatical and phonological abilities employed in this? For example, if regular speaker change is to take place, participants must be able to scan phrases to predict when an utterance is about to end. They must be able to distinguish between rhetorical pauses and turn relinquishing pauses. Although overlap is an integral part of interaction, conversation cooperation requires that interactional synchrony be maintained so that speakers cannot be interrupted at random. To follow the thematic progression of an argument, moreover, and to make one's contribution relevant, one must

be able to recognize *culturally possible lines of reasoning*. (My emphasis: ibid).

Gumperz gives an example of a Black student approaching an instructor about getting a recommendation. The student says: "Could I talk to you for a minute? I'm gonna apply for a fellowship and I was wondering if I could get a recommendation?" After the instructor tells him to come to his office and speak to him the student turns slightly to the other students in the room and says: "Ahma git me a gig!" (Gumperz, 1982a, p. 30).

Gumperz analyzes this situation as a case of metaphorical code switching whereby the student signifies that he is "just trying to get by" and is "still in control". Gumperz makes the point that people interpreted this example in different ways based on their cultural backgrounds. Whites with little experience with Blacks either refused to interpret the exchange "beyond saying that the speaker lapsed into dialect", or interpreted the code-switch as a political statement, that "this implied a rejection of the white instructor and of the academic enterprise." Other Whites interpreted the code-switch as "indicating that the speaker was addressing himself only to the other blacks in the audience." But the group consisting of Blacks and one White who "had spent a great deal of time in black circles" made the above interpretation of metaphorical code switching (Gumperz, 1982a, p. 31).

The point for Gumperz was that the student relied on the "audience's knowledge of grammar, of norms of appropriateness, and on the differences in their linguistic background to achieve his effect." His indirect approach "alludes to an entire body of culturally specific tradition and associations which are rooted in Afro-American culture and history. What he seems to be doing is taking part of the audience into his confidence and appealing to them as if to say 'If you can decode what I mean you must share traditions in which case you will understand why I behave the way I do'" (Gumperz, 1982a, p. 36).This analysis considers a wide range of contextual variables including, most importantly, the audience and cultural signification.

Now to an example from ethnomethodological conversation analysis. In Pomerantz's (1984) discussion of agreeing and disagreeing with assessments, she points out that there are different preference organizations. For example, one may agree by an "upgrade" such as a stronger evaluative term, one may disagree by not saying anything, and so on. Here is an example of disagreement with prior speakers' self-deprecations:

C:I have no dates I don't go:
  there is no sense in hanging onto the clothes.
J: (Are you -)((high pitch))
J:What do ya mean you don't have any da:tes ((low pitch))
C:Well: I just don't go out anymore that's all
J:Oh: that's ridiculous   (Pomerantz, 1984, p. 84).

Pomerantz (1984, p. 83) points out that "disagreements may include partial repeats that challenge and/or disagree with their priors." In this case C's final line is the partial repeat and J's final line is the disagreement. There is much which could be analyzed here in terms of discourse markers (see Schiffrin 1987b) or even prosodics, but what Pomerantz points out is the sequencing of C's partial repeat and then J's remark. It is the sequencing of turns which shapes the order – the disagreement is an assessment of a prior self-deprecating statement. There is therefore no need to talk about cultural norms of politeness or frames of expected behavior, or whether these are two women with similar backgrounds, etc, this kind of information is simply neither given nor considered. That this exchange is a partial repeat and a disagreement with an assessment is considered given and obvious in the text, therefore external context is not an issue.

Here then are different approaches to what one may consider relevant in interpretation of conversation. Here are also two different notions of common-sense rationality. For Gumperz this rationality is based on cultural norms; for conversation analysts the rationality seems to be more simply the ability to make inferences from sequential ordering.

Communication, Social Meaning and Communicative Competence

Gumperz's definition of communication is an interactive one: "Communication is a social activity requiring the coordinated efforts of two or more individuals. Mere talk to produce sentences, no matter how well formed or elegant the outcome, does not by itself constitute communication. Only when a move has elicited a response can we say communication is taking place" (Gumperz, 1982a, p. 1). How does a move elicit a response?

Frames, Schemata and Interpretation

According to Gumperz's model of conversational inference, one first has to have a general sense of what is going on, then one makes more specific judgements based on local inferences as the interaction proceeds. Each move elicits a response based on an inter-relationship between initial global inferencing and local inferences generated by each consequent exchange.

Gumperz places great emphasis on the preliminary interpretation. How does one arrive at this preliminary interpretation? Gumperz suggests that "conversationalists...rely on indirect inferences which build on background assumptions about context, interactive goals and interpersonal relations to derive frames in terms of which they can interpret what is going on" (Gumperz, 1982a, p. 2). The way the initial judgement is made is by framing the interaction in a global way. One has a set of expectations (Goffman 1974) about what is about to ensue.

The study of frames and schemata has a diverse history reflecting differences in disciplinary perspective be it cognitive psychology, social psychology, artificial intelligence, anthropology or interactional sociology. The concept of frames used by Gumperz (also by Tannen 1979; Tannen and Wallat 1987) seems to have evolved within Bateson's and Goffman's uses of the term.[9] For example, Gumperz (1982a, p. 131) cites Goffman 1974 in the following quote: "people make decisions about how to interpret a given utterance based on their definition of what is happening at the time of interaction. In other words, they define the interaction in terms of a frame or schema which is identifiable and familiar."

According to Gumperz one must first have some presupposition, some set of expectations, about what is ensuing before one can make sense of it. For example is this joking around or is this dangerously serious? (Cf. Bateson, 1970.) Though a frame is a set of expectations, expectations fluctuate with each new input of information as discourse proceeds. The relationship between an initial frame of a situation, ensuing frames and emerging information is therefore a complex and dynamic one.

In addition to Bateson, Alfred Schutz, and Schank and Abelson, are two of a number of theories of interpretation to which Gumperz makes reference in his book *Discourse Strategies*. By 1932, Alfred Schutz had developed the concept of interpretive schemes: "the completed meaning-configurations that are present at hand each time in the form of 'what one knows' or 'what one already knew'. They consist of material that has already been organized under categories. To these schemes the lived experiences are referred for interpretation as they occur" (Schutz, 1972, p. 84).

Interpretive schemes are therefore ways in which memory is organized in terms of experiential knowledge and to which one refers in order to make sense of present activity. These schemes are organized in terms of ideal types. The interpretation of meaning for Schutz is therefore an interaction between the past and present usually in anticipation of immediate or future action.

More recently with the development of artificial intelligence and computer technology, Roger Schank, Robert Abelson, and others, have developed models of cognitive processes which use a theory of schemata, whereby a person performs a series of inferential steps each in reaction to informational input and each in anticipation of more input.

Schank and Abelson devise a model of mental processing whereby one uses global and local organization of information to create a dynamic series of inferences. (See Brand 1984 for a discussion of this model.) One has experiences organized into "scripts": "a predetermined stereotyped sequence of actions that defines a well know situation" (Schank and Abelson, 1977, p. 41). One could have, for example a script of a speech activity such as talking about the weather or a speech event such as testifying as a witness in court. Within this script one would expect certain actors (Hymes' participants) certain props (the physical aspects of the situation) and certain actions to take place within a specific order of action. In a court for example one would expect a judge, one or more attorneys, possibly a jury, and other individuals such as a stenographer. One would expect some sort of tables and chairs and other objects such as a flag of the country one was in. And one would expect the court to be called to order and for one to answer questions directed at one. This then is a stereotypic notion of what testifying in court is like and would correspond more or less to an actual situation of testifying in court dependent on the context of situation.

Continuing with Schank and Abelson's model, more general than scripts are "plans". Plans are "explanations of sequences of actions that are intended to achieve a goal. The difference is that scripts are specific and plans are general" (Schank and Abelson, 1977, p. 72). An example which Brand (1984, p. 205) gives in his discussion of the model is: someone who eating in a restaurant is a routinized occurrence will have a script of eating in a restaurant, however "if eating in a restaurant is a rare occurrence in someone's life...then he has a general plan for doing so but not a stereotyped script. For such persons parts of the activity would not be routinized." If applied to a speech activity imagine a situation where someone has never participated in a particular religious ceremony, therefore does not know when to stand or sit, or speak or be silent, and therefore has no set expectations or script to follow. However, they might have a general notion of what religious ceremonies are like and therefore base their expectations and performances on this general "plan".

Now that the preliminary framing of the interaction has been accounted for in terms of some interpretive schema, how does ongoing interpretation take place? Or, what is it about communication which creates interpretive sequencing which in turn elicits particular moves? How does one infer from some sort of action some sort of meaning?

Conversational Conventions and Contextualization Cues

What aspects of communication are salient to interpretation? What do people use in communication to signal their intent? And what signals do people use to interpret intent?

For Gumperz the answer lies in a conventional theory of signs whereby a participant in an interaction is able to interpret the actions of another based on the interpretation of socio-cultural specific relations between signs and meanings. For Gumperz the signs which carry the most social meanings are those which have the most important role in the inferencing process. These he calls "contextualization cues".

Gumperz holds that there are a whole range of contextualization cues which can lead participants to interpret communication in the way that they do. Contextualization cues are "any feature of linguistic form that contributes to the signalling of contextual presuppositions. Such cues may have a number of such linguistic realizations depending on the historically given linguistic repertoire of the participants" (Gumperz, 1982a, p. 131). They may include "code, dialect and style switching processes,...prosodic phenomena...as well as choice among lexical and syntactic options, formulaic expressions, conversational openings, closing and sequencing strategies...(ibid)."

As the term implies, contextualization cues are contextually bound and "although such cues carry information, meanings are conveyed as part of the interactive process. Unlike words that can be discussed out of context, the meanings of contextualization cues are implicit (ibid)." In addition, "the cues involved here are basically gradual or scalar; they do not take the form of discrete qualitative contrasts" (Gumperz, 1982a, p. 132).

Gumperz suggests that contextualization cues channel interpretation "based on conventionalized co-occurrence expectations between content and surface style" (Gumperz, 1982a, p. 131). In this way, "what is involved is a departure from normal in one or another direction" (Gumperz, 1982a, p. 132). Contextualization cues are therefore "constellations of surface features of message form [which] are the means by which speakers signal and listeners interpret what the activity is, how semantic content is to be understood and *how* [in original] each sentence relates to what precedes or follows" (Gumperz, 1982a, p. 131). And, "the situated interpretation of the meaning of any one such shift in context is always a matter of social conventions" (Gumperz, 1982a, p. 132).

In concrete terms, a contextualization cue may be a phonetic, syntactic, lexical or stylistic variable. It may be formulaic routines (talk about the weather), formulaic expressions ("so nice to meet you"), or discourse routines such as openings and closings. It may be "ways of speaking" such as prosody – loudness, tempo, stress, intonation – silence, laughter, back channeling. It may be "code-switching". (See Gumperz 1982a.b. for examples of analyses of contextualization cues in actual conversations.)

The way that contextualization cues are involved in interpretation and the signalling of meaning is through a complex relationship with other linguistic and extra-linguistic cues. According to Gumperz, "the extralinguistic signals lie in the setting and the participants' knowledge of what preceded the interaction. There are at least three linguistic signals: first, the semantic content; second, the syntactic paradigm; and third, the contextualization cues such as prosody ..." (Gumperz, 1982a, p. 145). In addition to these factors, there are such things as the "physical setting, participants' personal background knowledge and their attitudes toward each other, socio cultural assumptions concerning role and status relationships as well as social norms associated with various message components ..." (Gumperz, 1982a, p. 153).

Contextualization cues are all conventionalized, that is though there is nothing innately conventional in their form, the ability to interpret meaning from their form is entirely a matter of convention. According to Gumperz miscommunication occurs when one either does not have the communicational competence of the other participant/s, or one has different conventions so that one is either unable to interpret signalling or one misinterprets signalling.

Gumperz and Cook-Gumperz (1982, p. 12) in their work on cross-cultural communication point out that one may have: "(1) Different cultural assumptions about the situation and about appropriate behavior and intentions within it. (2) Different ways of structuring information or an argument in a conversation. (3) Different ways of speaking." In addition, Gumperz has used work on cross cultural differences to demonstrate his claim that communicative competence is culture specific cognition. He does this by showing that miscommunication involving people from different cultures can be explained in terms of different communicative conventions, such as differences in interpretation of utterance intonation. Someone in one culture will expect a particular rising or falling utterance final intonation, for example, and when she encounters something different will interpret another's behavior evaluatively as being rude, impatient, evasive, or so on.

Gumperz gives a number of examples of this phenomena. Here are two, one with speakers of Indian English and the other with speakers of West Indian English interacting with British English speakers in England. In the first example, Gumperz tells of newly hired Pakistani and Indian women working at an airport cafeteria who when serving food would ask whether the person wants gravy or not by saying the word "gravy" with falling intonation. The women were perceived to be surly and uncooperative because the speakers of British English with whom they were interacting expect a politely phrased question to have rising intonation (Gumperz, 1982a, p. 173). The second similar example concerns a West Indian bus conductor who was perceived as being hostile and impatient when he requested fares by saying "exact change please" divided into two tone groups and with extra loudness, high pitch and falling intonation on "please". The expected prosody was "exact change please" as one tone group with a rising intonation on "please". (Gumperz, 1982a, p. 168-170). Gumperz notes that when these sorts of miscommunications occur they tend "to be seen in attitudinal terms. A speaker is said to be unfriendly, impertinent, rude, uncooperative, or fail to understand ..." (Gumperz, 1982a, p. 132).

Though interactional sociolinguistics is concerned with mental processes, the interpretation of action, intent, and so on, these mental processes are based on conventionalized assumptions and behavior which are not innate but have to be learned. Gumperz has stressed that the sorts of differences that the examples above demonstrate between speakers of different Englishes are "matters of basic cultural norms and of the interaction of prosody and syntax reflecting long established historical traditions that arise in distinct culture areas, and maintained through networks of interpersonal relationships." Conversational conventions "are learned only through prolonged and intensive face to face contact" (Gumperz, 1982a, p. 152).

Communication and Communicative Competence

For Gumperz communication is not defined in terms of the intent of the speaker (as it is defined for Grice), or in terms of the performance of utterance.

It is instead defined in terms of 1.) the coordinated efforts of two or more individuals, and 2.) the elicitation of response.

Searle disagreeing with communication defined as recognition of speaker intent makes the following distinction between representation and communication: "Characteristically a man who makes a statement both intends to represent some fact or state of affairs and intends to communicate this representation to his hearers. But his representing intention is not the same as his communicating intention. Communication is a matter of producing certain effects on one's hearers, but one can intend to represent something without caring at all about the effects on one's hearers" (Searle, 1983, p. 165). Following Searle, who in this case has a concept of communication similar to Gumperz's, communication may be defined as intentional behavior meant to produce some effect in those with whom one is communicating. Communication as (inter)action, is therefore purposeful and orientated towards achieving some goal. It is not the mere representation (or transmission) of ideas or information such as the representation of intent.

Gumperz has placed great emphasis on the manner in which conversational exchanges are coordinated within an interaction. The theoretical assumption seems to be that the closer the coordination, the more successful the communication, and the more problematic the coordination the less successful the communication. In referring to the coordination of framing a speech activity, Gumperz (1982a, p. 167) writes, "once a conversational rhythm has been established both participants can reasonably assume that they have successfully negotiated a frame of interpretation, i.e. they have agreed on what activity is being enacted and how it is to be conducted."

Another way of talking about conversational rhythm is the notion of "synchrony". According to Gumperz conversational synchrony – smooth automatically synchronized exchanges where participant rhythms are in unison – underlies successful communication. Lack of synchronization, such as problems in allocation of turn taking, dissimilar timing in such things as pausing, overlapping and speed of verbalization, is seen by Gumperz as importantly pointing to either unsuccessful communication or unsuccessful episodes within an overall interaction. Lack of coordination is like a methodological smoke detector leading the analyst to possible breakdown in communication.

It is not clear whether synchrony for Gumperz is the result of shared interpretive frames. Does one need coordination in the preliminary framing of the situation for synchrony to be possible? This would seem to be the case because Gumperz suggests that "if conversational inference depends on shared social presuppositions and if *conversational continuity is a function of the success of such inferences* [my emphasis], then the mere fact that two speakers can sustain on interaction over time is evidence for the existence of at least some common level of social knowledge and agreement on interpretation" (Gumperz, 1982a, p. 201,). It is also possible that synchrony helps to reinforce or create shared frames as interaction ensues.

Communication is more than referentiality. In order to communicate one has to first hold the attention of the person with whom one wants to communicate. One has to involve them. The success of communication is based on our ability to involve our fellow communicators. According to Deborah Tannen (1989) interpersonal involvement both creates meaning and is necessary for meaning in conversation. Involvement is based on emotionality, it is an appeal to momentary connectedness between separate individuals, what Schutz (1972, p. 163) has called "growing old together." In a conversation one needs to first get the other person's attention and then one needs to keep their attention through involving them in the mutual activity at hand.

Tannen has pointed out a number of ways in which involvement is created and maintained:

> Audiences are moved (1) by being swept along by patterns of sound and rhythm as well as by such patterns as repetition and parallelism, and (2) by the sense of identification that results from being required to participate in sensemaking. That is, in interpreting indirectness, ellipsis, tropes, imagery, and detail, the audience has to do a lot of filling in of meaning, and this participation contributes to the sense of a shared universe, and of coherence in the world, at the same time that it contributes to persuasion (...) (Tannen, 1990a, p. 7).

Eliciting a response is therefore a matter of creating and maintaining involvement.

Communicative competence is a form of knowledge which allows us to make judgements as to how to act and how to interpret actions within communicative contexts. Conversational coordination and conversational inferencing are matters of learned social behavior. For Gumperz communication is normative action:

> all verbal behavior is governed by social norms specifying participant roles, rights and duties vis a vis each other, permissible topics, appropriate ways of speaking and ways of introducing information. Such norms are context and network specific, so that the psycholinguistic notion of individuals relying on their own personal knowledge of the world to make sense of talk in context is an oversimplification which does not account for the very real interactive constraints that govern everyday verbal behavior (Gumperz, 1982a, p. 164).

How do these norms become part of an individual's communicative competence so that she is able to sustain involvement, or produce synchronous conversation with a range of people, or plan discourse strategies, or make inferences as to how communication is proceeding?

Social norms are not predetermined but are specifically introduced throughout each interaction depending on a complex interchange of variables having to do with the participants, the goals of the interaction, the level of interpersonal involvement, whether intent is cooperative or malicious, and so on. Given this range of contextual variation, it is Gumperz's position that the more similar two individuals backgrounds, the more similar their interpretive frames, the more likelihood there is for synchrony, and thus the less likelihood there will be for miscommunication.

Why would two or more people be able to produce synchronous exchanges? The answer would seem to be that they have similar socialization: they have been socialized in the same *style* of verbal behavior. Or, put another way, they have had similar experiences leading to similar memories.

Style, as was discussed in Chapter Three on Hymes, is a way of doing things. Tannen who has developed the notion of style to be explanatory in nature (communication or miscommunication may be defined in terms of the conflicting or nonconflicting styles of the participants) has described an individual's style as "a combination of features learned in interaction with others (hence, social) plus features developed idiosyncratically. Perhaps the impression of individual style results from the unique combination and deployment of socially learned features" (Tannen, 1984:10).

How a person got to acquire her particular style is an interesting topic, as it might shed some light on the exact nature of conventionality in communication, as well as add some insight to the question of the cultural nature of cognitive processes such as frames. It is however not a topic that is greatly pursued by either Gumperz or Tannen. The acquisition of the ability to interpret conventional cues, and the ability to perform in a particular style, seems to be assumed as evolving first within ones own family and then beyond the family with ones immediate network of contacts. In this manner, Tannen states that "each person's notion of what strategy is appropriate to apply is influenced by a combination of family background and other interactive experience" (Tannen, 1984, p. 13).

The relationship between social convention and norms, and individual behavior and interpretation is not explicated by Gumperz, but he does offer networks as an important means of constraining behavior and as having as important role in the evolution of interpretive schemata. According to Gumperz social networks are "associate classes of individuals with interactive experience" (Gumperz, 1982a, p. 41). They represent the patterned regularity of social interaction that an individual participates in. Some sociolinguistics such as Gal (1979) and Milroy (1983) have pointed to social networks, rather than class or ethnic group, as being the most important social institution affecting linguistic behavior. The argument is that those with whom one most closely associates most affect one's communicative choices.

Intersubjectivity

If Gumperz's interactional sociolinguistics is a theory of knowledge in the form of communicative competence, and if it is also a theory of interaction, then a number of questions are raised not only about the nature of this knowledge, but about the role this knowledge plays in interaction.

Gumperz's theory is based on the principle that similar competence in the form of similar frames is fundamental to successful communication, or at least dissimilar competence is a basis for unsuccessful communication. Must one have similar competence for successful communication? How similar does this competence have to be? And how is knowledge shared between participants? All of these questions raise the larger question of intersubjectivity.

Alfred Schutz was one of the earlier leaders of modern sociology to pursue the issue of intersubjectivity. Schutz held that one functions using interpretive schemes which are meaning configurations. Each individual is unique in their experiential history and therefore in their subjective consciousness. However people are able to communicate through intersubjectivity.

In developing his theory of common sense rationality Schutz expanded on Weber to develop the notion of ideal types and shared worlds. In this view, participants proceed until signalled otherwise as if they share the same assumptions about the world:

> We shall start out by simply accepting the existence of the social world as it is always accepted in the attitude of the natural standpoint, whether in everyday life or in sociological observation. (...) The object we shall be studying, therefore, is the human being who is looking at the world from within the natural attitude. Born into a social world, he comes upon his fellow men and takes their existence for granted without question, just as he takes for granted the existence of the natural objects he encounters (Schutz, 1972, p. 97,98).

From Schutz's point of view there is a starting point where participants are experientially equal and then adjustments are made as interaction evolves and the actualities of experiential differences become apparent. In fact, participants often begin with the stark assumption that they are not experiential equals, but the point Schutz was making here is that there are certain aspects of everyday life that are simply untouched by skepticism in ordinary interaction. One therefore is able to converse with someone without raising basic issues about the nature of reality. Without this tacit agreement as to a basic shared reality communication would not be possible.

Schutz mentions two ways in which we are able to achieve intersubjective understanding. One is through subjectivity: an individual interprets another's actions in terms of her own subjective experience. In this way intersubjectivity is not a matter of reaching mutual knowledge at all, it is simply the experiencing of someone else in terms of one's own experiences. Another way of reaching intersubjective understanding is through the concept of ideal types. An ideal type is a subjective generalization. One interprets behavior in terms of idealized categorization based on one's values and prior experience. In this way people who one doesn't know intimately remain anonymous to one, meaning that one really doesn't know who they are in actuality. Here is an example Schutz gives to illustrate this point: "When I mail a letter, I assume that certain contemporaries of mine, namely, postal employees, will read the address and speed the letter on its way. I am not thinking of these postal employees as individuals. I do not know them personally and never expect to." (Schutz, 1972, p. 184)

There is in a person's interpretive repertoire the notion of certain people who do certain things, or certain people who behave a certain way, or certain situations that go a certain way, and until presented with the particularities of the specific situation, particular person, particular activity etc., one makes interpretations on the basis of generalizations.

Another way of defining intersubjectivity different from that developed by Schutz is one which Taylor and Cameron (1987, p. 161) have described as the fundamental principle in "the study of verbal communication in modern times": it is the assumption that "communication is a means of bringing participants in it to a mutual awareness, a common perception, of an idea, an emotion, a representation, a governing structure and so on (ibid)." This definition of intersubjectivity is the transmission of something from one individual to another and is based on communication as the transmission of referentiality. This is in contrast to Schutz's model which is based on a notion of communication as a form of accomplished action.

What sort of intersubjectivity holds for interactional sociolinguistics? The position held by Schiffrin (1990, p. 122) that "conversation is an activity that allows the relevance of intersubjectivity to be interactively managed" is representative of the interactional perspective. Interactional sociolinguistics is also in agreement with Taylor and Cameron (1987, p. 15) that an account of intersubjectivity need not "look for intersubjectivity in the shared apprehension of a common event or object but rather in the social conformity of behavior and of the reflexive characterization of behavior" (Taylor and Cameron, 1987, p. 15).

Nevertheless, it is not entirely clear where Gumperz stands on this issue. On the one hand Gumperz (1982a, p. 6) indicates that when approaching data he "makes no assumptions about sharedness of rules or evaluative norms", and that though "being able to interact also implies some sharing" one "must not assume that sharing at all levels of either grammatical or social rules is necessary" (Gumperz; 1982a, p. 29-30). But on the other hand he seems to require some mutuality of knowledge, and miscommunication is defined in terms of lack of mutuality. He writes: "Experiences with conversational analysis so far suggest that it is at the level of perceiving and categorizing interutterance or intention relationships that interpretation is most sensitive to differences in social background" (Gumperz; 1982a, p. 36).

Gumperz makes use of notions such as background knowledge, shared frames, and synchrony. Though it is not entirely clear that participants in talk are actually attempting to create mutual perception, it can be read that way. And though the epistemic type of intersubjectivity defined by Taylor and Cameron above is based on a notion of communication, the traditional telepathic model, which is totally at odds with the interactive model of communication, Gumperz does have a concept of successful communication which seems to require the epistemic definition of intersubjectivity.

In this way, Gumperz holds the position that:

> Knowledge of the conversational activity entails expectations about possible goals or outcomes for the interaction, about what information is salient and how it is likely to be signalled, about relevant aspects of interpersonal relations, and about what will count as normal behavior. *A minimal requirement for successful communication is that participants share these expectations, i.e. that they can agree on the nature of the activity in which they are engaged.* [my emphasis] This implies they must also have a common system for signalling or negotiating shifts or transitions from one activity to another (Gumperz, 1982, p. 101).

How do participants agree? Do they both need to achieve shared knowledge? Does that lead to agreement? Or do they simply have to signal some kind of non-specific general social knowledge (such as "I am not going to cut your throat")? The level at which intersubjectivity is most important for Gumperz is at the level of presuppositions, shared expectations as to what is happening or going to happen. However, the pursuit of what the other person's expectations are, and whether they are mutually compatible with one's own, is a matter that is constantly in flux during the interaction. Gumperz's theory seems to require both an epistemic and normative concept of intersubjectivity. It is possible that Gumperz requires some kind of initial epistemic intersubjectivity in order for communication to get off the ground, then the more normative interactional type of intersubjectivity comes into play once the interaction has begun.

How similar does competence have to be for successful communication? How is knowledge shared? Gumperz notes that a theory of discourse strategies should begin by specifying "the linguistic and socio-cultural knowledge that needs to be shared if conversational involvement is to be maintained, and then go on to deal with what it is about the nature of conversational inference that makes for cultural, subcultural and situational specificity of interpretation" (Gumperz, 1982a, p. 3). There are really no definitive means of deciding how similar competence needs to be since the focus is with interaction and not something static.

If one accepts Gumperz's notion of communicative competence, then on the extreme end of possibilities if two people have dissimilar linguistic knowledge (speak two separate, distinct, and unrelated languages without a mutual *lingua franca*) as well as dissimilar socio-cultural knowledge (two completely different sets of norms of behavior) they cannot communicate without third party assistance. But the opposite does not seem to be necessarily true, that if two people have similar linguistic knowledge (speak the same variety right down to the same situational register) and similar socio-cultural knowledge (have the same ways of speaking) successful communication is guaranteed. There might be other factors such as willful uncooperativeness, or experiential differences leading to an inability to understand a particular topic at hand. Yet, given the assumption of cooperativeness, two individuals with similar linguistic ability and enough socio-cultural knowledge should be able to either ignore or repair whatever problems arise over the course of a conversation. Without a certain level of shared competence there would be at its most extreme either no conversation at all (though there could be some kind of communication through for example much expressive eye contact and gesture), or the conversation may proceed but without the participants having the means to either recognize or repair communicative problems.

Gumperz's position is that "Knowledge of the conversational activity entails expectations about possible goals or outcomes for the interaction, about what information is salient and how it is likely to be signalled, about relevant aspects of interpersonal relations, and about what will count as normal behavior" (Gumperz, 1982l, p. 101). The conversational activity (previously speech activity) is the basic unit in Gumperz's theory of communication. He has stated that the minimal requirement for successful communication is that participants agree on the nature of the conversational activity, so that both know for example that they are chatting about the weather and not having a political debate about perestroika. And he states that for there to be this agreement, participants "must also have a common system for signalling or negotiating shifts or transitions from one activity to another (ibid)."

Though at first glance Gumperz, seems to be requiring a minimal amount of similar communicative competence for successful communication, at closer range it is not quite so clear. If both participants need to share the same expectations as to activity type and need to have a common system for dealing with changes in activity types, this could require rather substantial amounts of shared knowledge.[10] Gumperz does not explicitly define what successful communication is, but consider his definition of communication and it would seem to require a large degree of coordination and response.

Coordination such as synchrony is quite clear, but how does one define what counts as a response? Must a response be public? What if your response to my remarks is to feel physical pain, is this part of communication? Certainly if my intention was to cause you pain one could say that I had succeeded in eliciting such a response but what if I hadn't intended to cause you pain? In contrast what if you recognize my communicative intent but do not respond?

Depending on what is meant by successful communication, Gumperz may be overstating his case when he states that "a minimal requirement for successful communication is that participants share these expectations." If successful communication is the type of epistemic intersubjectivity that Taylor and Cameron described above, then it is likely that one need the level of mutuality that Gumperz outlines. But if successful communication is something less, something more along the lines of recognition of intent, and the establishment of momentary involvement, then all of Gumperz's criteria for successful communication (coordination, response, shared frames) are not necessary. One can communicate with someone from a different culture using a language that neither know well and therefore have awful coordination, not very similar frames of experience, yet be able to communicate in the sense that one makes the other person respond to some need, some emotion, or be able to get something accomplished such as purchasing goods.

Part of the problem here is that what counts as successful communication and the role that intersubjectivity plays is based on the prior question of what may count as communication. For Sperber and Wilson, successful communication is simply a matter of recognizing intent: "Grice's greatest originality was not to suggest that human communication involves the recognition of intentions. That much...is common sense. It was to suggest that this characterization is sufficient: as long as there is some way of recognizing the communicator's intentions, then communication is possible. Recognition of intentions is an ordinary human cognitive endeavor" (Sperber and Wilson, 1987, p. 25).

For Herrnstein Smith (1988, p. 102):

> that which we call 'communication' is a historically conditioned social interaction, in many respects also an economic one and, like other or perhaps all economic transactions, a political one as well. It is historically conditioned in the effectiveness of any particular interaction depends on the differential consequences of the agents' prior verbal acts and interactions with other members of a particular verbal community. It is an economic interaction – and thus, one could say, transaction – to the extent that its dynamics operate on, out of, and through disparities of resources...between/among the agents and involve risks, gain, and/or losses on either or all sides. Communication is also a political interaction, not only in that its dynamics may operate through differences of power between the agents but also in that the interaction may put those differences at stake threatening or promising...either to confirm and maintain them or to subvert or otherwise change them.

In terms of intersubjectivity and the notion of successful or "genuine communication" in Habermas' sense she writes:

> there is no 'communication' in the sense either of a making common of something (for example, 'knowledge') that was previously the possession of only one party or in the sense of a transferral or transmission of the same (information, feelings, beliefs, and so on) from one to the other. What there is, rather, is a differentially consequential interaction: that is, an interaction in which each party acts in relation to the other differently – in different, asymmetric ways and in accord with different specific motives – and also with different consequences for each (Herrnstein Smith, 1988, p. 110).

For Sperber and Wilson one can rely on the "ordinary human cognitive endeavor" of recognizing intentions and communicate without benefit of mutual-knowledge, or similar communicative competence or linguistic fluency, or shared expectations, etc. For Herrnstein Smith there is no such thing as successful communication; that is, there is no ideal to which one may or may not say a particular communication conforms. Instead, communication can only be evaluated in terms of the evaluations of the participants themselves. These evaluations are dependent on the multiplex and fluid personal economies of the participants and will therefore not grant a unitary or single evaluation.

For both Sperber and Wilson and Herrnstein Smith therefore, mutuality is not needed in communication, and in fact for both, mutuality is denied. Sperber and Wilson reject the need for mutual knowledge in communication and Herrnstein Smith insists on the asymmetry of interaction. For Sperber and Wilson one need only deduce the intentions of one's fellow communicators for communication to have been said to have taken place. And for Herrnstein Smith what one has is the coming together of two individuals for varying self-interests.

What is lacking in either definition of communication is Gumperz's notion that communication is only communication when there is elicited response. For Sperber and Wilson the recognition of intent may be all the response that is necessary. For Herrnstein Smith it is assumed that since communication is interaction, there are responses, but this fact is part of interaction and has no special significance for communication.

For Gumperz the question of successful communication does seem to rest on some sort of mutuality and this mutuality seems to rest on some kind of intersubjectivity. Miscommunication is defined in terms of lack of mutuality, and communication is defined in terms of having and maintaining mutuality. Involvement which is central to Gumperz notion of communication seems to be related to intersubjectivity and successful communication. The more involved one is in a conversation the more likely one is to attempt or assume some sort of mutuality, not necessarily mutuality of knowledge but at least mutuality of purpose.

Conclusion

In this chapter interactional sociolinguistics has been discussed mainly in terms of the theory of interactional sociolinguistics developed by John Gumperz. This is a theory based on face-to-face communication and is concerned with the interpretation of social meaning in interaction. In this way it is distinguished from both the ethnography of communication and Labovian sociolinguistics in its concentration on individual processes rather than group trends. It is distinguished from received linguistics because it is discourse based and is concerned with "marginal" linguistic phenomena.

Gumperz's interactional sociolinguistics is grounded in the assumption of rational cooperative behavior whereby linguistic actions are seen as intentional. Linguistic actions are seen as belonging to a larger system of symbolic actions. Linguistic actions are therefore part of communicative behavior generally and are subject to general socio-cultural as well as specific interactive normative constraints. Meaning is arrived at through a complex process of interpretation of linguistic and nonlinguistic context bound cues which signal the intent of participants, and channel expectations as to the possible outcome of the interaction.

Gumperz presents an interesting combination of rationality and conventionality in his theory. His theory of communication is intentional and is based on rational processes of inferencing. However though these rational processes are mental and are therefore rational in that sense, they are ontologically tied to experience and are therefore based on cultural and context specific information rather than logical properties and they cannot be reduced to any one brain function or mental principle.

Moving away from the specific aspects of Gumperz's theory, what type of metatheory does he offer for sociolinguistics? It is a metatheory which is motivated by a cultural, temporal, and context-bounded approach to phenomena. It is therefore particularistic in nature. It chooses not to aim for predictive generalities but to account for singular occurrences within the context of their occurrence. It is therefore not motivated by received science's abstraction from particularity, but instead approaches with ethnographic curiosity ordinary phenomena. Though Gumperz's theory in practice is often rather limited in emphasis, such as the interpretation of intent, he has demonstrated that a linguistics of particularity is possible.

Notes

[1] Goffman's work on social interaction, in particular his works *The Presentation of Self* (1959), *Interaction Ritual* (1967), *Frame Analysis* (1974), *Replies and Responses*, and *Footing* (1981), has greatly influenced the work of particular interactional sociolinguistics including Gumperz, Tannen, Brown and Levinson, and Schiffrin. Harold Garfinkel developed a particular metatheory and way of doing sociology which he called ethnomethodology. See, Heritage 1984 for a detailed discussion of Garfinkel and ethnomethodology. Out of ethnomethodology developed conversation analysis, in particular the work of Harvey Sacks, and then Emanuel Schegloff and Gail Jefferson. Conversation analysis has had immense influence on the development on what is now the field of discourse analysis.

[2] Though Gumperz does mention Halliday, I haven't found reference to Firth. Nevertheless, Gumperz's particular linguistic emphasis was preempted by the London School, whether he was personally influenced by them or not.

[3] One may consider interactional sociolinguistics very broadly to be a field of study (the study of discourse, or face-to-face communication) or a separate linguistic paradigm (pragmatics or a linguistics of particulars). Tannen has pointed out that the study of discourse "embraces" at least nine disciplines (Tannen, 1989, p. 7). Considering interactional sociolinguistics in this way there cannot be an overall paradigm leader, but there are people who have seen to the development of specific ways of doing pragmatics or discourse based linguistics. In this way the specific work that Gumperz has done, in particular cross-cultural communication, and his particular method would be considered one way of doing interactional sociolinguistics or one area within interactional sociolinguistics – the study of communicative competence. Nevertheless, if one looks internally to linguistic theory and the development of different ways of thinking about and doing linguistics, Gumperz has developed a theory which goes way beyond his own work and which goes a long way to developing sociolinguistics as a separate paradigm.

[4] Gumperz's early work was ethnographic. (See, Gumperz 1971 for a collection of his earliest work.) Gumperz has stated that his book *Discourse Strategies* "grew out of approximately ten years of field studies of verbal communication in India, Europe and the United States(...) (Gumperz, 1982a, p. vii). In this way, his work can be seen as an expansion of the ethnography of communication to include the previously neglected level of the individual.

[5] That Gumperz's work is informed by the work of conversation analysts is clear for a number of reasons, the most obvious of which is his using their work to illustrate points in his own work. Harvey Sacks, who along with Garfinkel, did the earliest and most influential work in Conversation Analysis is frequently cited by Gumperz, as is Schegloff. Gumperz has proposed his

work as an improvement on Conversation Analysis. For example, in Gumperz's 1984 paper on communicative competence he shows how his analysis can account for particulars which Conversation Analysis cannot.

[6] This suggested extension of maxims was later formulated by Leech, 1983. Leech's extension has generated some controversy. So also has Sperber and Wilson's (1987) dismissal of the maxims in favor of the restating of the Cooperative Principle as the cognitive principle of relevance. See Brown and Levinson, 1987, for a brief discussion of the extension or contraction of Grice's maxims.

[7] The Maxim of Quantity is: 1. Make your contribution as informative as is required (for the current purposes of the exchange). 2. Do not make your contribution more informative than is required. Grice would argue that saying nothing is a violation of the Maxim because it disregards part 1. of the Maxim.

[8] Gumperz and Cook-Gumperz define the term evaluation as: "determination of how participants reflexively address the social activity that is being constituted by their ongoing talk" (Gumperz and Cook-Gumperz, 1982, p. 19).

[9] Goffman and Bateson are most frequently cited by both Gumperz and Tannen. Tannen's work on frames (1979) is also cited by Gumperz.

[10] This could require a substantial amount of knowledge because of the complex requirements of synchronizing one's exchanges in terms of pausing, turn taking, openings and closings, floor allocation, topic coordination, and so on. This in addition to knowing what sort of speech activity one is participating in.

Part Three — Paradigms: The Construct Level

6

Sociolinguistics and Utterance

> *In a linguistics of particularity, you have to have a particularity to start with.*
> A.L. Becker, 1988, p. 21

Introduction

This chapter is concerned with what is *linguistic* about sociolinguistics. As has already been discussed in the previous chapters, sociolinguistic disciplinary matrixes approach the relationship between sociolinguistics and linguistic theory in varying ways. Nevertheless, though each matrix differs from the other, they also differ from received linguistics in a significantly similar way. Whether attempting to stay within received linguistics as does Labov, or attempting to move away from received linguistics, as do Hymes and Gumperz, each sociolinguistic matrix approaches linguistics, though with diverse motivations, as the study of language as it is actualized in society. This is in opposition to strictly hypothetical, abstract, asocial, and/or mentalist approaches to linguistics. What this translates to in concrete terms is that the linguistic construct studied by sociolinguistics is utterance[1] – contextualized rather than decontextualized linguistic phenomena.

Sociolinguistics and Utterance

> *To produce an utterance is to engage in a certain kind of social interaction.*
> John Lyons, 1977, p. 725

> *An utterance has a variety of properties both linguistic and non-linguistic. It may contain the word 'shoe' or a reflexive pronoun, or a trisyllabic adjective; it may be spoken on top of a bus, by someone with a heavy cold, addressing a close friend.*
> Sperber and Wilson, 1986, p. 9

Definitions of Sociolinguistics

Typical definitions of sociolinguistics are of the type: "the study of language in relation to society", (Hudson, 1980, p. 1) or "the study of language as a social phenomenon" (Svejcer and Nikol'sij, 1986, p. 1). Or sociolinguistics is seen as the study of language in "social context", (Trudgill, 1974a) or the "systemic co-variance of linguistic and social structure" (Bright 1966, from Bell, 1976, p. 22). These types of definitions share the assumption that language is somehow social, but other than mentioning language they don't give any hint as to what is *linguistic* about sociolinguistics.

Here are some definitions which do: sociolinguistics "attempts to make a coherent statement about the relationship between *language use* and social patterns or structures of various kinds", (Romaine, 1982b, p. 1, emphasis added) and, sociolinguistics places "stress on *parole*, on the *speech act* in all its social dimensions" (Giglioli, 1972, p. 8, emphasis added). Again the concern is with language as societal, but now there is also some hint as to what type of linguistics sociolinguistics might be: sociolinguistics is concerned with, "language use", "*parole*", "the speech act".

How to further define sociolinguistics linguistically? Received linguistics is based on a distinction between form and function, between knowledge and use (e.g. Chomsky's competence and performance), between the linguistic and non-linguistic, and between the supra-individual linguistic system and individual behavior (e.g. Saussure's *langue* and *parole*.) Hymes and Gumperz reject received linguistic theory's separation of the linguistic from the non-linguistic, and instead consider the two to be interactively combined. On the other hand, Labov accepts the distinction and instead correlates the linguistic with the non-linguistic as separate systems. It is therefore not a prerequisite of sociolinguistic theory either to reject or embrace these sorts of dichotomies. There may be no agreement, for example, whether language use is part of competence or solely a matter of performance, or whether notions like competence and performance even have validity. Differences in regard to these types of fundamental issues will of course lead to differences in theories and methods of sociolinguistics.

But despite these real and potential differences, what is held in common is the view that actual language use is the concern of sociolinguistics. To say that sociolinguistics is concerned with language use, or with *parole*, or with the speech act says nothing about the relationship between form and function or *langue* and *parole*, etc., but it does identify a specific area of concern for sociolinguistics. But what does the study of "language use", "*parole*", "speech acts" mean concretely in linguistic terms? The answer to this question lies in the linguistic construct "utterance". Sociolinguistics can be defined linguistically as the *recontextualized* study of utterance.[2]

Sociolinguists have made the basic claim that in order to study language realistically (Labov, 1972a; Neubert, 1976), or completely (Hymes, 1974a) one has to study how language is used, and why it is used in particular ways and for particular purposes. When an individual uses language there are a range of factors involved, whether biological, physical, political, social, cultural, which are not linguistic in any traditional sense of the term linguistic. Immediately then studying language use takes one out of the realm of what is considered linguistic in received linguistics – the autonomous aspects of the language system.

When one considers the nature of language (as understood in linguistic theory) in the phrase "language use", when one considers the concrete manifestation of that which may be considered *linguistic* in "language use", what exists are contextualized, spatio-temporally constrained entities known in linguistic theory as utterances. "Language use" is a matter of performing utterances. Sociolinguistics as the study of language use generally, is specifically the study of utterance.

Definitions of Utterance

What is utterance? Throughout the history of linguistics one can find ample usages of the word "utterance". For example, Bloomfield defines a language as "the totality of utterances that can be made in a speech community" (Cited in Chomsky, 1986, p. 16). The term "utterance" is often used in a pre-theoretical sense as a general term for observable language. There are also different technical uses of the term having to do with either a type of unit, such as a particular size, or a type of process, such as an action.

Lyons has pointed out that utterance as a concept is ambiguous as to whether one is referring to a process or a product: "In one sense, it denotes, a particular type of behavior. In its other relevant sense, it denotes, not the behavior itself, but the products of that behavior: not speaking (or writing), but what is spoken (or written)" (Lyons, 1981b, p. 23). Sometimes the term utterance is used to refer to the spoken rather than the written. Brown and Yule make this distinction: "the features of spoken language...should be considered as features of utterances, and those features typical of written language as characteristic of sentences" (Brown and Yule, 1983, p. 18). Sometimes the focus of the utterance is on the act of speaking, such as Firth's 1937 definition: "the expenditure of bodily energy in muscular efforts, as a grouped pattern of bodily movements" (Firth, (1937) 1964, p. 27). Sometimes the focus of the utterance is on the act of comprehension, such as Moore and Carling's concern with the 'knowledge base': "each understanding of an utterance in turn has the effect of causing further reordering of the 'knowledge base'" (Moore and Carling; 1982, p. 112). Frequently the focus is on utterance as a social action: "every utterance and its hearing bear the marks of the framework of participation in which the uttering and hearing occur" (Goffman, 1981, p. 3). And frequently the focus of the utterance is on defining utterance as a unit of analysis. Harris, for example defined an utterance as "any stretch of talk, by one person, before and after which there is silence on the part of the person" (Z. Harris, 1960, p. 14).

None of the above definitions or applications of the notion utterance have mentioned context; that is, there is no explicit reference to context in the truncated quotes above. Nevertheless, any reading of Brown and Yule, Firth, Moore and Carling, Goffman, or Harris will demonstrate that context is very much at issue. Firth, who also used utterance in a less restricted sense to mean *text* generally, always frames utterance in terms of the "context of situation".

Moore and Carling's concern with the 'knowledge base' is a concern with the contextualized nature of knowledge and therefore the contextualized nature of comprehension. Brown and Yule are concerned with utterance in discourse with discourse itself being a contextually defined entity. Goffman places utterance within contexts such as the participation framework and the social situation. And Harris, in developing his structuralist approach, was aware that the distributional restrictions of utterances within a discourse are contextually defined within the unfolding discourse.

Lyons, who uses utterance to mean any type of language be it spoken, written or signalled, defines utterance meaning as context dependent. (Lyons, 1977a,b, 1981a,b.) Sperber and Wilson also define utterance meaning in terms of context: "The set of premises used in interpreting an utterance (apart from the premise that the utterance in question has been produced) constitutes what is generally known as the *context* (emphasis in original)" (Sperber and Wilson, 1986, p. 15).

Context

What is context? What is significant about context as a theoretical construct? Schiffrin (1987b) has pointed out the vagueness and overly general nature of context as a concept in linguistics. She has shown that this is partly because context is important to a cross section of branches within linguistics:

> For example, pragmatics focuses on how language is influenced by frames of mutual knowledge, discourse analysis on the influence of textual structures and conversational patterns, sociolinguistics on the influence of social situations and speaker/hearer identities, and the ethnography of communication on the influence of cultural constructs[3] (Schiffrin, 1987b, p. 11).

Contexts are therefore at least psychological, textual, social and cultural. Below are four definitions of context by Sperber and Wilson, Hymes, Lyons, and Givon.

Sperber and Wilson define context as:

> a psychological construct, a subset of the hearer's assumptions about the world. It is these assumptions, of course, rather than the actual state of the world, that affect the interpretation of an utterance. A context in this sense is not limited to information about the immediate physical environment or the immediately preceding utterances: expectations about the future, scientific hypotheses or religious beliefs, anecdotal memories, general cultural assumptions, beliefs about the mental state of the speaker, may all play a role in interpretation (Sperber and Wilson, 1986, p. 15,16).

Hymes includes in his typology of context: the situation – the physical and temporal locality; the participants – their relationships to each other and the goals of their interactions; the text – the content, form, genre and delivery of the message; and the social norms for interaction and interpretation.

Lyons defines context as "a theoretical construct, in the postulation of which the linguist abstracts from the actual situation and establishes as contextual all the factors which, by virtue of their influence upon the participants in the language-event, systematically determine the form, the appropriateness or the meaning of utterances" (Lyons, 1977b, p. 572). He uses Hymes' notion of communicative competence as the base for delineating what aspects of context are influential, his list of features is therefore similar to Hymes (Hymes' features are in parenthesis). Lyons includes appropriate knowledge of role and status (participants), the location (situation), formality level (key), medium (genre), subject matter (message form and content), province (setting and scene) (Lyons, 1977a, p. 574).

Givón (1989, p. 74-5) divides his typology of context into three categories: the generic focus – shared world and culture – including knowledge of the "so-called real world"; the deictic focus – shared speech situation – including knowledge of the immediate speech situation, knowledge of participant roles; and the discourse focus – shared prior text – including knowledge of the immediately preceding discourse, knowledge of discourse modality.

What do these four descriptions say about context? First it is important to note that no typology is complete. Givón makes this claim explicitly:

> One must, finally, own up to the existence of an irreducible residue, a recalcitrant *escape clause* concerning the open-endedness of 'context'. This residue can never be fully captured, however exhaustive and refined one's taxonomy may be. I refer here to the provision...which in principle admits any information at all as legitimate context...in natural communication, provided the speaker deems *it relevant* to the transaction – on whatever grounds – and *available* to the hearer, by whatever means (emphasis in original) (Givón, 1989, p. 76).

The open-endedness of context, due to the constantly changing and dynamic nature of perception, identity, the physical world and so on, has great significance for the integration of context into any linguistic theory.

All four typologies share a number of general factors. They all include linguistic (e.g. prior-text) and non-linguistic (e.g. physical location) factors. They all include culture whether in the form of beliefs, assumptions, expectations, or norms of behavior. And they all include the participants (e.g. their social relationship to each other, their shared and un-shared knowledge) without whom any discussion of context would be moot. Context is multi-dimensional, it includes the past (prior-text, memory, cultural norms, discourse routines, etc.) the present (the physical environment, the speech situation, etc.) and the future (hypotheses, hopes, desires, goals, fears, etc.), and it includes a range of "worlds" – worlds of discourse, worlds of experience, worlds of fancy, material worlds – so that one is simultaneously experiencing many times, many places and many selves in relation to others and in relation to the worlds one is inhabiting.[4]

According to Lyons context is a *theoretical* construct which is *systematic* in nature. Context here therefore is not any possible contextual occurrence, potential or otherwise, but only that which "the linguist abstracts from the actual situation and establishes as contextual all the factors which, by virtue of their influence upon the participants in the language-event, systematically determine the form, the appropriateness or the meaning of utterances.(...) All random variation is to be discounted in terms of the distinction of competence and performance" (Lyons, 1977b, p. 572). Context in this sense requires the linguist to know what is and what is not influential in the actual situation and is only that which can be demonstrated to have influenced the participants.

This is rather different from the open-endedness of Givón's concept of context. But since Givón speaks of context in terms of shared knowledge, one could argue that those aspects of context which are not shared would not be considered part of the specific context for the analysis of hand. In this way consider the following scenario: I am facing you when we are conversing, I can see something going on behind you which you are not aware of and this is affecting my processing of the conversation. One might then say that this was part of my context of situation and not yours and therefore not shared context. However since this fact was salient to me, though not to you, shouldn't it be considered as context nevertheless?

Under Lyons' definition of context it would be considered if it was systematically related to my interpretation of meaning in the conversation. Under Givón's proviso of shared knowledge it would seem to be excluded from the context at hand; that is, though it would obviously be part of some aspect of the context of situation, it would not count as part of our shared context.

Lyons is correct to point out that context as linguists use it, is a theoretical construct, an abstraction away from the plurality of contexts to some sort of construct, "context", which can be described in terms of a categories or features. However, the question remains; how does the linguist go about deciding what is and is not part of the theoretical construct "context"? Is it what is shared? what is relevant to one or all participants? what is salient to one or all participants? or simply what is salient or relevant to the linguist herself at the time of the analysis? There is the problem of relating the contexts that linguists reconstruct to the infinite, open-ended nature of context as it exists in the world.

Firth and Givon provide two ways of dealing with the multiplexity of contexts: Firth's "context of situation" and Givón's notion of multiplex contexts. Firth's (1937/1964, p. 182) context of situation within which utterance occurs is rather similar to the previous typologies above:

A: The relevant feature of participants ...
(i) The verbal action of the participants
(ii) The non-verbal action of the participants
B: The relevant objects
C: The effect of the verbal action

Note two interesting aspects of Firth's typology. One is that context is defined in terms of relevant features. The other is that the effect of the verbal action is considered part of the context. To redefine Firth in terms of contemporary theory context is a matter of relevance and interaction.

Firth viewed language in terms of a systemic approach, whereby there are levels of language, each a context for other levels and each occurring within "a serial contextualization of our facts, context within context, each one being a function, an organ of the bigger context and all contexts finding a place in what might be called the context of culture" (Firth, 1935, p. 33). For Firth the highest level of context is culture.

Givón, in looking at this problem of contexts within contexts, also takes a systemic approach using the notion of systems and meta-levels:

> The system, as a hierarchic entity, is made out of a progression of *levels*, each one acting as *meta-level* for the sub-levels embedded within it. Each meta level is thus the *context* for the sub-levels embedded within it. For purely practical reasons, if the system is to remain finite (i.e. describable within *finite* time, space and means), the last – highest – meta-level must remain *context-less*; it lacks its own meta-level (emphasis in original) (Givón, 1989, p. 3).

The highest meta-level remains context-less or else the system would not be finite. Therefore though context is open-ended in life-as-we-know-it, context as a theoretical construct is closed. Though Givón does not explain this notion of meta-level and sub-levels in much detail, here is an attempt to apply it.

Consider culture above in Firth's definition of context as the meta-level within which all other contexts are subsumed. Below this level, consider a disciplinary matrix as the meta-level for doing linguistic analysis; subsumed under this disciplinary matrix is the context of the particular analysis (for example, interactional sociolinguistic analysis of a conversation). This analysis is *itself* the meta-context for the context which is the focus of analysis (for example, the focus is on the role of formulaicity in conversational exchanges). And this in turn is the meta-context for the form of the analysis (for example, the types of formulaicity considered are formulaic greetings). In this sense, everything one does is both within a context and itself a context for something else.

As seen in the typologies, context is a matter of at least textual, social, physical, and cognitive properties. Just what these properties are and how they are related to each other in what is reconstructed as "context" is problematic. For Lyons the role of the linguist is to distinguish the contexts which belong to competence from those which belong to performance (see, Blakemore 1987 also for this distinction). The reconstruction of context is therefore a *linguistic* construct. For Firth and Givón it is a *cultural* construct. Here the emphasis is ultimately on the framing of perception and cognition is itself considered culturally framed. In Givón's words, "reality and/or experience are not absolute fixed entities, but rather *frame-dependent, contingent upon the observer's perspective* (emphasis in original)" (Givón, 1989, p. xvii). With Lyons the emphasis is on linguistic competence; with Firth and Givón it is more generally on the framing of reality and the effect that such framing has on knowledge. What may count as context is therefore quite different in these separate accounts.

Sperber and Wilson define context as a psychological construct, Lyons' refers to context in terms of appropriate *knowledge,* and Givón refers to context in terms of shared *knowledge.* Similarly, if context is acknowledged as an integral part of Hymes' notion of communicative competence, one can assume that Hymes also considers context in terms of *knowledge.* Context therefore can be defined as a psychological construct having to do with knowledge.

However, agreeing that context is psychological does not in itself mean agreement, as different theories of psychology can lead to very different notions as to what kind of psychological construct "context" is. In this way, granted that Sperber and Wilson, Lyons, Hymes and Givón agree to the psychological nature of context (that contexts are in some way a matter of knowledge, beliefs, expectations, etc.), it is still not the case that the psychological basis of context is the same for all four. For example, for Sperber and Wilson context is a part of a mechanistic process wedded to the normal deductive processing of the brain rather than socially motivated behavior. But for Hymes, context as a psychological construct is less a matter of mechanistic brain processes and more a matter of socio-cultural processes. For Hymes, the framing of reality is less a matter of natural deductive processes and more a matter of culturally situated learned behavior, and therefore communicative competence is to a great extent social knowledge.

Here is therefore a basic difference in psychological theory: Sperber and Wilson following a more innatist position and Hymes following a more constructionist position. For Sperber and Wilson individual psychology is more importantly based on innate biological properties, while for Hymes individual psychology is more importantly constructed in terms of social properties such as interaction between members in society.

In this way Sperber and Wilson (1986) grant social context a very minor role in their theory of relevance. Even though social factors make up an aspect of the psychological construct "context", the input of social factors to what is or is not relevant is downplayed by Sperber and Wilson, who choose instead to highlight the innate deductive properties of the brain. This is of course quite contrary to Hymes' position where the socio-cultural aspects of human psychology are integrated in communicative competence in a non-subservient way with other cognitive processes, and where such social aspects of context as the social relationship between participants, the social goals of the participants, and the social norms which define the speech event, are extremely important.

The issue here is whether one's theory of psychology is based on the social interactive and cultural nature of cognition or whether one grants priority to species specific or individualist brain processes. One can agree that context is situated in the mind of the individual who is using language and is therefore a psychological construct, yet have a very different sense of what is influencing or creating the construct: is it reducible to automatic brain processing such as Sperber and Wilson's principle of relevance, or is it complexly irreducible to any one overriding feature? If contexts are a matter of knowledge, previous knowledge and emerging knowledge, then how one defines context will have to rest on one's theory of epistemology – what knowledge is, how knowledge arises, and how knowledge is transmitted. A more careful analysis of context therefore requires a more careful rendering of prior concepts such as knowledge.

Part of the reason that the concept of context is so underdeveloped is that it is used as a descriptive construct without explication of the epistemology upon which it is based. In this way, Leech defines the context of an utterance as "any background knowledge assumed to be shared by s and h and which contributes to h's interpretation of what s means by a given utterance (Leech, 1983, p. 13)." There is no discussion as to what is meant by background knowledge or how speakers and hearers could share it.

Text and Context

All of the four descriptions of context discussed above include both linguistic and non-linguistic factors as comprising context; context is therefore in these formulations not something separate from text. This view of context is not the traditional view of the relationship between text and context. Traditionally in discussing, for example, the difference between semantic meaning and pragmatic meaning, it has been the case that semantic meaning is considered context independent while pragmatic meaning is considered context dependent. With the former one need be told no extra-linguistic information; one need not go outside the text for comprehension because meaning is stable and constant within the text. (See Leech, 1983, Levinson, 1983, Lyons, 1977a,b, 1981a,b, for a discussion of this semantic-pragmatic distinction.)

Text, in this view, is a strictly linguistic phenomenon: that which is said or written which is contained within the linguistic system – "the propositional meanings that are linguistically realized through units such as clauses or sentences and through the relations conveyed or implied through such units" (Schiffrin, 1994, p.364). And context is that which is non-linguistic and which influences the interpretation of the text, such as the cultural beliefs, social positioning and brain processes. Text and context in this sense are separate entities which may be related to one another to explain a particular interpretation of meaning. Another possible view is that text is somehow enveloped in context; rather than being separate and somehow correlated with context, text is embedded within context though not actually part of context. (See Schiffrin 1990b, p. 264 for a brief summary of differing perspectives on the relationship between text and context.)

There is an alternative view of the relationship between text and context which is not based on the tidy division of meaning into semantic and pragmatic meaning. If one does not accept the traditional distinctions between semantic and pragmatic meaning, such as not accepting that meaning can be context independent except in metalinguistic scientific discourse, then the text/context distinction becomes difficult to maintain. Even if one does accept that some distinction between text and context is valid, for example, allowing that certain types of text require more context than others for interpretation, explicating the relationship between the two is not always easy.

That text and context are often mutually related has been demonstrated traditionally in work on indexicals, deixis, and more recently in work on discourse cohesion and coherence. Schiffrin (1990b, 1994, Chapter 10), for example, has argued against the strict separation of text from context and against a simplistic distinction between context dependent versus context independent texts. She has analyzed the word "then", both as a temporal adjective and as a discourse marker, to demonstrate that the relationship between text and context is bi-directional. She has shown that "neither expressions nor utterances have a fixed relationship with the situation in which they occur. Contexts can impose themselves upon texts to different degrees – upon the messages conveyed, the meanings of expressions, the definition of and relationships between textual units (personal communication)." And texts can impose themselves upon contexts to different degrees as well: "because what is said helps to create a shared knowledge base, texts can change the cognitive domain of a context; similarly, what is said can alter (just as readily as it can reflect) a social relationship (personal communication)."

The fact that the text-context relationship is bi-directional and can be extremely embedded is significant in at least two ways. If this is the case then received linguistic theory's distinction between what is linguistic and non-linguistic is problematic, and therefore the ability to separate text from context as two separate and independent systems is also problematic. This makes context a more powerful theoretical construct since contexts are not something outside of language which can be ignored, but are embedded in language and can inform language use and interpretation.

Discourse

An important part of a definition of utterance is a definition of discourse. Indeed to understand utterance requires an understanding of discourse. Though "utterance" and "discourse" are not usually equivalent usages in either English or in linguistic theory, they are often at least parallel concepts, and to a great extent the same thing. This view is supported by Deborah Tannen's definition of discourse:

> Discourse – language beyond the sentence – is simply language – as it occurs, in any context (including the context of linguistic analysis), in any form (including two made-up sentences in sequence; a tape recorded conversation, meeting, or interview; a novel or play). The name for the field 'discourse analysis', then, says nothing more or other than the term 'linguistics': the study of language (Tannen, 1990a, p. 6).

Utterance, in the broadest sense as simply contextualized language, is therefore equivalent to discourse in this sense.

The term discourse has been used in many different ways to mean different things. (See Schiffrin 1987, Tannen 1989a, Potter and Wetherell 1987, for a discussion of different meanings of the term discourse.) Three uses of the term discourse are important for this chapter: 1) Discourse can mean "language in use" (Brown and Yule, 1983). Sociolinguistics is the study of "language in use", since the concrete realization of language in use is utterance, there is a meaningful relationship between discourse and utterance as well as between the study of discourse and sociolinguistics. Utterance and discourse are equivalent in this sense. 2) Discourse can mean a unit of language larger than the sentence. (See Tannen, 1984, 1990a.) The study of discourse in this sense is concerned with the coherent sequencing of utterances into the discourse unit. 3) Discourse can mean an ideological meta-schema which constrains, informs or controls the way one perceives reality, including the way one performs language, while at the same time, performing language affects perception of reality (MacDonell, 1986).

Starting first with the third sense of discourse: the interpretation of meaning begins with the framing of reality in the form of a set of expectations. Discourse, in this sense is a frame or schema. The context of inference makes inferencing possible yet at the same time is created by inference. The relationship between discourse and context is therefore reflexive. Gumperz explains this:

> We are faced with a paradox. To decide on an interpretation participants must first make a preliminary interpretation. That is, they listen to speech, form a hypothesis about what routine is being enacted, and then rely on social background knowledge and co-occurrence expectations to evaluate what is intended and what attitudes are conveyed (Gumperz 1982a, p. 170-1).

A preliminary judgement is made and then adjusted and readjusted as the interaction proceeds. Discourse as a frame is the context of the initial judgement, however context in the form of ongoing "information" about the world around us, the interaction, etc, create new frames of discourse.

Consider this example. Suppose you believe that all gay men are effeminate. This is your discourse frame which is the context for your initial framing of your conversation with a particular male who is masculine therefore you assume him to be heterosexual. Imagine that during the course of this conversation he makes reference to his male lover of ten years, this information (if you can process it at all since your initial discourse frame may overwhelm your ability to absorb this new information into your interpretive schema) may very likely cause your discourse frame that all gay men are effeminate to collapse. This then serves as a new context for the rest of your interaction.

Now to the second meaning of discourse – discourse as a unit beyond the sentence. Zelig Harris (1960) suggested that the goal of the structural analysis of discourse is to be able to distinguish between a random sequence of utterances and a coherent meaningful sequence of utterances. (This is a position also held by Grice.) Harris (1960, p. 14), defined the utterance as "any stretch of talk, by one person, before and after which there is a silence on the part of the person." This definition of utterance may be equivalent to a turn of talk which takes place in a larger discourse such as a conversation.

Harris' structural model whereby utterances belonging to a larger discourse may be composed of a number of smaller units (sentences) is not an uncommon one. Allerton, for example, accepts Harris' distinction defining an utterance as a turn, "a contribution by one speaker to a discourse, the contribution being bounded on both sides either by a change of speaker or by the beginning or end of the discourse (...). Thus some soliloquies would be discourse consisting of a single utterance." And he defines discourse as a "conversation or text involving one or more speakers, bounded on both sides either by a considerable period of silence or by the arrival or departure of all participants. Since this is our highest unit of all, the vagueness involved in its definition is perhaps defensible" (Allerton, 1969, p. 30).

Discourse in the sense of a unit of language larger than the sentence is therefore made up of utterances (whether utterances are defined as smaller, larger and or the same size as sentences). Utterances as contextualized phenomena means that how utterances relate to other utterances within the overall discourse and to the world outside the discourse is also a matter of context.[5]

The ambiguity which Lyons assigns the term utterance as to whether it is a product or a process also applies to discourse. Lyons states that utterance in one sense "denotes a particular kind of behavior. In its other relevant sense, it denotes, not the behavior itself, but the products of that behavior: not speaking (or writing), but what is spoken (or written)" (Lyons, 1982b, p. 25). Discourse may be seen as action – the act of discoursing – or as a product of action – a unit of language. It would seem that discourse as the construction of reality, a type of meta-schema, relates to discourse as process, and discourse as a unit of analysis larger than the sentence relates to discourse as a product.

Utterance and Linguistic Theory

> *Utterances are physical events. Events are ephemeral. Utterances die in the wind.*
> Hurford and Heasley, 1983, p. 15

> *A sentence is neither a physical event nor a physical object. It is conceived abstractly, a string of words put together by the grammatical rules of a language. A sentence can be thought of as the ideal string of words behind various realizations in utterances and inscriptions.*
> Hurford and Heasley, 1983, p. 15

The Sentence/Utterance Distinction

The question for linguistic theory is not so much whether linguistic theory studies utterances or not, because all linguistics no matter what the source of data ultimately studies utterances. This is because (at least in terms of ordinary reality) all human actions take place within a particular spatio-temporal context. Therefore whether one is introspecting about a sentence, whether one is reading a sentence, whether one is speaking, one is performing utterances. All behavior is contextualized including the context of metalinguistic scientific discourse. The question for a linguistic theory is thus whether utterances are decontextualized either into an utterance type or sentence, for example, or whether utterances are left contextualized, and what the processes of decontextualization or recontextualization are.[6]

Received linguistics has made the distinction between the autonomous linguistic system (such as *langue* or competence) and language use (such as *parole* or performance). One way this distinction has been maintained is through the distinction between sentences, which belong to the autonomous linguistic system, and utterances which belong to the extra-linguistic realm of use. A number of interesting linguistic distinctions have been made in this way, for example, the distinction between phonetics and phonemics, and the distinction between semantics and pragmatics. Another way the autonomous linguistic system and language use distinction has been maintained is through the notion of distinct linguistic levels, whereby sentences and utterances belong to different levels of the same linguistic system.

The sentence/utterance distinction raises a great number of questions. What is the relationship between sentences and utterances? Are sentences derived from utterances? Are utterances derived from sentences? If utterances and sentences are phenomena existing on distinct levels, are these levels real? If they are real, are phenomena on different levels the same or different phenomena? How does one get from one level to the next? And does this process from level to level create change?

Levinson (1983, p. 19) defines the sentence/utterance distinction in this way: "... a sentence is an abstract theoretical entity defined within a theory of grammar, while an utterance is the issuance of a sentence, a sentence-analogue, or sentence fragment, in an actual context." This is a received linguistic formulation of the distinction. Danes makes the same distinction when he defines a sentence as "an abstract pattern which represents one of several formal grammatical units of a given linguistic system", and utterances as "realizations (implementations) of sentence patterns in the act of communication. In contradistinction to the abstract sentence pattern, the utterance refers to a concrete piece of reality, to a particular situation and is an organic constituent of a discourse (text)" (Danes, 1970, p. 133). Likewise, Leech suggests that "it is convenient to reserve terms like sentence...for grammatical entities derived from the language system, and to reserve the term utterances for *instances* of such entities, identified by their use in a particular situation (emphasis in original)" (Leech, 1983, p. 14). Lyons, also maintains the same distinction:

> Sentences in the more abstract sense are theoretical constructs, which are postulated by the linguist, in order to account for the acknowledged grammaticality of certain potential utterances and the ungrammaticality of others. They may or may not have some kind of psychological validity in the production and interpretation of language-utterances. But they certainly do not occur as the inscribed, and transcribable, products of utterances (Lyons, 1981b, p. 196).

Sentences

From the distinctions made above, a sentence is a formal grammatical construct which belongs to a particular theory of grammar. The grammarian can decide what a sentence is in terms of the internal needs of the grammar. This type of definition of a sentence does not tell us what a sentence is except to say it is whatever the theory says it is; which apart from being circular, is rather unhelpful a definition. Lyons (1977b, p. 629) has pointed out that, "linguists tend to spend far less time these days discussing the nature of sentences. But this is not because there is now some generally accepted criterion, or set of criteria, in terms of which it can be decided what is and what is not a sentence. The reason is simply that linguists have been less concerned recently with questions of definition" (Lyons, 1977b, p. 629).[7]

Two well-known works, Ries 1931 (first published in 1894) and Fries 1952, have highlighted the difficulty of defining the sentence. Ries came up with 140 different inadequate definitions, and then added his own: "A sentence is a grammatically constructed smallest unit of speech which expresses its content with respect to this content's relation to reality" (Fries, 1952, p. 17, translation by Fries). Fries starts out his chapter "What Is a Sentence?" by stating that "more than two hundred different definitions of the sentence confront the worker who undertakes to deal with the structure of English utterances" (Fries, 1952, p. 9).[8] Definitions of sentences have typically clustered around the notions of thoughts or propositions, completeness, and or independence. There is the long standing definition of a sentence as a group of words expressing a complete thought. (Fries traces this definition to predate Priscian c. 500 A.D. Fries, 1952, p. 9.) And the relatively more recent definition (held for example by Meillet, Jespersen and Bloomfield) of the sentence as a complete and independent formal unit not subsumed by a larger grammatical category. (See Fries, 1952, p. 20 for these definitions.)

Sentences have also been defined in terms of comprising certain formal properties. In this way Linell defines the sentence as having the following "formal-structural properties":

a) a sentence must be limited by an onset and an end that are structurally clearly manifested,
b) a sentence must, at least in some languages, e.g. English, contain both a subject and a predicate
c) a sentence must exhibit certain other properties which enable it to occur as an independent unit. (...)
d) a single sentence may contain several clauses, e.g. subordinate clauses (Linell, 1982, p. 67).

According to Linell, a sentence therefore is an independent formal unit with a formally defined beginning and ending, and which may contain smaller units within it. That the onset and end which would limit a sentence is not given us above, and that the subject and predicate might not be universally necessary, and that "certain other properties" in (c) are also not delineated points to the danger of attempting to define the sentence in a typological way.

Defining the sentence is therefore problematic in at least two ways. If the sentence is defined as an abstract theoretical linguistic construct there is the problem of relating the abstraction to the observable behavior. Lyons makes this point when he criticizes Chomskyian linguistics (pre-government and binding theory) for failing "to give an account, even in principle, of the way the sentence as a theoretical construct within the linguist's model of the language-system is related to the sentence as a contextualized product of language-behavior" (Lyons, 1977b, p. 629). If the sentence is defined concretely in terms of comprising of certain necessary constituents, there is the problem of generality, whereby the sentence cannot be defined universally but has to be defined language variety by language variety or possibly even more situationally restricted. The first problem is relating the platonic object to the actual phenomenon that people experience, and the second problem is generalizing from the sentence as a relative construct to the sentence as a universal construct. This is therefore a problem of universals and particulars.

The Relationship Between Utterances and Sentences

In the received distinction between utterances and sentences, utterances are actions rather than abstractions. Utterances have also been traditionally defined in terms of units of speech larger than the sentence. In this sense, an utterance as a single act of speech (Bloomfield, 1933; Harris, 1960) is a functional or interactional unit rather than a syntactic unit. Fries, for example, defines the utterance unit as "those chunks of talk that are marked off by a shift of speaker" (Fries, 1952, p. 23). Utterances are therefore of varying durations and forms. Fries goes on to posit that a sentence is a free utterance unit, that is, "it is not included in any larger structure by means of any grammatical device" (Fries, 1952, p. 25). This notion of sentences and utterances is not driven by a linguistic theory which requires the separation of acts of speech (performance) from some deeper underlying form (competence) and therefore the question of the derivation of sentences or utterances does not come up. This is of course not the case with current received theory.

Leech maintains that "an utterance may be a sentence-instance, or sentence-token; but strictly speaking it cannot be a sentence." (Leech, 1983, p. 14, see also Lyons, 1977a,b, 1981a,b and Levinson, 1983, for the same position.) An utterance can be the instantiation of a sentence (for example, when a sentence is uttered) or a sentence-token (the instantiation of a sentence-type, for example, the utterance of an interrogative) but it can not be a sentence because a sentence only exists in the abstract.

Lyons has devised an elaborate system which distinguishes between sentences and utterances, and between levels of sentences and utterances. He distinguishes between system-sentences, text-sentences, sentence-types, sentence-tokens, utterance-types, utterance-tokens, utterance-acts and utterance-products (Lyons, 1977a,b).

Lyons suggests that "each of the well-formed strings that is generated by the grammar will be a system-sentence of L; and it will be correlated with a text-sentence of L" (Lyons, 1977b, p. 387). System sentences:

> are abstract theoretical constructs, correlates of which are generated by linguists model of the language-system in order to explicate that part of the acceptability of utterance-signals that is covered by the notion of grammaticality; text-sentences are context dependent utterance signals (or parts of utterance signals,) tokens of which may occur in particular texts" (Lyons, 1977b, p. 622).

System-sentences are generated by the rules of the grammar and exist only as a formal unobservable abstraction (for example, X-double bar to X-bar to N-double bar, or earlier S - NP,VP). Text-sentences, however, are "a sub-set of actual or potential utterances" (Lyons, 1977b, p. 385). A text-sentence is therefore an utterance-product, brought into being by an utterance-process, which may be phonic or graphic in nature. How does one get from the abstract unobservable level to the concrete observable level?

According to Lyons, "every actual utterance is spatiotemporally unique, being spoken or written at a particular place and at a particular time (...)" (Lyons, 1977b, p. 570). System-sentences, on the other hand, "can be regarded as maximally decontextualized utterance-signals" (Lyons, 1977b, p. 625). A system-sentence is therefore a decontextualized utterance. Nevertheless, Lyons holds that the system-sentence is more basic than the text-sentence and "does not depend for its validity upon the occurrence, as acceptable utterances of the language in question, of strings of words in one-to-one, order-preserving correspondence with the strings of words that are held to be well-formed system-sentences (ibid.)" The fact that what a grammar posits as "sentences" and what is observed as utterances do not correspond is therefore not an argument either against the validity of the posited "sentences" or the claim of the sentence's ontological priority.

Still at issue is how to get from system-sentences to utterances (though we know how to get from utterances to system-sentences – by decontextualization.) Apparently the act of uttering a system-sentence produces the concrete manifestation of the system-sentence: the utterance in the form of the text-sentence. However, since system-sentences technically cannot be uttered, and since technically sentences cannot be utterances, how then are utterances derived from system-sentences? If the text-sentence is at a level between the abstract sentence level and the concrete utterance level, an utterance type or a potential utterance, for example, it is possible that this is the level at which grammatical form is paired with context and then becomes actualized as an utterance (the received notion is that an utterance is the pairing of a sentence with a context). This is not explicated by Lyons, except by his contention that form (apparently syntax) has priority over all other linguistic levels.

Thus, despite Lyons' typology of separate levels, and a proliferation of terminology, one is still not informed as to how one gets from one level to the next, if system-sentences are decontextualized utterances, how it is logically possible to claim therefore that utterances are derived from sentences. To follow this line of reasoning one must accept the competence-performance distinction, one must accept that sentences are part of competence while utterances are part of performance, and one must accept that competence is ontologically prior to performance.

If sentences are simply an abstract theoretical construct dreamed up by linguists then there is no point in talking about sentences as if they exist outside of scientific linguistic discourse because what exist in actuality are utterances which linguists idealize and abstract from. However, if instead sentences are seen as real and are real in a way which is different from utterances, then the sentence-utterance distinction becomes something more than a linguistic fabrication. The competence-performance distinction and the autonomy of syntax have been recently supported as psychologically real by the notion of modularity, i.e. that the mind/brain has separate faculties for separate tasks and that there is a specific language faculty which computes linguistic competence only. (See e.g., Fodor 1983, Newmeyer 1983.)

In this way, Blakemore (1987) argues for a distinction between semantic and pragmatic meaning, between the psychological reality of linguistic knowledge and non-linguistic knowledge. Though she does not concern herself with the sentence/utterance distinction (and is in fact concerned with utterances), if one follows her claim that there is a real distinction between strictly linguistic knowledge and non-linguistic knowledge, and sentences are defined as being strictly linguistic, then one could claim that sentences are real (they encode only linguistic knowledge) and are different from utterances which encode both linguistic and non-linguistic knowledge. However the modular interaction between linguistic and non-linguistic knowledge could not explain how utterances are derived from sentences unless the autonomous linguistic module is somehow more powerful than the non-linguistic modules.[9]

The question here is whether different levels are real and if they are, do phenomena on different levels undergo change as they are processed from level to level? It is not always clear whether generative grammatical models are being posited as actual models of human competence or models of the linguist's grammar; that is, a concise formal display of a general theory. Even though we know Chomskyian generative grammar is supposed to be psychologically real it is not always clear whether one should interpret a model as linear or not. Nevertheless, it would seem that the pre-modular transformational approach was positing a progression from deep structure (phrase structure rules and the lexicon) to surface structure with the phonetic realization as the final stage. Despite the lexicon being in deep structure little attention was paid to the lexical basis of the grammar, and syntax was presented at the highest level with an intervening but unexplicated level of semantics, then specific transformational rules were applied to generate the surface structure output, the phonetic realization of the deep structure sentence. (Chomsky 1957, 1965; Sells 1985; van Riemsdijk and Williams 1986). Such a model would seem to posit syntax as ontologically prior to everything else, but it is not at all clear how the different levels are represented in the mind or what is being processed. The post-modular approach places great weight on the lexicon (and therefore lexical-semantics) and is concerned more with S-structure rather than D-structure (Chomsky 1981; Sells 1985; van Riemsdijk and Williams 1986). This is a much more complexly interrelated system and one which does not obviously lead to linear processing, as for example, the logical form and phonetic form may be considered simultaneously. What if modularity is a matter of simultaneous instantaneous processing, whereby the different modules process in inter-relation to each other depending on the contextual demands of the moment? One would therefore be unable to realistically speak of one element of the module being ontologically prior to another.

Sentences are "the purely-linguistic properties of utterances...a common linguistic structure...shared by a variety of utterances which differ only in their non-linguistic properties" (Sperber and Wilson, 1986, p. 9). To accept that utterances are derived from sentences one has to accept that the abstract grammar is not simply the invention of the grammarian but is instead psychologically real, and therefore that sentences are psychologically real. Furthermore, one has to accept, that sentences, in addition to being psychologically real, are ontologically prior to utterances. One has to further accept, therefore, that although actual linguistic grammars are based on performance data, that is, sentences are decontextualized utterances, the competence that grammars isolate is ontologically prior to the performance data from which it comes.

What if one does not accept the psychological primacy of sentences? Hopper, for example, has strongly objected to the validity of the sentence: "the problems with the sentence exist at every level – historical, ontogenetic, psychological, and universal-grammatical" (Hopper, 1983, p. 131). Many linguists have claimed that the sentence is actually a literary construct, that without writing, and the illusion of stability, permanence and objectivity that scripts allow, the development of the sentence would be doubtful given that in reality utterances are anything but stable and permanent. (See e.g. Linell 1982; R. Harris 1980, 1981; Taylor and Cameron 1987; Moore and Carling 1982.) Roy Harris (1980, p. 18) states that the sentence is a "linguistic abstraction for which there is only one conceivable archetype so far in human history; the sentence in writing." Linell supports this:

> I very much doubt that linguistic structuralism would have evolved in the way it has, if linguists had studied the varying, quasi-continuous speech behavior instead of the spatially arranged objects of written texts, and if they had not had access to the possibilities of organization and systematization inherent in writing...as a meta-language (Linell 1982, p. 51).

Whether the sentence as a construct is only possible because of literacy or not, it is certainly a construct with written features being amongst other things uni-dimensional and linear.[10]

Now to the two-sided problem of the sentence, which Hopper includes in his list of problems above: its universality and its psychological reality. There is a problem in explaining how one gets from the unutterable abstract construct (what Lyons calls the system-sentence) to that which people actually utter (the sub-set of utterances that Lyons calls the text-sentence). Even if one could claim that the sentence is psychologically real, that the brain is programmed to generate forms from abstract rules, an utterance is much more than forms generated by abstract rules.

To say that an utterance is derived from a sentence, then, is to give precedence to grammatical form over all other factors contributing to utterance including the context: memory processes, cultural beliefs, expectations, social norms, prior-text, the participants, etc. This kind of reasoning has led to the practice of using editing rules or transformations to claim that utterances are fragmented or disorganized surface manifestations of the higher level sentence structure. (See Taylor and Cameron 1987 for a discussion of this practice.) However, making an utterance conform to grammatical notions of a well-formed sentence does nothing to explain or describe the utterance as itself. The psychological reality of the sentence therefore, if it exists, exists at such a removed level from that of the contextualized utterance that it becomes incoherent to speak of utterances being derived from sentences. The universalist theory of sentences, which is devised to be a model of species endowed ideal brain computations, is therefore not sufficient for explaining utterances (something which it was not devised to do).[11]

There is a flip-side to this problem: the universality of the concrete notion of sentence. The universalist approach to sentences is too abstract to account for utterances. However, approaches which do attempt to define sentences as concrete entities, and therefore as closer to utterances, run into the problem of universality. That is, the sentence as defined as a typology will find languages varieties which do not typically have all the elements in the typology. One could therefore only speak about the sentence in a specific language variety or the sentence in a specific situation, or a specific type of sentence, but not "The Sentence" as a concrete universal. (See Chomsky 1986, Botha 1989 for arguments against typological syntax as universals.)

The relationship between the sentence and utterance in this concrete notion of sentence is more obvious since here sentences are empirically derived from utterances; that is, the linguist extrapolates from a body of data those structures which are most typical and those less typical. (See e.g. Comrie 1981, Shopen 1985, Givón 1984.) Since different language varieties have different norms of structure, in this sense, though one may choose otherwise, there is no *a priori* theoretical necessity to have all utterances ultimately conform to any universal structure, nor to posit higher structures from which utterances are derived. Instead, explanations for different sentence structures can be historical, developmental, communicational, and so on.

What exists in the rejection of the priority of the sentence, and the rejection of the derivation of the utterance from the sentence, is also partly a matter of differences in approach to grammar and the theory of linguistics. In the case of Hopper, for example, there is a rejection of what he terms an *a priori* approach to grammar and the adoption of an emergent approach to grammar. (Hopper, 1986). Utterances are emergent phenomena. They emerge within a complex web of often competing and contradictory worlds, selves, forms and functions.[12] Utterances are not sentences, not because of some theoretically necessary distinction in scientific linguistics, but because utterances are more than sentences. They are not strictly linguistic phenomena and therefore cannot be fully accounted for by linguistic constructs such as the sentence.

As noted earlier, one of the ways of defining discourse is in terms of a unit larger than a sentence. Given the inability of received linguistic theory to relate the abstract sentence to the actualized utterance, it is questionable whether this is a useful definition of discourse.[13] The sentence is a purely linguistic construct based on the notions of separation of the linguistic from the non-linguistic, universality and context independence. Discourse/utterance is not a purely linguistic construct; it is contextually defined and it is not based on the separation of the linguistic from the non-linguistic. Furthermore, utterances are dialogic and sentences are not. Defining discourse in terms of the sentence implies that the sentence is in some way fundamental or even valid for the analysis of discourse – that, for example, discourse is a collection of sequenced sentences. But, the type of inferencing which goes into the understanding of discourse is not simply a sequential process nor is inferencing processed on the sentence level. Discourse is processed in both "top-down" and "bottom-up" ways; that is, it requires both global and local inferencing strategies and therefore cannot be understood simply in structuralist terms of linguistic building blocks be they sentences or any other linguistic unit. (See Conner-Linton 1989 for a discussion of top-down and bottom up discourse processing.)

Utterances as Units of Analysis

An utterance is more than a sentence, i.e. an utterance is more complex than a sentence having both linguistic and non-linguistic properties and functions. The abstract notion of the sentence is insufficient to account for utterance. It is therefore not surprising that the sentence as a syntactic unit has been shown to be inadequate for the study of discourse, whether by discourse is meant language in context, language use, or language beyond the sentence level. Schiffrin, for example, in choosing not to use the sentence as the unit of analysis in her work on discourse markers points out that sentences are often "difficult to identify in everyday conversation", and that "sentences are not the unit most germane to understanding language use and social interaction" (Schiffrin, 1987b, p. 32). The search for units of analysis which are reflective of interactional demands, or cognitive constraints, or are able to account for structure beyond the sentence, has led to a wide range of utterance based units.

The traditional definition of an utterance as being bounded by silence on both sides can be seen as an interactive unit such as a turn at a talk. If "silence" is considered to be a pause on the part of the speaker which does not necessarily signal either a potential or real end of turn, the utterance can be defined as a phonological unit marked by, for example, suprasegmental patterns of rising and falling intonation. These phonological units have been called at different times: breath groups, tone groups, intonation units, and idea or information units.

An interesting question arises in defining these phonological units: what do they represent? Chafe has been a leader in the development of one member in this type of unit, the information unit, which is delineated by phonological properties and which correlates with cognitive processes. Information units are marked by intonation patterns and pausing, and reflect the ability of the mind to process only a certain amount of information at a given time. (See Chafe, 1977, 1980, 1987.) This type of unit allows for a parsing of spoken speech which is adequate for capturing the contours of actual speech while simultaneously capturing the cognitive processing that bursts of speech reflect. This therefore gives the analyst a unit which is useful methodologically in that it allows for a systematic means of parsing speech, while at the same time makes a theoretical statement about the relationship between cognitive processing (for example, the organization of information, the retrieval of information or the planning of up-coming talk) and speech processing.

The utterance unit most related to the sentence which is an alternative to sentence grammar is the clause. This is the unit of choice of many functional grammarians, for example, Halliday's more recent work on functional grammar (Halliday 1985), and Dik (who segments his clauses in terms of predicates and arguments, see e.g. Dik, 1979). The fundamental difference between the functional and formal approach is not the size of the unit (sentence versus clause) but the difference in focus.

The modern functional approach to sentence level structure can be traced back to the Prague school and the functional sentence perspective.[14] The Prague school's functional approach, according to Danes (1970, p. 133): "follows from the recognition of the instrumental character of language...and is manifested in the lasting interest in the problems of meaning, in the linguistics of *parole*, in stylistics, in the analysis of text, as well as in practical application (standardization, etc.)." From the Prague school come the functional categories of theme (something one is talking about) and rheme (what one says about it), categories analogous to topic and comment (see Li and Thompson, 1976). The Prague school also developed the notions of functional load and the placement of old and new information which has also been influential in the development of the functional analysis of grammatical structure. (See, for example, Givón 1984, 1989)

In functional grammars and functional approaches to structure there are units which often conform to the sentence in size but which are defined not only in formal syntactic terms but in relation to function, in particular the arrangement of information in communication. In this way word order, for example, may be seen in terms of the relative weight of information which needs to be communicated, with the foregrounding or backgrounding of new or old, shared or unshared information. Some functional linguists maintain that syntax is derived from these sort of informational demands. (See, for example, Siewierska 1988.)

As mentioned by Schiffrin above, the sentence is not an adequate unit to account for interaction; those doing interactive analyses have therefore had to devise alternative units, some more closely tied to linguistic structural properties than others. Goffman, for example, makes the following observations:

> Now clearly, a sentence must be distinguished from its interactional cousin, namely everything that an individual says during his exercise of a turn at talk. (...) Obviously the talk of a turn will sometimes coincide with a sentence (or what can be expanded into one), but on many occasions a speaker will provide his hearers with more than a one -

sentence-equivalent stretch. Now the problem with the concepts of sentence and talk during a turn is that they are responsive to linguistic, not interactional, analysis (Goffman, 1981, p. 22).

Goffman goes on to suggest the loose term "move": "any full stretch of talk or its substitutes which has a distinctive unitary bearing on some set or other of the circumstance in which participants find themselves" (Goffman, 1981, p. 24). Moves take place in language games (term borrowed from Wittgenstein) and are dialogic in nature. A move, according to Goffman, may be made up of uttered sentences, but this is not what is of interactional significance; rather, what is of interactional significance is how one move can be seen as some sort of reaction to another's move or as participating in some language game.[15]

An important development in the history of utterance units is the speech act. The term speech act was first used descriptively to simply mean an utterance, the act of speaking or the product of speaking. (See Lyons 1977b, p. 484.) The utterance in this sense was of no particular size since it was not being analyzed as a unit. The later technical development of the term speech act is associated first with Austin (1962) and then more restrictively and more bound to theory with Searle (1969). Austin introduced the notion of speech act to refer to the fact that speech is not simply referential or used for the expression of ideas, but that speech does things, that is, language is used to accomplish actions. He proposed the notion of performatives, particular types of utterances which are used to do things such as promising, threatening, requesting. In keeping with Austin's ordinary language position that speech acts (i.e. utterances) occur in contexts, Austin proposed that performatives could be felicitous or infelicitous depending on certain aspects of the context, and he distinguished between the conventional force of an utterance and its effect on the hearer. (For further detail of speech act theory, see Austin 1962, Levinson 1983.)

What is of interest here is that Austin's attempt at categorizing different types of speech acts is functional in approach. Despite Searle and others attempts at formalizing speech acts so that they are linguistically derived and sentence like (see Levinson 1983 for a discussion of performative verbs), and indeed Austin's own work on performative verbs, Austin was proposing an utterance unit based on how people use language rather than on the grammatical properties of language. One could then identify and group utterances as doing similar things, e.g. this is a request here and again here, and so forth. But once one recognizes that roles in utterance are not simply speaker-hearer and that utterance meaning is not simply a matter of intention, recognizing whether something is or is not a particular speech act, becomes much more complex than Austin's original theory. Speech acts, in the non-technical sense of actions performed for some purpose, nevertheless remain an interesting way of considering the utterance as a unit of analysis.

As already noted, a discourse may be seen as an ideologically framed utterance which can be expressed in metalinguistic terms, such as having a chat about the weather or flattering your mother-in-law. A discourse or utterance in this sense is also a language game (Wittgenstein), speech activity (Levinson, Gumperz) discourse routine (Hymes) or genre (Bakhtin). Utterance in this sense is a cultural unit of analysis and though it may be referred to metalinguistically, and may be partially analyzed in terms of linguistic factors (for example, the preference for certain linguistic structures) it is not a linguistic unit.

In summary, what exists then are the primary frames which situate the utterance, defining an activity as a particular type of activity or grouping of activities. Within this context of utterance are then a range of interactive and functional utterance units such as moves, turns and speech acts. There are also units more closely related to sentence structure, functional sentence and clausal perspectives. And there are phonological units which are related to cognitive processes.

This brief overview of ways in which utterances have been used or defined as units of analysis reflects the different purposes which analysts have in mind. Is one interested in the psychological reality of utterances and their relation to brain processes? Is one interested in utterances and how they reflect, enforce or constrain the moral social order? Is one interested in utterances as cultural framing? Is one interested in utterances as coding grammatical relations? Utterances as units of analysis are therefore motivated by the theoretical interests of the linguist using them.

Utterance and Linguistics of Particularity

> The methods and results of linguistics, in spite of their modest scope, resemble those of natural sciences, the domain in which science has been most successful.
>
> Leonard Bloomfield, 1933, p. 509

> I don't want to replace scientific linguistics with anything else, I want to look at something which I think is important to do but which can't be handled within scientific linguistics.
>
> A.L. Becker, 1988, p. 20

> The idealization to 'perfect knowledge' excludes from the domain of investigation what seems to us to be close to the heart of the problem of explaining language, namely, that we are dealing with a subject matter which in its operation appears to be necessarily imperfect, incomplete, open and only admitting of partial regularities.
>
> Moore and Carling, 1982, p. 64

Scientific Linguistics and Utterance

The debate as to whether linguistics is a science or not is longstanding and well mired in the ideological machinery of academia. This contentious question will not be addressed here. (See Lass 1980 for an argument against linguistics as a science and Pateman 1987 for an argument for linguistics as a science.) What is of concern here is scientific linguistics, received linguistics based on certain normal science assumptions which were discussed in Chapter Two in terms of Markova's Cartesian Framework.

In Chapter Two it was shown that the metatheoretical basis of normal science requires discrete categories governed by the rule of the excluded middle. An object cannot be both itself and something else, or both itself and not itself; therefore contradiction and contradictory behavior is excluded from or idealized away in normal science. Normal science requires that objects be classified in terms of essential non-variant properties. Received linguistics therefore excludes those properties which are considered unessential to the linguistic system. And the goal of normal science is to generalize, predict and reduplicate.[16]

Throughout this study there is reference to the received linguistic tenet that the linguistic system (*langue* or competence) is separate and ontologically prior to the uttering of actual language (*parole* or performance). This separation is based on the normal scientific distinction between the scientific object (the abstract, platonic or real object) and the ordinary object as perceived by or referred to meta-linguistically by the non-scientist. This distinction is sometimes referred to as the pre-theoretical (everyday intuitions about something) and the theoretical (scientific claims about something). (See e.g, Lyons 1977b for a use of this distinction in grammatical classification.) This chapter has shown how the derivation of this larger distinction (between the scientific and non-scientific) embodied in the linguistic/non-linguistic distinction has become formulated in the sentence/utterance distinction.

Roy Harris describes the relationship between scientific linguistics and utterance in this way:

> Those working within this tradition [scientific linguistics], while not denying in principle that the specific contexts in which utterances occur affect their interpretation, have usually taken the view that it is not the business of the linguist to account for such matters. A language in their view is to be treated as a system of decontextualized verbal signs organized into complexes called 'sentences', and mastery of a language is interpreted as mastery of the decontextualized system. Some such idealization, it is claimed, is theoretically essential if there is to be a science of language (Harris, 1981, p. 32).

Because they encompass the totality of human experience utterances are contradictory, variant, changeable and particularistic. It is only sensible, therefore, that normal science has chosen to turn them into sentences which are formal, rule governed, non-variant, constant and universal.

The allocation of language use (*parole* or performance) to the periphery of scientific linguistics, and the inability of scientific linguistics to incorporate context and contextualized phenomena, has led some linguists to search for frameworks outside of normal science. Hymes has suggested the adoption of a revolutionary science which would be pluralistic rather than positivist and which would not be based on the scientific/non-scientific dichotomy. Becker

(1988) has looked to the humanities for the development of a particularistic linguistics. Givón (1989) has turned to mystical traditions such as Philosophical Taoism as an antidote to normal science and as a philosophical frame for pragmatics. And the new science of Chaos is being investigated for its applicability to linguistics as it is a dynamic scientific approach fundamentally based on multi-dimensionality.[17]

Utterances as Particulars

What does it mean to say that utterances are particulars and why does this make utterance a problem for scientific linguistics? Bakhtin suggests that "linguistics and the philosophy of language acknowledge only a passive understanding of discourse...it is an understanding of an utterance's neutral *signification* and not *its actual meaning* (emphasis in original)" (Bakhtin, 1981, p. 281). The actual meaning of an utterance is much more broad and complex than any linguistic meaning that can be abstracted from it:

> The living utterance, having taken meaning and shape at a particular historical moment in a socially specific environment, cannot fail to brush up against thousands of living dialogic threads, woven by socio-ideological consciousness around the given object of an utterance: it cannot fail to become an active participant in social dialogue. After all, the utterance arises out of this dialogue as a continuation of it and as a rejoinder to it – it does not approach from the sidelines (Bakhtin, 1981, p. 276,277).

Utterance as contextualized phenomena "brush up against thousands of living dialogic threads", threads which are living in our memories and threads which are present and emerging in our context of situation at the time of our utterance.

On the question of universals and particulars; particulars are individuals, entities which are singular and distinguished in their singularity from other entities, while universals are general, not dependent on the senses, unchangeable, all-encompassing, and unify one entity with another.(See, Loux 1970 for an ample discussion.) The problem with relating particulars and universals is in relating things which are similar yet different to each other; that is, if two particulars have certain similarities, are they therefore instances of the same universal? This is an important question for analyzing utterance: are two utterances two instances of the same sentence, the same word, the same phonological contour, the same discourse strategy?

Utterance occurs in contexts and two utterances are never the same in the sense that no two configuration of contexts are ever the same. Context is open-ended and communication has certain emergent properties (such as creativity) related to this open-endedness. Utterances occur within unique spatio-temporal boundaries. It is safe to say therefore that utterances are particulars.

Utterances are linguistic and non-linguistic in nature. Utterance entails the totality of human being, requiring and using capabilities, processes and functions of the body and the mind, and involving all aspects of the way humans exist in and experience the world – biological, socio-cultural, material etc.[18] It is utterance that brings all these actions, processes, doings and beings together through how one learns to perform utterances and how one experiences utterances. It is in this way that utterances as particulars may be related to each other. To discuss this, consider Wittgenstein's notions of language games and family resemblances. This discussion will be framed by Volosinov/Bakhtin's notion of the socially grounded dialogic nature of utterance.[19]

Utterance takes place in a context of situation itself comprising a complex interplay of contexts. The context of situation places a number of demands on the participant many of which are contradictory (for example, maintaining a particular presentation of self as a nice person and firing someone from a job). When alone and participating in private dialogue with our selves we are faced with a rush of conflicting choices, desires, needs, what to do next, what to say next, who to be next. We plan, we rehearse, we remember, we play with language, we theorize about the world. When participating in public dialogue with others we are faced with the same rush of conflicting choices, etc., but we are also constrained by the demands of the social situation, the constraints of interaction and social order, the constraints of what we are trying to accomplish, the constraints of prior-text, the constraints of our communicative competence, and so on. Yet at the same time, though our behavior is constrained by the context of situation, it is still not determined; as context remains open-ended and because of the volitional, creative and what one might call the irrational aspects of human behavior, i.e. the ability to behave in novel, unwarranted, improvisional, unpredictable, fantastic ways. The context of situation is therefore neither absolutely relative nor absolutely determined. Utterance and utterances are therefore neither absolutely relative nor absolutely determined. (See Mazor, 1989 for a development of this argument.)

Utterances are therefore particulars in that no two are the same, i.e. each is experienced differently by those experiencing them and no two can be replicated; but, given that utterance takes place within time, space and dialogic social traditions, utterances are particulars which can be placed within a comparative context. One is therefore able to relate one particular to another without necessarily having to derive the particular from a universal or having to decontextualize the particular to reflect essential universal properties.

Wittgenstein made the rather simple point that one learns to use language by using it; that is, one learns to play certain language games such as asking a question or making a joke, by participating in language games such as asking questions and making jokes. The more games one plays and the more variations on these games that one is exposed to, the greater one's familiarity with the rules of usage which guide language games. How to play and what the rules are is something one is constantly learning and remembering as each game is situationally located and somewhat different. There is no way to assure therefore that even a tried and true discourse routine will always work. The joke that always works may fall flat, the politeness strategy that usually wins you admiration may leave you unnoticed, and one will find oneself in situations where one simply does not know which game to play or how to play it.

Within the language game there are a range of potential moves that one can make given what one is trying to achieve, given the rules of the game, the instruments of the game and one's ability to play the game. One may relate this to the notions of speech activities and discourse strategies. It is one's communicative competence which will inform one how to play the game and how one is doing, if one is managing at all. One may also relate this to Bakhtin's (1986) notion of genre – typical situations of speech communication – again the more familiar one is with the genre, the more knowledge one has of options and the more one is able to make informed choices.

When one participates in language games, one figures out not only the "rules" of usage but also the preferred forms and structures of usage: phrases, idioms, metaphors, syntactic structures, narrative structures, turn-taking structures, etc. In our memories are whole utterances, sequences of utterances, collections of utterances – bits of songs, poems, myths, wise-sayings, religious instructions, things one has heard others say, read others write, things one has said or written oneself – and these utterances are enveloped in our memory with a range of emotions and ideas and concepts which are often not known to one until they are recalled through action. Playing language games is a dialogic process of bringing up the past and making it presently relevant.

Wittgenstein brought his notion of family resemblances to the debate over universals and particulars and it provides a way out of the universals/particulars bind. (See also Bambrough in Loux 1970 for this view of Wittgenstein.) Wittgenstein argued that two things are similar not because they must agree in some essential way, or that they must have the same properties, but because they resemble each other. This is a non-discrete notion of membership in a category, that is, something is more or less like something else rather than it is or isn't a member. In this way no two things will be the same yet a vast array of things may be said to have likeness. No two utterances will be the same but many utterances will share certain likenesses depending on the context of focus that the analyst brings to them.

Linguistics of Particularity

A.L. Becker, who has coined the phrase linguistics of particularity (see, for example, Becker 1984, 1988), in describing his own road to a linguistics of particularity, relates the following amusing anecdote: "It was Pike who said to me when he left Michigan, What you should really work on is particularity.

What is linguistics when it focuses on particularity? It was a nice challenge, although I really had no idea what he meant" (Becker, 1988, p. 17). It is a challenge which remains and is still a very difficult one to grasp. Becker proposes a linguistics of particularity as the close analysis of particular instances of discourse (Tannen, 1989, p. 34) and notes that the study of discourse "is of necessity the study of particularity" (Becker, 1984, p. 435).

This study is in agreement with Becker's assertion above regarding discourse, and the use of the phrase "linguistics of particularity" reflects Becker's development of the term, but my use of the phrase "linguistics of particularity" is not derived from Becker's usage nor his particular way of doing linguistics. The term "linguistics of particularity" is used here to contrast with the emphasis on universals and the essentialism which exists in received linguistics.

Except for the more recent development of interactional sociolinguistics, sociolinguistics has traditionally been unable to account for individual behavior. Variation has been seen in terms of general patterns which could be traced to social factors such as class or gender membership, or cultural factors such as ritualized norms of behavior. Utterances became statistical regularities or socially stipulated behavior, and why a particular individual used a particular form at a particular time and place was ignored or could not be explained. Oddly enough sociolinguistics, which was studying language use and included the notion of context in its theory, was unable to explain individual behavior, while generative grammar, which was devised as the study of universals, was capable of explaining individuals. If linguistics is to be able to account for actual observable language as it exists for those using language then linguistics needs to come to terms with particularity, otherwise linguistics will remain many steps removed from its subject matter.

A linguistics of particularity is concerned with how each utterance is an individual and then how individuals are related to other individuals. This is in reverse to received practices which start with universals and then decontextualize individual differences to prove universal properties. To understand the uniqueness of utterance, as well as to be able to understand how one utterance might resemble another, requires attention to detail. Borrowing a simplistic rendition of the Butterfly Effect from the science of Chaos, very small inputs can have significant effects. The Butterfly Effect, so named to account for the chaotic nature of weather and the difficulty of weather prediction, metaphorically states that a butterfly moving its wings in Beijing can cause a storm in Kansas. This notion implies at least two things which have importance for us: the potential significance of seemingly insignificant factors and the inter-connectedness of systems.

Context is a dynamic system of interconnected and fluctuating smaller, more restrictively defined, less encompassing contexts. Small differences in context can lead to rather significant differences in meaning and behavior. A linguistics of particularity calls for an understanding of a great number of separate processes and an understanding of how they function and interact. Memory, perception and the ordering of information are key to understanding context and how certain contexts are more relevant than others. Also key is the development and management of identity and social placement, and the acquisition and mastery of texts and language games. All of these key factors are interrelated. A linguistics of particularity thus has to be able to identify the individual contexts and relate them to each other.

My answer to Pike's question "what is linguistics when it focuses on particularity?" is the study of utterance. What this means concretely is the study of language as it is lived, a phenomenon which is open-ended, contextual, volitional, dialogic, and intimately connected to all aspects of life both private and public. A linguistics of particularity requires the development of an approach which defines utterance not in reductionist terms of essentialist universals but in terms of situated contextualized resemblances; that is, utterance can only be defined in terms of something else, some context, some other utterance; it is not an abstract independent entity. (Recall Gumperz's definition of contextualization conventions in this manner.)

There are foundations of a linguistics of particularity which have been there for a very long time. In the recent history of sociolinguistics, Hymes and Gumperz have provided the metatheoretical basis for such a theory, and some of the details.[20] Nevertheless, sociolinguistics needs a better understanding of context and how contexts are related, as well as the need to continue to develop ways of talking about utterance which are not wedded to sentence-based grammar. There is certainly a great amount of work already done and being done in such areas as the philosophy of language, pragmatics, discourse analysis, psycholinguistics, functional grammar. The key is not to get ghettoized within the narrow confines of any one disciplinary matrix.

Notes

1 Part of the problem of trying to talk about utterance and utterances is that both English and scientific linguistics as meta-languages are greatly lacking. Because of the ideology of prior-text one is forced to either invent words or invent reformulations of words which then immediately identify one as marked, as being outside of normal discourse and place one within a particular ideological framework whether one chooses to be there or not. I use the term utterance in a difficult and not always clear way partly because alternatives such as languaging or discourse or discoursing do not capture the range of uses I need, or have similar problems to utterance, and partly because utterance is ambiguous in English. I use utterance to mean the act of uttering, the process of interpreting uttering, discourse in the meta-schematic sense of discourse as an ideological frame, and the product of uttering. Utterance is meant therefore as a general term which encompasses rather than separates out these different aspects of utterance. I use the terms "an utterance" or "utterances" to refer to products, a unit or units of analysis which may or may not be real to language users.

2 I use the term "recontextualized" study of utterance because all linguists, sociolinguists included, decontextualize utterances by the very fact of writing them down and studying them linearly. Therefore one is in a sense always inventing some new context and relating it to the possible context of the utterance one is attempting to analyze. However, one can propose a recontextualized study of utterances by first taking into account the various levels of decontextualization that occur in the analysis of language by placing it within the particular context of analysis, that is by defining it metatheoretically. One can then go on to account for context (in terms of recontextualization; the original context cannot be captured), in terms of both the contexts inevitably decontextualized in analysis and the context of situation of the analyst. The meta-context within which recontextualization takes place is the focus of the analyst herself, is she looking at turn-taking? is she looking at subjacency? is she looking at pronouns?

3 Schiffrin points out that these categorizations of different types of linguistics overlap and are not discrete.

4 This perspective on the self in relation to the world is of course not a position that one need hold. It is, for example, built on a dialectic or conflict model of self. See Harré 1984 for a discussion of the social foundations of personal psychology.

5 Schiffrin's discourse model (1987), for example, may be seen in terms of potentially inter-related contexts. In this way the participation framework, ideational structure, action structure, exchange structure, and information state would act as contexts within the larger discourse context, so that a

change in the exchange structure or the information state, for example, could explain a change in meaning.

6 All data used by linguists is performance data whether gathered in a speech community or derived from introspection. All data is then decontextualized to a lesser or greater degree depending on the focus of the linguist. It is the focus of the linguist that is the context for recontextualization.

7 That Lyons continues to think there is a problem was recently demonstrated in his Keynote Address at GURT 1990, when he claimed that current received linguistic theories do not bother to define the construct sentence despite it being fundamental to received linguistics.

8 Note Fries' use of sentence and utterance in this quote. For Fries an utterance is an interactive unit which may contain one or more syntactic units – sentences. It is interesting to note that in most traditional (pre-generative) definitions of the sentence there is no sentence/utterance distinction of the type outlined above. Sentences are simply units of some sort which appear in utterances.

9 The transformational and post-transformational generative models are based on very different assumptions despite their schematic similarities. See van Riemsdijk and Williams, 1986, p. 172 for four models from the Standard Theory to the T-model of grammar. If one considers phonetic realization in the earlier models and phonetic form and logical form in the later models as utterances then it would seem that they are indeed at the lowest level, how they are derived from the higher levels is another question, one that these models might not be concerned with.

10 The sentence and its literary features is well evidenced in the metalanguage of linguistics. The linearity and uni-dimensional nature of language is assumed much as one would see it on the written page so that sounds are presented as discrete units in linear order just like alphabetic orthography. It becomes near impossible to represent speech sounds as having non-linear dimensions and to represent the kind of variations that do occur. Representing contours, varying length, timing, voice quality etc. is very difficult given received linguistic practices and the nature of alphabetic orthography. The metalinguistic practice of representing language schematically in trees and algebraic equations is also a product of the graphic tradition. And the metalanguage of linguistics is filled with movements, transformations, branching, dislocations etc. which are also related to the graphic medium where some object may stay still and other objects are placed around it. In actuality, sounds are not heard as discrete units nor does sound and meaning progress in a linear way.

[11] See e.g. van Riemsdijk and Williams for a discussion of generative grammar as sentence grammar: "'Sentence grammar' is the theory of sentences as objects, not of their uses in larger frameworks such as discourse or logical argument." (van Riemsdijk and Williams; 1986, p. 184).

[12] One could argue that sentences are also emergent in that grammar is emergent. However, what is being considered sentences in this case are utterances rather than sentences in the received sense.

[13] I have chosen to use the term utterance rather than discourse in this study partly because of this sentence-based definition of discourse. Because of the sentence/utterance distinction, utterance more clearly defines language in context as something quite distinct from sentence and therefore sentence grammar.

[14] Though the Prague school functional analysis has become known as the Functional Sentence Perspective, Danes has explained that it is really a functional utterance perspective (Danes, 1970, p. 134).

[15] As has been noted in previous chapters, there are other utterance units of analysis such as those typical of conversation analysis which are concerned with interactive sequencing in discourse – turns, pairs, sequences, and so forth. (See, e.g. Atkinson and Heritage 1984.)

[16] Pateman (1987) has argued that this view of normal science is positivist rather than realist and that one can escape from these problems of normal science through his version of realism. This might be so but whether linguistics as a normal science is heavily positivist or not, it does adhere in a significant way to these principles.

[17] The science of Chaos has not been rigorously and broadly applied to linguistics but certain aspects taken from the popularization of the field (see Gleik 1987) have been bandied about as possible answers to questions of variability in linguistic behavior. See, for example, Bowers 1990. The science of Chaos is a mathematical theory based on universal deterministic principles of randomness. It is based on rather different geometric principles than normal science being a non-linear science working with dynamic phenomena (such as weather systems) on multidimensional planes. In the science of Chaos disorderly data is not discounted or made orderly through homogenizing variation, instead patterns are sought within disorder. What is especially interesting for recontextualized linguistics is the notion that very small variations in input can have great effects on output (the Butterfly effect) and the notion that open-ended systems are not completely unconstrained – "Behavior that produces information (amplifies small uncertainties) but is not utterly unpredictable" (Bowers, 1990, p. 7).

[18] By body and mind here is not meant any Cartesian duality but simply the difference between, for example, communicative body movements such as hand or facial gestures, placement of body in relation to other bodies and objects, etc., and unobservable brain processes. The role that utterance/discourse plays in such things as learning/deciding who one is (at any given time), the storing of information about a great number of things including ones experiences, the communication of identity, emotions, desires, etc. is a very important one that can always use further study.

[19] There is disagreement as to whether Bakhtin and Volosinov were the same person or not. (See, Cazden 1989 for a brief discussion of this question.) Works under both names state quite clearly a view of language as an ideological system in a continuous dialogue between the past and the present based on a social conflict model. They are of course not the first to have such a view of society or language in society nor am I necessarily in total agreement with them, I use them here for convenience sake since their position is well known and it supports what I am saying.

[20] Labov has added greatly to the study of language, especially in the areas of historical linguistics, social grammars, and the study of narrative. However, I would not include Labov as directly contributing to a linguistics of particularity since his own work decontextualizes from the utterance to the abstract linguistic system, and since his metatheory is essentialist rather than relativist.

7

Conclusion

...'radical questions'... cannot be resolved by an appeal to the normal operating procedure of the discipline to which they are put. (...) They cannot be answered within the normal paradigm because it is precisely the normal paradigm which is under consideration. 'Radical questions' are radical in that they question the taken for granted foundations of the discipline from within which they are asked. The primordial questions of 'What is this phenomenon?' and 'How is it to be approached' are asked on a bridge unsecured at either end: a bridge moreover, which traverses an abyss whose walls are sheer paradox.

Melvin Pollner, 1987, p. 2

Sociolinguistic Disciplinary Matrixes: A Comparison

This section will briefly compare the three disciplinary matrixes already presented in terms of the questions asked in Chapter One: Did leading practitioners in the disciplinary matrixes set out to make their approach more or less like received linguistics? Did they see the goal of sociolinguistics as belonging to "normal" or "revolutionary" science? What theories of language can be isolated from these theories of sociolinguistics? What is the relationship between their definitions of sociolinguistics and their approaches?

Developments in sociolinguistics may be understood in terms of how close or how far sociolinguistic leaders wanted their theories to be from other received theories. This positioning of sociolinguistics in relation to other received theories may be seen in turn as partly motivated by the sociolinguist's support or lack of support for normal science.

Hymes distanced himself ideologically (if not always in practice) from normal science and received linguistics. This may be demonstrated by one of Hymes many statements to this effect: Sociolinguistics "cannot leave normal linguistic theory unchallenged nor limits challenge to reform, because its own goals are not allowed for by normal theory, and cannot be achieved by 'working in the system'. (...) Its task is the thoroughgoing critique of received notions and practices (...)" (Hymes, 1974a, p. 197).

Labov, on the other hand, positioned himself well within received linguistics and normal science. Labov's realism is typical of normal science. Labov defined sociolinguistics in terms of linguistics proper: "'general linguistics', dealing with phonology, morphology, syntax and semantics"

(Labov, 1972a, p. 184). The development of variable rules was a conscious attempt to contribute to received linguistic theory.

Gumperz, though with less ideological advocacy than Hymes, may also be seen as distancing himself from received linguistics and normal science. He does this by developing a theory of language which concentrates heavily on linguistic features which are considered marginal by received theory, and by his embracing of "common sense" rationality as the object of analysis rather than scientific reasoning. Nevertheless, it is not clear how far Gumperz does intend to distance himself, as it is not clear whether he is calling for moderate reforms or whether he is rejecting normal science.

Hymes' theory of language is a functional one whereby form and function are in a dialectic relation, whereby form and function are not independent of each other. Gumperz's theory of language is also similar in this regard. Labov, in contrast, follows an autonomous theory of language whereby form and function are separate, though often correlatable in terms of co-occurrence. The linguistic system and social system are separate entities but they are related within the world of language use. Another way to differenciate these theories of language is to categorize Hymes and Gumperz as developing theories of *communicative* competence, but Labov as developing a theory of *linguistic* competence.

All three theories of language, however, do locate language in society and are therefore social theories of language. They do not, however, adhere to the same theories of society. For Gumperz, social meaning does not adhere in a text, or in an institution, but is negotiated interaction. For Labov, language is a social fact which is imposed on the individual in concourse with other social institutions such as class and gender. For Hymes, social meaning is to be found in the culturally defined patterned use of language.

How does a definition of sociolinguistics relate to the development of specific theory and method? Labov has defined sociolinguistics in terms of linguistics proper and therefore his work has concentrated on segmental grammatical features. Grammar for Labov, however, is located in the community and therefore analysis takes place at the level of a speech community rather than the individual. Labov has also defined sociolinguistics in terms of a particular sort of empiricism and thus his method reflects this fact. Data is therefore collected from speakers and identified in terms of a speech community.

Gumperz has defined sociolinguistics in terms of understanding communicative competence: the specific knowledge a participant uses in the interpretation of communication. His theory is therefore focussed on inferential processing and his method is directed at analyzing the communicative competence of individuals.

Hymes has defined sociolinguistics in terms of a theory of language as the organization of speech. Narrowly speaking, it is a theory of communicative competence (Hymes does not concentrate on this aspect of his theory though he does posit it.) Broadly speaking, it is a theory of the relationship between language functions and social functions. Since it is also a theory based on the fundamental principle that different language varieties and societies do not function in the same way, the method is ethnographic and case specific. However, unlike with Gumperz, analysis is not done in terms of individual competence but in terms of a general structural context of situation within which the individual is a participant.

Sociolinguistics Revisited

Sociolinguists should address the question of whether or not there is anything more to their field than a common interest in diversity of language and in its social foundations and concomitants. Perhaps there is not an actual field of study, but only a perspective. Perhaps 'sociolinguistic' is an adjective for such a perspective, not part of the name of a subject-matter or discipline.

Dell Hymes, 1984, p. 41

What then is sociolinguistics? What is the current state of sociolinguistics? And, what are some of the questions to consider for future developments in sociolinguistics? There is no unified theory of sociolinguistics, or even for that matter, a shared metatheory. There is a shared sociolinguistic subject matter – "utterance" – but this would not necessarily delimit sociolinguistics from other types of linguistics such as psycholinguistics which also study utterance.[1]

Sociolinguistics has never been defined internally; that is, it has not been defined by its own practioners in terms of a unified theory, or shared metatheory, but instead has been defined in relation and in reaction to the external forces of received linguistics. In this way particular sociolinguists who might in fact not have had much in common came together to fight against a common foe (asocial autonomous linguistics) or were lumped together as "other" by received linguistics.

Hymes writing about sociolinguistics presents just this scenario:

Labov might fear that other linguists would feel excused from attention to the issues if they were called something other than plain 'linguistics'. Fishman might come to feel that predominately linguistic interests left in shadow the issues of policy and societal institutions that 'sociology of language' might better suggest. Hymes might come to feel that identification of 'sociolinguistic' with Labov's methods for the study of on-going change in urban settings left 'ethnolinguistic' still needed to label long-standing anthropological concerns and perspectives. *But for a time the sense of a need, and opportunity, to establish a study of language on a social basis predominated, together with a sense of a need for allies in the effort* (Hymes, 1984, p. 40, my emphasis).

Despite the real differences between those practicing sociolinguistics, a coalition was formed out of a sense of need for allies to counterattack the establishing of a linguistic paradigm which was not based on a social theory of language.

DONCASTER COLLEGE LEARNING RESOURCE CENTRE

One may say that sociolinguistics has suffered from the fate of all coalitions; at some point the disparate beliefs, self interests, and power of the members of the coalition can no longer be subsumed under unity and the coalition first frays, then splits, then eventually becomes irrelevant. Meanwhile individual members continue their self motivated pursuits.

Again Hymes (1984, p. 41):

> In brief, Ferguson, Gumperz and Labov continued to be certain kinds of linguist. Bernstein, Fishman, Goffman (and Cicourel, Grimshaw) continued to be certain kinds of sociologist. The pattern applied to my own case. I continued to be an Americanist, and the major new direction of my own research came to be the discovery of patterns of narrative structure and performance in long-familiar American Indian texts.

Hymes (ibid) comments on the current state of sociolinguistics that

> the present situation seems one of tradition, not consolidation. Individual scholars may be consolidating the lines of work that brought them into the general field, but the field itself remains only loosely connected. It would not be possible to say that something was *the* [in original] leading problem of method or theory in sociolinguistics. One would have to fall back on describing the interests and lines of work of particular scholars, or groups of scholars.

I agree with Hymes that the state of sociolinguistics is one of tradition rather than consolidation. But it is more consolidated in practice now than it was twenty years ago in that a blurring of methodology (ways of doing sociolinguistics) has taken place. One can for example find ethnographic method applied in community studies of the type associated with Labovian linguistics, interactional discourse analysis applied to data gotten from Labovian sociolinguistic methods such as the sociolinguistic interview, quantitative methodology applied to interactional sociolinguistic data, and so on.

Novices in the field of sociolinguistics are socialized into the exemplars of a particular tradition in sociolinguistics. These particular traditions (the disciplinary matrixes here discussed are three of these traditions) are based on a specific historical context of which the novice is usually unaware. But the needs of the novice are not the same needs as those who founded the tradition, nor the next generation of practitioners in the tradition who followed the founders, because the historical context has changed. What brought together Hymes, Labov, Gumperz, Fishman, et al. in the 1960's might still be of current relevance, but the focus has changed. There are now so many different options for doing linguistics, whether it is sentence based or discourse based. If one thinks of sociolinguistics as some sort of coalition, what might be possible coalitions for the 1990's?

Hymes' quote which opened this section is helpful to reconsider to help answer this question, maybe sociolinguistics is not a discipline, not a subject matter, but instead a perspective. Yet, sociolinguistics may be considered *both* as a discipline with a particular subject matter and as a perspective. Hymes suggested that the goal of sociolinguistics is the development of a multidisciplinary approach which can work towards a unity which is yet to come. If one considers a coalition as some sort of "multidisciplinary" union then the notion of multidisiciplinary is useful to the discussion of coalition.

Sociolinguistics as a multidisciplinary approach may be considered from two different angles. One angle may be that various fields share the same overriding metatheoretical approach. An example of this type of multidisciplinary approach may be Structuralism, or more recently, the Science of Chaos where certain general principles are applied across disciplines. For example, Structuralism has been applied to anthropology, linguistics, literary criticism, and the Science of Chaos to physics, mathematics, economics, meteorology, biology.

Another multidisciplinary approach might instead be that various disciplines are interested in the same phenomenon. In this way there would be no overriding metatheory or any particular overriding theory. Instead, one would have a pluralism of approaches concerned with explaining a similar phenomenon. To an extent this has already happened in the study of utterance/discourse where there are diverse approaches from various branches of psychology, sociology, philosophy, literary criticism, linguistics, as well as models taken from theories of economics and history. This type of pluralism can be seen, for example, in the development of speech act theory, discourse analysis and interactional sociolinguistics. Tannen (1989), in defining discourse as the study of language in context, supports this contention when she claims that discourse analysis includes at least nine disciplines.

Sociolinguistics as what Hymes is calling a "perspective", and what I call a metatheory, is not sociolinguistics as it has become known or as it has been practiced but something much broader. Given the previous discussion of "Hegelian" versus "Cartesian" linguistics it would fall under "Hegelian" linguistics. That is, sociolinguistics is linguistics done within what Markova called the Hegelian Framework, whereby linguistic phenomena are considered dynamic, contextualized, dialogic, and where the social and interactive nature of language, knowledge and existence is stressed. Certainly one need not call this *perspective* "Hegelian", and indeed one should not since it is inaccurate; however, it is the *principles* isolated in this perspective which could apply across disciplinary boundaries.

Coalition can be built around a common subject matter. In this case the subject matter is "utterance". Linguistics as theories of utterance, rather than sentence, is another means by which people with disparate interests may come together (as in the case of discourse analysis.)

What might the redefinition of sociolinguistics as "Hegelian" (as opposed to "Cartesian") linguistics or as the study of "utterance" rather than "sentence" add to the study of language? And what might be some of the interesting issues which such an approach might involve?

Cartesian linguistics (received linguistic theory) is incapable of dealing with contextualized phenomena. Linguists have made attempts to devise means of describing and analyzing these types of phenomena whether in terms of functional units or interpretive processes. With a "Hegelian" metatheory one can concentrate on the development and refinement of a discourse – a way of envisioning and of talking – and a theory of contextualized phenomena which does not have to resort to essentialist universals. Linguistics as the study of utterance, as Hymes has said in regard to linguistics as socially constitutive linguistics, requires the rethinking of the foundations of linguistics itself. It means the rethinking of linguistic categories and units and how language is analyzed. As Bakhtin has said, utterance is the "living utterance", we live language we don't just "use" language or even "perform" language. The study of utterance requires an understanding of how language is lived.

In terms of the types of questions such an approach would engender, there are many which sociolinguistics has already considered, such as the relationship between language and social meaning, language and communication, between language and identity, between language and social order. But in addition there is the need for a better understanding of the individual and the way language is lived within the individual life both in terms of the more private manifestations of language such as thinking, dreaming, strategizing and the more public manifestations of language such as interacting, signifying, doing. The act of utterance is an individual act and therefore needs to be understood individually. There needs to be therefore a better understanding of the relationship between the individual and the various parts of her personal economy: the individual in relationship to her audience, or speech network, or any societal group which is recognizable and salient to her or others with whom she is relating. (See Herrnstein Smith, 1988 on the "scrappiness" of the individual.) This requires a better understanding of the social nature of mind, the social nature of language and the acquisition of both.

Starting at the level of shared metatheoretical assumptions which guide work done across disciplinary boundaries, one can build a pluralistic coalition of people who have diverse interests and who do work within a variety of traditions, but who share a fundamental attitude towards the way language should be studied. The proliferation of descriptive labels (such as "sociolinguist", "discourse analyst", "applied linguist", "psycholinguist") which may apply to a linguist are often less a matter of information on what sort of language theory a person holds, and more a matter of political allocation of resources within the academy. What a sociolinguist is can only be defined in terms of other linguists. Sociolinguists have been correct in both attempting to *avoid* the use of the term sociolinguist and in *claiming* the term sociolinguist. In the case of avoidance there is the insistence that a *sociolinguist* is a *linguist* and that no group has a singular claim to the title of linguist. And, in the case of acceptance there is the insistence that sociolinguistics is a specific sort of linguistics not to be confused with other (particularly asocial) forms of linguistics. There is a dilemma here with both a need to claim the rightful legitimacy of sociolinguistics as an approach to the study of language and the need to identify this approach. Which will seem more important to emphasize at a given time depends on the historical context.

The term sociolinguist is important if it can be identified with a specific perspective and theory of language; if not it is not worth the marginalization and relegation to secondary citizenship which it implies. Rather than fruitless attempts at delimiting sociolinguistics as a field, instead linguists of varying sorts can find common ground in a common metatheory and/or a common subject matter. This is a way in which we can achieve Hymes' (1974a, p. 209) vision when he says that "Linguistics as sociolinguistics, if it will, can envisage and work toward a unity that is yet to come."

Notes

[1] It could be argued that the difference between a psycholinguistic study of utterance and a sociolinguistic study is that the former focuses on how utterances are created and inferred located within the individual, while the latter focuses on utterances located in the social relationships between individuals. However, this sort of delimitation is not entirely successful, since for explanatory purposes, sociolinguistic study would still need to incorporate intra individual psychological processes, and psycholinguistic study would need to take into account the interactional and social nature of such processes.

References

Addis, L. (1989). *Natural Signs. A Theory of Intentionality.* Philadelphia: Temple University Press.

Agar, M. (1982). "Toward an Ethnographic Language." *American Anthropologist* **84**, 779-95.

Ammon, U., Dittmar, N. and K. Mattheier (Eds.), (1987). *Sociolinguistics. An International Handbook of the Science of Language and Society.* Berlin: Walter de Grupter.

Anderson, S. (1985). *Phonology in the Twentieth Century. Theories of rules and theories of representations.* Chicago: University of Chicago Press.

Andresen, J. (1985). "Why do we do linguistic historiography?" *Semiotica* **56**, 3/4, 357-370.

Andresen, J. (1987). "Historiographic observations on a current issue in American linguistics." In Aarsleff et al (Eds.), *Papers in the History of Linguistics.* Philadelphia: John Benjamins Publishing Co. 647-56.

Andresen, J. (1990). *Linguistics In America 1769-1924. A Critical History.* New York: Routledge.

Aracil, L. (1978). "Sociolinguistics: Revolution and Paradigm." *Sociolinguistic Newsletter* **9;2,** 3-8.

Arbib, M.A. and Hill, J.C. (1988). "Language Acquisition: Schemas Replace Universal Grammar." In J. Hawkins (Ed.), *Explaining Language Universals.* Oxford: Basil Blackwell 56- 72.

Atkinson, J.M. and Heritage, J.C. (Eds.), (1984). *Structures of Social Action: Studies in conversation analysis.* Cambridge: Cambridge University Press.

Austerlitz, P. (Ed.), (1975). *The Scope of American Linguistics.* Lisse: The Peter de Ridder Press.

Austin, J.L. (1962). *How To Do Things With Words.* Cambridge; MA: Harvard University Press.

Bailey, C-J. (1973). *Variation and Linguistic Theory.* Arlington, VA: Center for Applied Linguistics.

Bailey, C-J. (1981). "Theory, description and difference among linguists (or, what keeps linguistics from becoming a science.)" *Language and Communication* **1;1,** 39-66.

Bailey, C-J and Harris, R. (Eds.), (1985). *Developmental Mechanisms of Language.* Oxford: Pergamon Press.

Bailey, R. (1985). "Negotiation and meaning: Revisiting the context of situation." In Benson and Greaves (Eds.), *Systemic Perspectives on Discourse, Vol. II.* Norwood; NJ: Ablex 1-17.

Baker, G.P. and Hacker, P.M.S. (1984). *Language, Sense And Nonsense.* Oxford: Basil Blackwell.

Bakhtin, M.M. (1981). *The Dialogic Imagination. Four essays by M.M. Bakhtin.* Edited by Michael Holquist. Translated by Caryl Emerson and Michael Holquist. Austin: University of Texas Press.

Bakhtin, M.M. (1986). *Speech Genres and Other Late Essays.* Edited by Caryl Emerson and Michael Holquist. Translated by Vern Mcgee. Austin: U. of Texas Press.

Bates, E. (1976). *Language in Context: The acquisition of Pragmatics.* New York: Academic Press.

Bates, E. and MacWhinney, B. (1982). "Functionalist approaches to grammar." In E. Wanner and L. Gleitman (Eds.), *Language Acquisition: The state of the art.* Cambridge: CUP 173-218.

Bates, E. and MacWhinney, B. (1987). "A functionalist approach to the acquisition of grammar." In Dirven and Fried (Eds.), *Functionalism in Linguistics.* Philadelphia: John Benjamins Publishing Co. 209-264.

Bateson, G. (1970). *Towards an Ecology of Mind.* New York: Ballantine Books

Baugh, J. and Sherzer J. (Eds.), (1984). *Language in Use: Readings in Sociolinguistics.* Englewood, NJ: Prentice Hall.

Bauman, R. (1974). "Speaking the light: the role of the Quaker minister." In R. Bauman & J. Sherzer (Eds.), 144-160.

Bauman, R. and Sherzer, J. (Eds.), (1974). *Explorations in the Ethnography of Speaking.* Cambridge: Cambridge University Press.

Becker, A.L. (1984)."The linguistics of particularity: Interpreting superordination in a Javanese text." *Proceedings of the Tenth Annual Meeting of the Berkeley Linguistics Society.* Berkeley, CA: University of California, Berkeley 425-36.

Becker, A.L. (1988). "Language in particular: A lecture." In D. Tannen (Ed.), *Linguistics in Context: Connecting Observation and Understanding.* Norwood, NJ: Ablex. 17-35.

Bell, A. (1984). "Language style as audience design." *Language in Society* **13,** 145-204.

Bell, R.T. (1976). *Sociolinguistics. Goals, Approaches and Problems.* London: B.T. Batsford Ltd.

Benson, J. and Greaves W. (Eds.), (1982). *Systemic Perspectives on Discourse. 2 Vols.* Norwood; NJ: Ablex.

Bernstein, B. (1971). *Class, Codes and Control, Vol. One.* New York: Schocken Books .

Bernstein, B. (1973). *Class, Codes and Control, Vol. Two.* London: Routledge and Kegan Paul.

Bernstein, B. (1981). "Codes, modalities, and the process of cultural reproduction: A model." *Language in Society* **10,** 327- 363.

Bilmes, J. (1986). *Discourse and Behavior.* New York: Plenum Press.

Blakemore, D. (1987). *Semantic Constraints on Relevance.* Oxford: Basil Blackwell.

Bloomfield, L. (1933). *Language.* New York: Holt, Rinehart and Winston.

Blount, B.G. (1981). "Sociolinguistic theory in anthropology." *International Journal of the Sociology of Language* 31, 91- 108.

Botha, R.P. (1989). *Challenging Chomsky. The Generative Garden Game.* Oxford: Basil Blackwell

Bourdieu, P. (1977). "The economics of linguistic exchanges." *Social Sciences Information* 16;6, 645-688.

Bourgeous, P and Rosenthal, S. (1983). *Thematic Studies in Phenomenology and Pragmaticism.* Amsterdam: B. R. Gruner.

Bowers, R. (1990). "Mountains are not cones: what can we learn from Chaos?" Paper given at GURT, Washington DC, 15 March.

Brand, M. (1984). *Intending and Acting. Toward a Naturalized Action Theory.* Cambridge; MA: MIT Press.

Brekle, H. (1986). "What is the history of linguistics and to what end is it studied? A didactic approach. "In T. Bynon and F. R. Palmer (Eds.), *Studies in the History of Western Linguistics.* Cambridge: Cambridge University Press 1-10.

Bright, W. (Ed.), (1966). *Sociolinguistics.* The Hague: Mouton.

Brown, C. (1974). *Wittgensteinian Linguistics.* The Hague: Mouton.

Brown, G. and Yule, G. (1983). *Discourse Analysis.* Cambridge: CUP.

Brown, P. and Levinson, S. (1978) (1987). *Politeness Some Universals in Language Usage.* Cambridge: Cambridge University Press.

Brown, R.H. (1987). *Society as Text. Essays on rhetoric, reason and reality.* Chicago: University of Chicago Press.

Bynon, T. and Palmer, F. R. (1988). *Studies in the History of Western Linguistics. in Honor of R. H. Robins.* Cambridge: Cambridge University Press.

Cameron, D. (1985). *Feminism and Linguistic Theory.* New York: St. Martin's Press.

Cameron, D. (1990). "Demythologizing sociolinguistics: why language does not reflect society." In J. Joseph and T. Taylor, *Ideologies of Language.* New York: Routledge 79-93.

Cameron, D. and Coates, J. (1985). "Some problems in the sociolinguistic explanation of sex differences." *Language and Communication.* 5;3, 143-151.

Carrol, J.B. (Ed.), (1956). *Language Thought and Reality: Selected writings of Benjamin Lee Whorf.* Cambridge, MA: MIT Press.

Cazden, C. (1989). "Contributions of the Bakhtin Circle to 'Communicative Competence'." *Applied Linguistics* 10;2, 116- 127.

Chafe, W.L. (1974a). "Language and Consciousness. "*Language* 50, 11-133. (1974b). "The flow of thought and the flow of language." In Givón (Ed.),, *Discourse and Syntax.* New York: Academic Press.

Chafe, W.L. (1976). "Giveness, contrastiveness, definiteness, subjects, topics, and point of view." In Li (Ed.), *Subject and Topic.* New York: Academic Press. 25-55. (1988). "Information Flow in Speaking and Writing." To appear in the Proceedings of the Conference on Literacy and Linguistics, held at the University of Wisconsin, Milwaukee, April 8-10, (1988).

Chloupek, J. and Nekvapil, J. (Eds.), (1987). *Reader in Czech sociolinguistics.* Philadelphia: John Benjamins.

Chomsky, N. (1957). *Syntactic Structures.* The Hague: Mouton.

Chomsky, N. (1965). *Aspects in the Theory of Syntax.* Cambridge, MA: MIT Press.

Chomsky, N. (1966). *Cartesian linguistics: A chapter in the history of rationalist thought.* New York: Harper and Row.

Chomsky, N. (1968). *Language and Mind.* New York: Harcourt, Brace.

Chomsky, N. (1972). "Empirical issues in the theory of transformational grammar." In S. Peters (Ed.), *Goals of Linguistic Theory.* Englewood Cliffs: Prentice Hall

Chomsky, N. (1975). *Reflections on Language.* New York: Random House.

Chomsky, N. (1980). *Rules and Representations.* New York: Columbia University Press.

Chomsky, N. (1986). *Knowledge of Language. Its nature, origins and use.* New York: Praeger.

Cicourel, A.V. (1973). *Cognitive Sociology: language and meaning in social interaction.* London: Penguin.

Cole, P. (Ed.), (1978). *Syntax and Semantics 9: Pragmatics.* New York: Academic Press.

Cole, P. (1981). *Radical Pragmatics.* New York: Academic Press.

Cole, P. and Morgan, J.L. (Eds.), (1975). *Syntax and Semantics 3: Speech Acts.* New York: Academic Press.

Comrie, B. (1981). *Language Universals and Linguistic Typology. Syntax and morphology.* Oxford: Basil Blackwell.

Conner-Linton, J. (1989). "Crosstalk: A multi-feature analysis of Soviet-American spacebridges." Doctoral Dissertation University of Southern California.

Cook, D.J. (1973). *Language in the Philosophy of Hegel.* The Hague: Mouton.

Cook-Gumperz, J. (1986). *The Social Construction of Literacy.* Cambridge: Cambridge University Press.

Coulthard, M. and Montgomery, M. (Eds.), (1981). *Studies in Discourse Analysis.* London: Routledge and Kegan Paul.

Currie, H. (1981). "Sociolinguistics and American linguistic theory." *Intl.J.Soc.Lang.* **31**, 29-41 ("Introduction" 5-10.)

Currie, H. (1984). "An expanded abstract of notes on personal involvement in sociolinguistics." *Sociolinguistics* **16;2**, 10- 16.

Danes, F. (1970). "One instance of Prague School methodology. Functional analysis of utterance and text." In Garvin (Ed.), 132-146.

Danes, F. (1974). *Papers on Functional Sentence Perspective.* The Hague: Mouton.

De Camp, D. (1970). "Is a sociolinguistic theory possible?" In Alatis (Ed.),, *Report of the 20th Annual Round Table Meeting on Linguistics and Language Studies.* Washington, DC: Georgetown Press.

Dik, S. (1978). *Functional Grammar.* Amsterdam: North-Holland.

Dik, S. 1983 (Ed.), *Advances in Functional Grammar*. Dordrecht: Foros.

Dinneen, F. (1989). "Ferdinand de Saussure (1957-1913)." *Georgetown Journal of Languages and Linguistics* **1;1,** 31-53.

Dirven, R. and Vilem, F. (Eds.), (1987). *Functionalism in Linguistics.* Philadelphia: John Benjamins Publishing Co.

Dittmar, N. (1976). *Sociolinguistics: a critical survey of theory and application.* London: Edward Arnold.

Downes, W. (1983). *Language and Society.* London: Fontana.

Durkheim, E. (1938). *Rules of Sociological Study.* Glencoe, Illinois: The Free Press.

Durmuller, U. (1980). "American sociolinguistics (1980)." *Sociolinguistic Newsletter* **11;2,** 1-6.

Fasold, R. (1978). "Language variation and linguistic competence." In D. Sankoff (Ed.), *Linguistic Variation: Models and Methods.* New York: Academic Press 85-95.

Fasold, R. (1983). "Linguistic Analyses of the Three Kinds." In D. Sankoff (Ed.), *Diversity and Diachrony.* Philadelphia: John Benjamins Publishing Co.

Fasold, R. (1984). *The Sociolinguistics of Society.* Oxford: Basil Blackwell.

Fasold, R. (1985). "Perspectives on sociolinguistic variation (Review Article)." *Language in Society* **14,** 515-526.

Fasold, R. (1989). "The quiet demise of the variable rules." Paper presented at NWAVE 18, Duke University, North Carolina.

Fasold, R. (1990). *The Sociolinguistics of language.* Oxford: Basil Blackwell.

Fasold, R. and Schiffrin, D. (Eds.), (1989). *Language Change and Variation.* Philadelphia: John Benjamins Publishing Co.

Fasold, R. and Shuy, R. (Eds.), (1975). *Analyzing Variation in Language.* Washington, DC: Georgetown University Press.

Firth, J.R. (1957). *Papers in linguistics 1934-1951.* London: Oxford University Press.

Firth, J.R. (1964). *The Tongues of Men* [1937] and *Speech* [1930]. London: Oxford University Press.

Firth, J.R. (1968). *Selected Papers of J.R. Firth 1952-(1959).* Edited by F.R. Palmer. London: Longman.

Fishman, J.A. (1965). "Who speaks what language to whom and when?" *La Linguistique* 67-88.

Fishman, J.A. (1968). *Readings in the Sociology of Language.* The Hague: Mouton

Fishman, J.A. (1971a). *Sociolinguistics: A brief introduction.* Rowley, Mass.:Newbury House.

(1971b). *Advances in the sociology of language.* Two Volumes. The Hague: Mouton.

Fodor, J.A. (1983). *The Modularity of Mind.* Cambridge; MA: MIT Press.

Foley, W.A. and van Valen, R. (1984). *Functional Syntax and Universal Grammar.* Cambridge: Cambridge University Press.

Foucault, M. (1972). *The Archaeology of Knowledge.* New York: Pantheon Books.

Freedle, R. (Ed.), (1977) (1982). *Discourse Production and Comprehension.* Norwood, NJ: Ablex Publishing Co.

Friedrich, P. (1986). *The Language Parallax. Linguistic relativism and poetic indeterminacy.* Austin: University of Texas Press.

Fries, C.C. (1952). *The structure of English. An introduction to the construction of English sentences.* New York: Harcourt, Brace.

Gal, S. (1979). *Language Shift: Social determinants of linguistic change in bilingual Austria.* New York: Academic Press.

Garfinkel, H. (1967). *Studies in Ethnomethodology.* Englewood Cliffs, NJ: Prentice Hall.

Garvin, P. (1970). *Method and Theory in Linguistics.* The Hague: Mouton.

Gazdar, G. (1979). *Pragmatics.* New York: Academic Press.

Giesbers, H. (1985). "Sociolinguistics and Ideology." *Sociolinguistics* **15,2**, 2-12.

Giglioli, P. (Ed.), (1972). *Language and social context.* Harmondsworth: Penguin Books.

Giles, H. and H. Scherer (Eds.), (1979). *Social Markers in Speech.* Cambridge: Cambridge University Press

Givón, T. (Ed.), (1979a). *Discourse and Syntax.* NY: Academic Press.

Givón, T. (1979b). *On Understanding Grammar.* New York: Academic Press.

Givón, T. (1984). *Syntax. A functional-typological introduction.* Philadelphia: John Benjamins.

Givón, T. (1989). *Mind, Code and Context. Essays in Pragmatics.* London: Lawrence Erlbaum Associates, Publishers.

Gleick, J. (1987). *Chaos. The making of a new science.* New York: Viking.

Goffman, E. (1959). *The Presentation of Self In Everyday Life.* NY: Doubleday.

Goffman, E. (1967). *Interaction Ritual: essays on face-to-face behavior.* New York: Doubleday.

Goffman, E. (1974). *Frame Analysis. An essay in the organization of experience.* Cambridge, MA: Harvard University Press.

Goffman, E. (1981). *Forms of Talk.* Philadelphia: U. of Penn. Press.

Goldman, A. (1988). *Empirical Knowledge.* Berkeley: U. of Ca. Press.

Greenberg, J. (1963). *Universals of Language.* Boston: MIT Press

Greenberg, J. (1986). "On being a linguistic anthropologist." *UM Annual Review of Anthropology* **15**, 1-24.

Grice, H.P. (1957). "Meaning." *Philosophical Review* **66**, 377-88.

Grice, H.P.(1968). "Utterer's meaning, sentence-meaning, and word meaning." *Foundations of Language* **4**, 1-18

Grice, H.P. (1975). "Logic and conversations." In Cole and Morgan (Eds.), *Syntax and Semantics 3: Speech Acts.* New York Academic Press. 41-58.

Grice, H.P. (1989). *Studies in the Way of Words.* Harvard: Harvard U.Press.

Grimshaw, A. (1981). *Language as Social Resource.* Stanford: Stanford University Press.

Gumperz, J. (1971). *Language in Social Groups.* (Introduced by A. S. Dil.) Stanford: Stanford University Press.

Gumperz, J. 1977). "Sociocultural knowledge in conversational inference." In M. Saville-Troike (Ed.), *Linguistics and Anthropology.* Georgetown University Round Table on Languages and Linguistics

Gumperz, J. (1977). Washington, DC: Georgetown University Press.

Gumperz, J. (1982a). *Discourse Strategies*. Cambridge: Cambridge University Press.

Gumperz, J. (1982b). *Language and Social Identity*. Cambridge: Cambridge University Press.

Gumperz, J. (1984). "Communicative competence revisited." In D. Schiffrin (Ed.), *Meaning, Form, and Use in Context: Linguistic Applications*. Washington DC: Georgetown University Press.

Gumperz, J. and Cook-Gumperz (1982). "Introduction: Language and the communication of social identity." In Gumperz (1982b).

Gumperz, J. and Hymes, D. (Eds.), (1964). "The Ethnography of Communication." *American Anthropologist* 66 (6) Part II.

Gumperz, J. and Hymes, D. (Eds.), (1972) (1986). *Directions in Sociolinguistics*. Oxford: Basil Blackwell.

Gutting, G. (Ed.), (1980). *Paradigms and Revolutions. Appraisals and applications of Thomas Kuhn's philosophy of science*. Notre Dame, Indiana: University of Notre Dame Press.

Halliday, M.A.K. (1970). "Language structure and language function." In Lyons (Ed.), *New Horizons in Linguistics*. Harmondsworth: Penguin Books. 140-166

Halliday, M.A.K. (1973). *Explorations in the Functions of Language*. London: Edward Arnold.

Halliday, M.A.K. (1978). *Language as Social Semiotic*. London: Edward Arnold.

Halliday, M.A.K. (1985). *A Short Introduction to Functional Grammar*. London: Edward Arnold.

Halliday, M.A.K. and Fawcett, R. (1987). *New developments in systemic linguistics. Volume 1: Theory and Description*. London: Francis Pinter.

Halliday, M.A.K. and Hasan, R. (1976). *Cohesion in English*. London: Longman Group.

Harré, R. (1984). *Personal Being. A theory for individual psychology*. Cambridge: MN: Harvard University Press.

Harré, R. (1985). *The Philosophy of Science*. Oxford: Oxford U. Press.

Harré, R. (1989). "Language games and texts of identity." In J. Shotter and K. Gergen (Eds.), *Texts of Identity*. London: Sage.

Harris, R. (1980). *The Language-Makers*. London: Duckworth

Harris, R. (1981). *The Language Myth*. London: Duckworth.

Harris, R. (1987). *Reading Saussure*. La Salle, IL: Open Court.

Harris, R. (1988a). *Language, Saussure and Wittgenstein: how to play games with words*. London: Routledge.

Harris, R. (1988b). (Ed.), *Linguistic Thought in England 1914-1945*. London:Routledge.

Harris, R. and Taylor, T. (1989). *Landmarks in Linguistic Thought the Western tradition from Socrates to Saussure*. New York: Routledge.

Harris, Z. (1951) (1960). *Structural Linguistics*. Chicago:UC Press.

Hasan, R. (1985). "Meaning, context and text: Fifty years after Malinowski." In Benson and Greaves (Eds.), (1985), 16-49.

Hawkins, H. (1988). "Explaining Language Universals." In H. Hawkins (Ed.), *Explaining Language Universals*.Oxford: Basil Blackwell 3-28.

Heath, S. Brice (1983). *Ways with Words: Language, life and work in communities and classrooms*. Cambridge: Cambridge University Press.

Heritage, J. (1983). "Recent Developments In Conversation Analysis." *Sociolinguistics* **15**;1, 1-19.

Heritage, J. (1984). *Garfinkel and Ethnomethodology*. Cambridge: Cambridge University Press.

Herrnstein Smith, B. (1988). *Contingencies of Value. Alternative Perspective for Critical Theory*. Cambridge, MA: HUP.

Hickmann, M. (1987). *Social and Functional Approaches to Language and Thought*. NY: Academic Press.

Hopper, P. (1988). "Emergent Grammar and the A Priori Grammar Postulate." In Tannen (Ed.), *Linguistics in Context: Connecting Observation and Understanding. Lectures from the 1985 LSA, TESOL and NEH Institutes*. Norwood; NY: Ablex.

Hudson, R.A. (1980). *Sociolinguistics*. Cambridge: Cambridge University Press.

Hudson, R.A. (1989). *Review of Linguistics: The Cambridge Survey (4 vols.)* Edited by Frederick Newmeyer. *Language* **65**;4, 812-819.

Hurford, J. and Heasley, B. (1983). *Semantics: A Coursebook*. Cambridge: Cambridge University Press.

Hymes, D. (1962). "The ethnography of speaking." In T. Gladwen and W. Sturtevant (Eds.), *Anthropology And Human Behavior*. Washington, DC: American Anthropological Association.

Hymes, D. (1964a). "Introduction: Toward Ethnographies Of Communication." In Gumperz and Hymes (1964).

Hymes, D. (1964b). Introduction in D. Hymes (Ed.), *Language In Culture and Society*. New York: Harper and Row.

Hymes, D. (1966). "Two types of linguistic relativity." In Bright (Ed.), (1966), 114-167.

Hymes, D. (1967). "Models of the interaction of language and social setting." *Journal of Social Issues* **23**;2, 8-28.

Hymes, D. (1973). "The origin and foundations of inequality among speakers." *Daedalus* **102**;3, 59-85.

Hymes, D. (1974a). *Foundations In Sociolinguistics. An Ethnographic Approach*. Philadelphia: University of Penn. Press.

Hymes, D. (1974b). "Introduction, Traditions and Paradigms." In D. Hymes (Ed.), *Studies In The History Of Linguistics, Traditions And Paradigms*. Bloomington: Indiana University Press. 1-38.

Hymes, D. (1974c). "Ways of speaking." In Bauman and Sherzer 433-51.

Hymes, D. (1980). *Language In Education: Ethnolinguistic Essays*. Washington, DC: Center for Applied Linguistics

Hymes, D. (1983). *Essays In The History Of Linguistics Anthropology*. Philadelphia: John Benjamins Publishing Co.

Hymes, D. (1984). "Sociolinguistics: stability and consolidation." *Int. Journal of Soc. of Lang.* **45**, 39-45.

Hymes, D. (1986). "Discourse: scope without depth." *International Journal Sociology of Language* **57,** 49-89.

Hymes, D and Fought J. (1981). *American Structuralism.* The Hague: Mouton.

Joseph, J. (1987). *Eloquence and Power. The Rise of Language Standards and Standard Languages.* Oxford: Basil Blackwell.

Joseph, J. (1989). "Demythifying Saussure." *Linguistics* **27,** 341-352.

Joseph, J. (1990a). "Ideologizing Saussure: Bloomfield and Chomsky's readings of the Cours de Linguistique Generale." In J. Joseph and T. Taylor (1990), 51-78.

Joseph, J. (1990b). "Arbitrary equals Social does not equal Rational: On the evolution of Saussure's linguistic worldview." Paper given at GURT Presession on History of Linguistics, 14 March.

Joseph, J and Taylor, T. (Eds.), (1990). *Ideologies of Language.* New York: Routledge.

Kachru, B. (1981). "Socially realistic linguistics: the Firthian tradition." *Intl.J.Soc.Lang.* **31,** 65-19.

Kay, P. (1978). "Variable Rules, community grammar and linguistic change." In D. Sankoff (Ed.), 1978 71-82.

Kay, P. and McDaniel, K. "On the logic of variable rules." *Language in Society* **8,** 151-187.

Kay, P. and McDaniel, K. (1981). "On the meaning of variable rules: Discussion." *Language in Society* **10,** 251-258.

Katz, J.J. (1981). *Language And Other Abstract Objects.* Totona, NJ: Rowman and Littlefield.

Key, M.R. (Ed.), (1980). *The Relationship of Verbal and Nonverbal Communication.* The Hague: Mouton.

Khubchandani, L. (1973). "An overview on sociolinguistics." *Sociolinguistic Newsletter* **4,2,** 2-8.

Koerner, K. (1973). *Ferdinand De Saussure: Origin And Development Of His Linguistic Thought In Western Studies Of Language: A Contribution To The History And Theory Of Linguistics.* Branschweig: Friedrich Vieweg.

Koerner, K. (1986). "Aux sources de la sociolinguistique." *Linguisticae Investigationes* **10;2,** 381-401.

Kuhn, T.S. (1962). *The Structure of Scientific Revolutions.* Chicago: University of Chicago Press.

Kuhn, T.S. (1977). *The Essential Tension Selected Studies in Scientific Tradition and Change.* Chicago: University of Chicago Press.

Labov, W. (1963). "The social motivation of a sound change." *Word* **19,** 273-309.

Labov, W. (1966). *The Social Stratification of English in New York City.* Washington, DC: Center for Applied Linguistics.

Labov, W. (1969). "Contraction, deletion, and inherent variability of the English copula." *Language* **45,** 715-62.

Labov, W. (1971). "Some principles of linguistic methodology." *Language in Society* **1,** 97-120.

Labov, W. (1972a). *Sociolinguistic Patterns.* Philadelphia: University of Pennsylvania Press.

Labov, W. (1972b). *Language in the inner city: Studies in the black English vernacular*. Philadelphia: U. of Penn. Press.

Labov, W. (1972c). "The internal evolution of linguistic rules." In R. Srockwell and R. Macauley (Eds.), *Historical linguistics and generative theory*. Bloomington: Indiana University Press. 101-171.

Labov, W. (1972d). "Where do grammars stop?" In Shuy, R. (1972). 42-88.

Labov, W. (1975). "Empirical foundations of linguistic theory" In Austerlitz (Ed.), *The scope of American linguistics*. Lisse: Peter de Ridder Press. 77-134.

Labov, W. (1980a). "Is there a creole speech community?" In A. Valdman and A. Highfield *Theoretical Orientations in Creole Studies*. 369-388.

Labov, W. (1980b). "The social origins of sound change." In Labov (Ed.), *Locating Language in Time and Space*. New York: Academic Press.

Labov, W. (1981). "Resolving the Neogrammarian controversy." *Language* **57**, 267-309.

Labov, W. (1982). "Objectivity and commitment in linguistic science: The case of the Black English trial in Ann Arbor." *Language in Society* **11**, 165-201

Labov, W. (1984). "Field methods of the project on linguistic change and variation." In Baugh and Sherzer (Eds.), (1984).

Labov, W. (1987a). "The overestimation of functionalism." In Dirven and Fried. 311-332.

Labov, W. (1987b). "The community as educator." In Judith Langer (Ed.), *Language, Literacy and Culture: Issues of society and schooling*. Norwood NJ: Ablex 128-146.

Labov, W. (1989). "The exact description of a speech community." In Fasold and Schiffrin (Eds.), (1989), 1-57.

Labov, W. and Harris, W. (1986). "De facto segregation of Black and White Vernaculars." In D. Sankoff (Ed.), (1986), 1-24.

Lakoff, R. (1972). "Language in context." *Language* **48**, 907-927.

Lass, R. (1980). *On Explaining Language Change*. Cambridge: CUP.

Lavandera, B. (1978). "Where does the sociolinguistic variable stop?" *Language in society* **7**, 171-83.

Lavandera, B. (1988). "The study of language in its socio-cultural context." In Newmeyer (Ed.), *Language: the sociocultural context*. Cambridge: Cambridge U. Press. 1-13.

le Page, R.B. and Tabouret-Keller, A. *(1985). Acts of Identity.* Cambridge: Cambridge University Press.

Leech, G. (1983). *Principles of Pragmatics*. London: Longman Group.

Lehmann, W. (1981). "Historical linguistics and sociolinguistics." *Intl.J.Soc.Lang.* **31**, 11-27.

Levinson, S. (1979). "Activity types and language." *Linguistics* **17;5/6**, 365-99.

Levinson, S. (1983). *Pragmatics*. Cambridge: Cambridge U. Press.

Levinson, S. (1988). "Putting linguistics on a proper footing: Explorations in Goffman's Concepts of Participation." In *Erving Goffman: Exploring the interactive order*. Cambridge: Polity Press

Li, C. (Ed.), (1976). *Subject and Topic*. New York: Academic Press.

Lindberg, C. E. (1979). "Is the sentence a unit of speech production and perception?" In Mey (Ed.), *Pragmalinguistics Theory and Practice.* The Hague: Mouton. 51-60.

Linell, P. (1982). *The Written Bias in Linguistics.* Linkoping: University of Linkoping Department of Communication Studies.

Luntley, M. (1988). *Language, Logic and Experience. The case for anti-realism.* La Salle, IL: Open Court.

Lyons, J. (Ed.), (1970). *New Horizons in Linguistics.* Harmondsworth: Penguin Books.

Lyons, J. (1977). *Semantics.* (2 vols.) Cambridge: CUP.

Lyons, J. (1981). *Language Meaning and Context.* London: Fontana.

Margolis, J. (1986). *The Persistence of Reality I. Pragmaticism without foundations. Reconciling Realism And Relativism.* Oxford: Basil Blackwell.

Margolis, J. (1987). *The Persistence of Reality II. Science without unity. Reconciling the Human and Natural sciences.* Oxford: Basil Blackwell.

Markova, I. (Ed.), (1978). *The Social Context of Language.* New York: Wiley.

Markova, I. (1982). *Paradigms, Thought and Language.* London: John Wiley and Sons.

Mayzor, M. (1989). "Really relativism: Dialectic interpretations of Saussure." *Language and Communication* 9;1, 11-21.

Mey, J. (Ed.), (1979). *Pragmalinguistics Theory and Practice.* The Hague: Mouton.

Meyer, M. (1986). *From Logic to Rhetoric.* Philadelphia: John Benjamins.

Miller, D. (1981)."Language and theory." *Intl.J.Soc.Lang.* 31, 43-64.

Milroy, L. (1980). *Language and Social Networks.* Oxford: Basil Blackwell.

Milroy, L. (1985). "What a performance! Some problems with the competence-performance distinction." *Australian Journal of Linguistics* 51, 1-17.

Milroy, L. (1987). *Observing and Analyzing Natural Language. A critical account of sociolinguistic method.* Oxford: Basil Blackwell.

Moore, T. and Carling, C. (1982). *Understanding Language: Towards a post Chomskyan linguistics.* London: The Macmillan Press.

Muysken, P. (1985). "Twenty years of sociolinguistics?" *Sociolinguistics* 15,2, 12-20.

Neubert. A. (1976). "What is sociolinguistics? Three postulates for sociolinguistic research." *Archivum Linguisticum* 7;2, 152-160.

Newmeyer, F. (1980). *Linguistic Theory in America. The first quarter-century of transformational Generative Grammar.* New York: Academic Press.

Newmeyer, F. (1983). *Grammatical Theory. Its limits and its possibilities.* Chicago: University of Chicago Press.

Newmeyer, F. (1986). *The Politics of Linguistics.* Chicago: University of Chicago Press.

Newmeyer, F. (Ed.) (1988). *Language: the socio-cultural context.* Cambridge: Cambridge University Press.

Palmer, F. R. (1976). *Semantics. A new outline.* Cambridge: CUP.

Parret, H. (1974). *Discussing language.* The Hague: Mouton.

Parret, H. (1983). *Semiotics and Pragmatics an Evaluative Comparison of Conceptual Frameworks.* Philadelphia: John Benjamins.

Pateman, T. (1983). "What is a language." *Language and Communication* **3,2,** 101-127.

Pateman, T. (1987). *Language in Mind and Language in Society. Studies in Linguistic Reproduction.* Oxford: Clarendon Press.

Peng, F. (1982). "The place of sociolinguistics in language sciences" *Sociolinguistic Newsletter* **13,1,** 16-33.

Pike, K. (1967). *Language in relation to a unified theory of the structure of human behavior.* The Hague: Mouton.

Pinkard, T. (1988). *Hegel's Dialectic. The exploration of possibility.* Philadelphia: Temple University Press

Pollner, M. (1987). *Mundane Reason. Reality in everyday and sociological discourse.* Cambridge: Cambridge U. Press.

Pomerantz, A. (1984). "Agreeing and disagreeing with assessments: some features of preferred/dispreferred turn shapes." In Atkinson, J.M. and Heritage, J.C. (Eds.), *Structures of Social Action: Studies in conversation analysis.* Cambridge: Cambridge University Press 57-101.

Potter, J. and Wetherall, M. (1987). *Discourse and Social Psychology, Beyond Attitudes and Behavior.* London: Sage Publications.

Pride, J.B. (1970). "Sociolinguistics." In Lyons (Ed.), *New Horizons in Linguistics.* Harmondsworth: Penguin Books.

Pride, J.B. (1971). *The Social Meaning of Language.* London: Oxford University Press.

Rescher, N. (1987). *Scientific Realism. A critical Appraisal.* Dordrecht: D. Reidel Publishing Co.

Ricento, T. (1987). "Clausal ellipsis in multi-party conversation in English."*Journal of Pragmatics* **11,** 751-775.

Ries, J. (1894) [1931]. *Was ist ein Satz?* Marburg: N.G. Elwert.

Roark, A. (1986). "Structure discovered in Chitchat." *The Los Angeles Times,* November 20, **22,** 26-7.

Romaine, S. (1981). "The status of variable rules in sociolinguistic theory." *Journal of Linguistics* **17,** 93-119.

Romaine, S. (1982a). *Socio-Historical Linguistics.* Cambridge: CUP

Romaine, S. (1982b). *Sociolinguistic Variation in Speech Communities.* London: Edward Arnold.

Romaine, S. (1984a). *The Language of Children and Adolescents.* Oxford: Blackwell

Romaine, S. (1984b). "On the problem of syntactic variation and pragmatic meaning in sociolinguistic theory." *Folia Linguistica* **18;3-4,** 409-437.

Sacks, H. (1984). "Notes on methodology." In Atkinson and Heritage (Eds.), 1984, 21-28.

Sampson, G. (1980). *Schools of Linguistics.* Stanford: Stanford University Press.

Sankoff D. (Ed.), (1978). *Linguistic Variation: Models and Methods.* New York: Academic Press. (Ed.),

Sankoff D. (1986). *Diversity and Diachrony.* Philadelphia: John Benjamins Publishing Co.

Sankoff, D. and Labov, W. (1979). "On the uses of variable rules." *Language in Society* **8**, 189-222.

Sankoff, G. (1980). *The Social Life of Language*. Philadelphia: University of Pennsylvania Press.

Sapir, E. (1921). *Language*. New York: Harcourt, Brace and World. (1929). "The status of linguistics as a science." *Language* **5**, 207-214.

Saussure, F. de (1966). *Course in General Linguistics*. Translation by W. Baskin. New York: McGraw-Hill.

Saville-Troike, M. (1982). *The Ethnography of Communication*. Oxford: Basil Blackwell.

Schank, R. and Abelson, R. (1977). *Scripts, Plans, Goals, and Understanding: an Inquiry into Human Knowledge Structures*. New York: John Wiley and Sons.

Schegloff, E.A. (1982). "Discourse as an interactional achievement: some uses of "uh huh" and other things that come between sentences." In Tannen (Ed.), *Analyzing Discourse: Text and talk*. Washington DC: Georgetown University Press. 71-93.

Schieffelin, B. and Ochs E. (1986). *Language Socialization Across Cultures*. Cambridge: Cambridge University Press.

Schiffrin, D. (Ed.), (1984). *Meaning, Form, and Use in Context: Linguistic Applications*. Washington DC: Georgetown University Press.

Schiffrin, D. (1985a). "An empirical basis for discourse pragmatics." Talk presented at Ferguson-Greenburg Lecture Series; Stanford University.

Schiffrin, D. (1985b). "Conversational coherence: The role of well." *Language* **61**, 640-67.

Schiffrin, D. (1987a). "Discovering the context of an utterance." *Linguistics* **25**, 11-32.

Schiffrin, D. (1987b). *Discourse Markers*. Cambridge: Cambridge U. Press.

Schiffrin, D. (1987c). "Sociolinguistic approaches to discourse: toward a synthesis and expansion." Keynote address at NWAVE XVI, University of Texas, Austin.

Schiffrin, D. (1988). "Conversation analysis." In Newmeyer (Ed.), *Language: the socio-cultural context*. Cambridge: Cambridge University Press.

Schiffrin, D. (1990a). "The Principle of Intersubjectivity in Communication and Conversation." *Semiotica* **80(1/2)**, 121-151.

Schiffrin, D. (1990b). "Between text and context: Deixis, anaphora, and the meaning of *then*." *Text* **10(3)**, 245-270.

Schiffrin, D. (1990c). "The language of discourse: Connections inside and out." *Text* **10(1/2)**, 97-100.

Schiffrin, D. (1994) *Approaches to Discourse*. Oxford: Basil Blackwell.

Schutz, A. (1970). *Alfred Schutz: on Phenomenology and Social Relations*. Chicago: University of Chicago Press.

Schutz, A. (1972). *The Phenomenology of the Social World*. London: Heinemann

Searle, J. (1969). *Speech Acts*. Cambridge: Cambridge U. Press.

Searle, J. (1979). *Expression and Meaning*. Cambridge: Cambridge U. Press.

Searle, J. (1983). *Intentionality. An essay in the philosophy of mind*. Cambridge: Cambridge University Press.

Searle, J. (1985). *Minds, Brains and Science.* Cambridge, MA: Harvard U.P.

Sells, P. (1985). *Lectures on Contemporary Syntactic Theories.* Stanford: Center for the Study of Language and Information.

Sherzer, J. (1977). "The ethnography of speaking: A critical appraisal." In M. Saville-Troike (1977), 43-58.

Shopen, T. (Ed.), (1985). *Language Typology and Syntactic Description. Volume I: Clause Structure. Volume II: Complex Constructions.* Cambridge: CUP

Shotter, J. and Gergen, K. (Eds.), (1989). *Texts of Identity.* London: Sage.

Shuy, R.W. (Ed.), (1973). *Sociolinguistics, Current Trends and Prospects.* Washington DC: Georgetown University Press.

Shuy, R.W. (1984). "The decade ahead for applied sociolinguistics." *Int. Journal of Soc. of Language* **45,** 101- 111.

Shuy, R.W. (1988). "The social context of the study of the social context of language variation." Keynote address at GURT, March, (1988).

Siewierska, A. (1988). *Word Order Rules.* London: Croom Helm.

Silverstein, M. (1987). "The three faces of function: preliminaries to a psychology of language." In Hickmann (Ed.), *Social and Functional Approaches to Language and Thought.* NY: Academic Press 17-38.

Singh, R. (1989). "A closer look at so-called variable processes." In R. Fasold and D. Schiffrin 1989, 367-380.

Sperber, P. and Wilson D. (1986). *Relevance: Communication and cognition.* Oxford: Basil Blackwell.

Strawson, P.F. (1950). "On referring." *Mind* **59,** 320-44.

Stubbs, M. (1983). *Discourse Analysis. The sociolinguistic analysis of natural language.* Oxford: Basil Blackwell.

Suppe, Frederick (1989). *The Semantic Conception of Theories and Scientific Realism.* Chicago: University of Ill. Press.

Svejcer, A.D. (1986). *Contemporary Sociolinguistic Theory, Problems, Methods.* Philadelphia: John Benjamins.

Svejcer, A.D. and Nikol'sij, L.B. (1986). *Introduction to Sociolinguistics.* Philadelphia: John Benjamins.

Tannen, D. (1979). "What's in a frame? Surface evidence for underlying expectations." In Freedle (1979), 137-81.

Tannen, D. (1982). *Spoken and Written Language: Exploring Orality and Literacy.* Norwood: Ablex. (Ed.),

Tannen, D. (1984a). *Coherence in Spoken and Written Discourse.* Norwood: Ablex.

Tannen, D. (1984b). *Conversational Style: Analyzing talk among friends.* Norwood, NJ: Ablex.

Tannen, D. (1986). *That's Not What I Meant! How Conversational Style Makes or Breaks Your Relations With Others.* New York: William Morrow and Company Inc.

Tannen, D. (1987). "Towards a poetics of talk: repetition in conversation." *Language* **63;3,** 574-605. (Ed.),

Tannen, D. (1988). *Linguistics in Context: Connecting Observation and Understanding.* Lectures from the 1985 LSA, TESOL and NEH Institutes. Norwood: Ablex.

Tannen, D. (1989). *Talking Voices: Repetition, dialogue and imagery in conversational discourse.* Cambridge: CUP.

Tannen, D. (1990a). "Ordinary conversation and literary discourse. Coherence and the poetics of repetition." In E. H Bendix *The Uses of Linguistics.* Annals of the New York Academy of Science.

Tannen, D. (1990b). "Discourse analysis: The excitement of diversity." *Text* **10(1/2)**, 109-11.

Taylor, T. (1990a). "Review of *The Politics of Linguistics* by Frederick Newmeyer." *Language* **66;1**, 159-162.

Taylor, T. (1990b). "Showing the fly the way out of the fly- bottle. Or why theorists who ignore the history of linguistic ideas do so at their peril." Paper Given at ICHoLS V, Galway.

Taylor, T. (1992) *Mutual "Misunderstanding." Scepticism and the Theorizing of Language and Interpretation.* Durham and London: Duke University Press.

Taylor, T. and Cameron, D. (1987). *Analyzing Conversation. Rules and Units in the Structure of Talk.* Oxford: Pergamon Press.

Trudgill, P. (1974a). *Sociolinguistics. An introduction to language and society.* Harmondsworth: Penguin Books.

Trudgill, P. (1974b). *The Social Differentiation of English in Norich.* Cambridge: Cambridge University Press.

Trudgill, P. (1984). *Applied Sociolinguistics.* London: Academic Press.

van de Craen, P. (1985). "The status of sociolinguistics as a science." *Sociolinguistics* **15,2**, 28-41.

van Dijk, T.A. (Ed.), (1985). *Handbook of Discourse Analysis.* (4 vols) London: Academic Press.

van Dijk, T.A.(1981). *Studies in the Pragmatics of Discourse.* The Hague: Mouton.

van Dijk, T.A. (1990). "The future of the field: Discourse analysis in the 1990's." *Text* **10(1/2)**, 133-156.

van Dijk, T.A. and Kintsch, W. (Eds.), (1983). *Strategies of Discourse Comprehension.* New York: Academic Press.

van Riemsdijk, H. and Williams, E. (1986). *Introduction to the Theory of Grammar.* Cambridge, MA: MIT Press.

Vaughn-Cooke, F. (1987). "A Critical Analysis of the Divergence Hypothesis: A response to William Labov." Paper presented at NWAVE 16 Georgetown University, Washington DC.

Verburg, P. (1974). "Vicissitudes of paradigms." In, Hymes (Ed.), *Studies in the History of Linguistics, Traditions and paradigms.* Bloomington: Indiana U. Press. 191-232.

Vgotsky, L. (1978). *Mind in Society.* Cambridge, MA: Harvard University Press.

Vision, G. (1988). *Modern Anti-Realism and Manufactured Truth.* London: Routledge

Volosinov, V. (1929) (1986). *Marxism and the Philosophy of Language.* Cambridge, MA: Harvard University Press.

Wardhaugh, R. (1986). *An Introduction to Sociolinguistics.* Oxford: Basil Blackwell.

Weinreich, U., Labov, W. and Herzog, M. (1968). *Empirical Foundations for a Theory of Language Change.* New York: Columbia University.

Whitney, W. D. 1887. *Language and the Study of Language. Twelve Lectures On the Principles of Linguistic Science.* New York: Charles Scribner's.

Widdowson, H.G. (1988). "Poetry and Pedagogy." In Tannen (1988), 185-197.

(1989). "Knowledge of language and ability for use." *Applied Linguistics* **10;2,** 128-137.

Williams, H. (1989). *Hegel, Heraclitus and Marx's Dialectic.* New York: Harvester Wheatsheaf.

Wittgenstein, L. (1953). *Philosophical Investigations.* Oxford: Basil Blackwell.

Wolfram, W. (1991). *Dialects and American English.* Englewood Cliffs, NJ: Prentice Hall.

Wolfson, N. (1976). "Speech Events And Natural Speech: Some Implications For Sociolinguistic Methodology." *Language in Society* **5,** 189-209.

Index